This Book must be returned to
the Library on, or before, the
last date shown below

FOUR WEEKS ONLY	-5. JUN 01 2 3 5 1
19 JAN 1976	
30.JUN93	
This item is due for return on 3 Sept 96	
UNIVERSITY LIBRARY 3 0 JUN 2008 ANN GGL 01	

30/-
U308

BOOKBINDING BY HAND

BOOKBINDING BY HAND

for Students and Craftsmen

by

LAURENCE TOWN

Formerly a Senior Lecturer in Crafts
St. John's College, York

with a preface by
A. G. DOVE

FABER AND FABER
24 Russell Square
London

First published in mcmli
by Faber and Faber Limited
24 Russell Square, London, W.C.1
Second edition mcmlxiii
Printed in Great Britain by
Latimer Trend & Co Ltd Whitstable

To

EVELYN

but for whose patience and
fortitude as wife to a craftsman, there could have been
neither bookbinder nor book

PREFACE

Few people have had a wider and more varied experience in the printing and binding of books by hand than has the author of this work; fewer still have taught these crafts to so wide a range of pupils and no one could display a keener interest either as a craftsman or as a teacher. His pupils have included boys of low general intelligence, students in 'Emergency' training colleges for teachers, set up to train mature men after war service, students following regular teacher training courses and members of evening institutes where serving teachers sought to consolidate or to extend their professional stock-in-trade, or amateurs developed an absorbing hobby. At all these levels his work was successful, not only in the development of technical skill, but also in arousing a real and lively interest in the work and in fostering a true spirit of craftsmanship.

Like all successful teachers, he prepared his work most carefully and in doing so he evolved copious notes on procedure and detailed instruction sheets for the guidance of pupils working at different stages. The production of the present book provides a natural sequence to this, for it not only codifies and expands the utilitarian teaching aids but it also manifests the spirit in which the teaching was done and preserves something of the atmosphere which pervaded Mr. Town's classes. In the result, this book gives most helpful guidance and instruction to anyone wishing to follow the ancient craft of bookbinding and, perhaps when he is himself a master of the craft, to teach it to others and it also creates a climate conducive to a real love of the craft. If

PREFACE

by its use readers achieve even a tithe of the sense of satisfaction and of the real joy which have so obviously come to Mr. Town in the easy and confident exercise of his own highly developed technical skill and in the broad and deep interest which he has found in the production of books, the publication of this work will be fully justified.

It has been my privilege to have close contact with Mr. Town's work over many years and it was always a pleasure to visit his classes. To read his book recalls memories of these visits and of the work seen, from single section books which brought a real sense of satisfaction in achievement to boys in a 'non-selective' school—those remaining after a double 'creaming' for grammar and for central schools—to the other end of the scale where bindings in full leather with tooled lettering and appropriate decoration, the work of adult students, ranking with the work of professional artist-craftsmen.

It will not surprise readers to learn that Mr. Town continues to practise his craft in retirement. What could be more conducive to health and happiness than continued submission to the exacting disciplines of a traditional craft, coupled with the joy which comes from the making of useful and beautiful things? Like all true craftsmen he is always willing to share his knowledge with anyone who shows genuine interest and for him the writing of this book was obviously a labour of love; it is certainly both instructive and pleasurable to study it.

A. G. Dove

August 1962

CONTENTS

CONTENTS

CONTENTS

13

FOREWORD

The guidance to be derived from a study of this book on the ancient craft of the bookbinder will depend to some extent on the assumption that the student has spent some little time in doing preliminary work leading up to the binding of books. This work is necessary in order that a background of skill and knowledge be acquired in the important processes of pasting, gluing, cutting, and measuring. Familiarity with the tools and equipment is also gained in this way. In the case of pupils entering a Secondary Modern School with no such preliminary training, the course should be planned so that a large portion of the first year is spent upon such work. Bookbinding proper could then be carried forward in the second and following years. Where pupils have spent the last year in the Junior School doing this introductory work, it is possible to begin with bookbinding when they enter the Secondary Modern School. Adults who are keen to learn this craft would do well to run through a short preliminary course before beginning to bind their first books. To those who desire to become master-craftsmen I should recommend a close study of the historical side of this delightful craft. It forms a good mental background, and is especially helpful when design for tooling is reached. A course also in general design for crafts, including lettering, is invaluable.

This book is written primarily with the teaching of bookbinding in schools always in mind, and many of the processes have been modified slightly to fit the needs and ability of children, but without sacrificing the essential methods of the practised craftsman. Wherever possible the orthodox method is described

15

alongside its modification. These deviations have grown out of long experience in the teaching of senior boys and adult students, and the ideas so obtained have proved their value by the results achieved under practical working conditions. A word remains to be said concerning the diagrams in this book. I have adopted the method of placing all such drawings in the text as near to the matter referred to as possible. This plan proves to be far more convenient for the reader in every way. Until the necessary experience has been gained, the student will find invaluable help and guidance from a table of styles and processes which has been placed at the end of the book.

Every teacher of bookbinding should endeavour, as far as lies within his power, to become a master-craftsman himself. By being a practising binder of books, he will acquire a sensitive appreciation of the difficulties experienced by his pupils, and to him will be opened out a world of experiment, research, and joy in achievement that is in itself a full reward for the effort entailed.

I cannot bring this foreword to a close without acknowledging the debt I owe to the many friends who have encouraged me by their appreciation during the last twenty years; to all the students I have taught for their enthusiasm and fellowship, and for their firm but kindly insistence which gave birth to the idea of this book; an insistence which kept alive the long task of writing it, and convinced me that it might fill a need in the teaching and practice of a fascinating craft.

My thanks are also due to my friend and tutor, Mr. Charles Turner, whose passion for sound and beautiful craftsmanship, together with his great kindness, is ever before me as an example to follow, and a fine tradition to be faithfully handed on. If there be any merit in these pages I gladly and gratefully ascribe it all to his laying of so sound a craft foundation. Finally I am very sensible of much courtesy from the publishers in the production of this work.

LAURENCE TOWN

York, December 1950

FOREWORD TO THE SECOND EDITION

More than twelve years have passed since this book was first issued and the addition of twelve more years of experience in the practice of this beautiful and satisfying craft has only served to further convince me that humility of approach to any creative activity is a necessary factor in the life of any true craftsman. With the growth of knowledge and experience there comes the ever-increasing consciousness that there are still wider fields to investigate and that life is not long enough to reach such an ever-widening horizon. The revision of this book is an effort to bring into its pages something of the experience gained since 1950 and to correct any details which had been overlooked at that time. To claim anything like completeness for this treatise would be gross presumption on my part and a betrayal of the true spirit of craftsmanship. I can only hope that it may serve to help all who desire to find the joy that comes to those who create something of beauty, in these 'mechanized' days, under their own two hands.

I must thank all those who have unconsciously helped me in this work by writing to me, not only from this country but from many parts of the world, giving me suggestions for improvement in the book or asking questions where clarity was not present in the text. I am grateful, for the same reason, to all my past students, who performed a similar service orally in my classes. My thanks also to fellow-members of the Guild of Contemporary Binders, who by their example and common interest have served to spur me on to greater efforts in my own work and to battle more successfully against the narrowing influence of advancing years. To Mr. A. G. Dove, whose friendship, interest and encouragement, through our common love of good craftsmanship, has been an inspiration to me for many years, I express my appreciation and thanks for the preface he has written for this edition. Lastly, I am even more sensible now of the continued help and courtesy of the publishers.

LAURENCE TOWN

Welburn, York 1962

CHAPTER 1

Tools and Materials

This list of tools and equipment should be regarded as a minimum requirement for a class of about fifteen students. If the list can be increased, that is all to the good, and makes for more efficient work, but under the conditions obtaining in many schools it may not even be possible to acquire this modest list. In such a case I have prepared a second list of simple tools with which a reasonable standard of bookbinding may be attained. These tools, together with essential materials, are indicated by asterisks in the following list. Experience has also shown that in far too many cases teachers attempt to do bookbinding with larger classes than the number mentioned above, and again experience proves this to be wasteful of time, materials, and the teacher's energy.

Although this book has been written primarily to assist teaching in schools, I must not forget the many keen students in all walks of life who take up this craft individually. Such students must adapt the following list to their own requirements, e.g. only one cobbler's knife, one backing hammer, one knocking-down iron and so on, through the entire list. When I equipped myself, on first taking up this craft, I bought or made an absolute minimum of equipment, viz. a second-hand press, a home-made cutting press and plough, odd pieces of plywood and old drawing boards for pressing boards, etc. I added to this, or replaced with new equipment, a little at a time, as I could afford it. Once the main equipment is acquired it should, with care, last a lifetime.

*One dozen ordinary cobbler's knives.

*Two backing hammers.

One knocking-down iron.

*A number of old flat-irons, with or without handles.

One standing press with plenty of 'daylight'. 'Daylight' is the distance between the platen and the bed when the press is fully opened.

*One second-hand steel nipping press. These can often be found in offices and banks where they were used for letter-copying. The owners are often very willing to sell them. One with a platen of about 15″ by 10″ is very useful. Second-hand dealers often have them for disposal. New ones, of course, are on sale if funds will allow.

One dozen bright pressing tins. Duraluminium is to be preferred.

*Twenty thick strawboards. These are used for cutting upon when using a knife and straightedge. A whole strawboard cut into four parts, i.e. approximately 15″ by 12″, is a convenient size, and 2 to 3 lb. board gives a convenient thickness.

*A good number of pressing boards. These must be in various sizes, and should be a little larger than the book sizes in common use. Boards measuring 9″ by 6″, 12″ by 8″ and 15½″ by 10½″ are the sizes most commonly used, but larger books must be catered for too. Half-Imperial drawing boards are useful for very large books. If such boards cannot be purchased ready made, then old drawing boards can be sawn up into the sizes needed. These are often full of holes made by drawing pins, but if they are covered with stiff paper or thin strawboard the difficulty is surmounted. Odd pieces of three-ply board make useful pressing boards, provided it is not too thin.

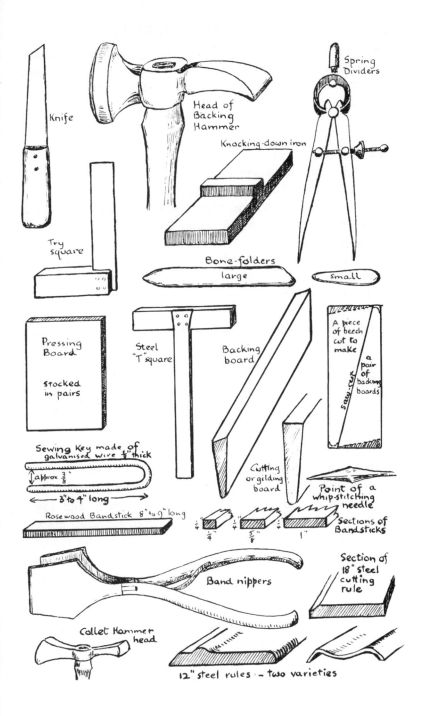

Knife

Head of Backing Hammer

Spring Dividers

Knocking-down iron

Try square

Bone-folders large

small

Pressing Board

stocked in pairs

Steel "T" square

Backing board

A piece of beech cut to make a pair of backing boards

saw-cut

Sewing Key made of galvanised wire ⅛" thick

approx ⅜"

3" to 4" long

Cutting or gilding board

Point of a whip-stitching needle

Rosewood Bandstick 8" to 9" long

¼" ¼" ⅝" 1"

Sections of Bandsticks

Band nippers

Section of 18" steel cutting rule

Collet Hammer head

12" steel rules – two varieties

One board cutter with a knife at least 12″ long, but longer if funds will allow the extra expense. Reference to catalogues of supplying firms will be necessary here.

*One pair of spring dividers. These should be not less than 6″ between the points when fully opened. A pair of 8″ and one of 10″ would be a great asset for larger books.

Six large bone folders.

*Six small bone folders.

*Six try-squares. Steel ones are best, but wooden ones would do. In any case these squares must be tested for truth.

One steel T square. These are expensive and difficult to obtain, and must not be regarded as a necessity. Its size should be about 12″ by 6″.

One cutting press with plough and stand. Two would be a great advantage.

*One worn tenon saw.

*Twelve sewing presses, three of which should be large ones. They can all be made in the handicraft department, and the cross-bar should be made adjustable as shown in Chapter 5.

*Three pairs of backing boards—8″, 10″, and 13″. These can be made from beech.

Three pairs of cutting boards in similar sizes to the backing boards.

Three pairs of gilding boards—6″, 8″, and 10″ long.

*Six pairs of scissors, and three pairs of bookbinder's shears.

*Two glue pots and brushes. These should be at least 1 pint capacity. A waterless electric gluepot is on the market made by Barlow, Whitney & Co., but it is expensive.

*Two paste pots and brushes.

Four finishing presses—see suppliers' catalogues.

*Two dozen bookbinder's needles and one dozen whip-stitching needles.

*Three yards $\frac{1}{8}$″ galvanized wire for making sewing keys.

*One second-hand cutting press of a large size for backing (or a converted vise).

*One awl.

One dozen penknives. These are useful in many ways where the ordinary knife proves too large.

*A bandstick or two, and some small sponges.

*One pair of band-nippers—chromium plated if possible.

*A few rulers, and three or four 18″ steel rules with a bevel.

*One dozen 12″ cutting rules.

*Two pairs of trindles.

*Four paring knives—two ordinary ones, and two of the French variety.

*Four metal adjustable spokeshaves.

*Two paring stones. Old marble table-tops are useful, but litho stones are to be preferred.

*Two oilstones—one coarse and one fine.

One special backing hammer for raised bands. It is similar to a collet hammer. See also p. 145 for a simpler shape.

Two agate burnishers—one tooth and one flat. Bloodstones are better but they are too expensive for school use.

Other items may be needed in the course of the work, but they will be mentioned as they arise.

In addition to the list above, a certain amount of consumable stock will be needed to commence bookbinding. This stock will be renewed from time to time as required, but the following items should prove sufficient for a good beginning.

*Half a ream of 11 lb. large post bank paper. Whatman's 13 lb. writing bank for very good work.

One cwt. of 2 lb. strawboard.

*One cwt. of 1½ lb. strawboard.

*Half-cwt. of 1 lb. strawboard.

Quarter-cwt. of 12 oz. strawboard.

*Quarter-cwt. of 8 oz. strawboard.

(Note on boards: For adult classes, and for the very best types of work, it will be necessary to obtain 'greyboards' and 'millboards'. Both types are sold in similar thicknesses to the strawboards, but are much tougher and more durable. Suggested 'grey boards' are ·116″, ·080/090″, ·064″, ·048″.)

*One ream of coloured cartridge paper or cover paper. The cover paper should not be too heavy for beginners.

*One ream of white cartridge paper (Imperial). For better work I prefer double-faced 'offset' cartridge no heavier than 45 to 60 lb. per ream.

*One roll of unbleached linen tape—stiffened. Let it be 1″ wide so that it can easily be cut to any width required, e.g. $\frac{1}{2}$″, $\frac{1}{4}$″, etc. For the individual binder $\frac{5}{8}$″ stiffened tape will be adequate, if cut down the middle to make $\frac{5}{16}$″ tape.

*Half a pound of unbleached linen thread, 2 cord 16.
 Quarter-pound of unbleached linen thread, 2 cord 25.

*One pound ball of Best Netting Twine, No. 8 cord 4, soft finish, from The British Linen Thread Co., Glasgow.

*A small quantity of Italian line in several thicknesses up to about $\frac{1}{8}$″ for use in the very best work, and for French head-caps.

*One ball of very thin hempen string for general purposes.

*One quire of fine sandpaper, and one each of medium and coarse.

*Six yards of mull.

*Six yards each of binder's cloth in about six colours.

*14 lb. of good cake glue. For good work flexible glue is the best, and is prepared for use in a few minutes. I have found 'Bookbinder's Specially Prepared Flexible Skin Glue' as supplied by Messrs. Laycock's Ltd., of William Street Works, Ashton-under-Lyne, or 'Lentus Grade A, Flexible Glue' from Messrs. Bardens of Bury, Lancs., to be very good.

 One stone of white flour.

 4 lb. of ground alum.

*14 lb. of cold-water paste powder.

 One large double pan for the making of flour paste.

 The question of leather will be discussed at a later stage when describing its use in binding.

Paper Sizes

Before beginning to bind, or re-bind, a book it is necessary to know something about the methods by which the sections have been printed and folded, and the various sizes of papers used. Paper is made in several standard sizes, each of which has its own particular name, e.g. Imperial, Demy, Crown, Royal, etc. Many of these names came originally from the device on each sheet known as the watermark. A study of ancient watermarks is of great interest, but it cannot be discussed fully here. One of the most obvious is that of the fool's cap and bells, and from that device worked into a certain size of paper we have the name 'foolscap', which has now come to indicate a definite size of paper. The most common sizes in printing practice are as follow:

Imperial	$30'' \times 22''$	Medium	$23'' \times 18''$
Foolscap	$17'' \times 13\frac{1}{2}''$	Double F'cap	$27'' \times 17''$
Crown	$20'' \times 15''$	„ Crown	$30'' \times 20''$
Post	$19\frac{1}{4}'' \times 15\frac{1}{2}''$	„ Post	$31\frac{1}{2}'' \times 19\frac{1}{2}''$
Demy	$22\frac{1}{2}'' \times 17\frac{1}{2}''$	„ Pott	$25'' \times 15''$
Royal	$25'' \times 20''$	Super Royal	$27'' \times 21''$

Books in Sheets

When a book has left the hands of the printer it is in the form of SHEETS or QUIRES and looks like the accompanying diagram. Of course the number of pages printed on one sheet varies considerably in modern practice, but for our purpose I have selected one printed '8 up', i.e. 8 pages to a side. The first pile of sheets would contain all the sheets paged 1 to 16, the second pile those paged from 17 to 32, and so on. Each pile is composed of sheets bearing the same SIGNATURE, and these signatures are printed letters—or in some cases numbers—placed in the tail margin of the first page of each section. In the case of the page printed '8 up', such signatures would therefore occur on pages 1, 17, 33, 49, and so on. This is a very important point to bear in mind when pulling an old book to pieces, as will be seen later when the section on 'pulling' is dealt with. The signature letters run from A to Z, but J, V, and W are usually left out. When the alphabet is exhausted, and still there are sheets requiring a signature, the usual method is to begin again with Aa, Bb, Cc, Dd,

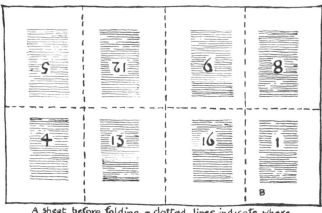

A sheet before folding – dotted lines indicate where folds will occur

etc. if the book is one of several volumes the volume number is placed in front of the signature, e.g. 1A, 1B, etc. Many binders and printers of very cheap modern editions use numbers instead of letters, and care must be taken to avoid confusion with the page numbers. The writer has never seen any explanation of the omission of J, V, and W, but it seems reasonable to conclude that the custom comes down from the early days of printing when the influence of books written in Latin was strong. There was no J or W in the Latin alphabet, and the use of V would be liable to confusion with the Roman numerals then used for pagination.

All plates, maps and the like are placed in a pile by themselves ready for insertion in the appropriate places in the folded sections.

Gathering

In order to make a book, one sheet is taken from each pile of signatures, beginning at sheet A and going through the book sheets until one has been taken from every pile. This is called GATHERING, and, before the advent of modern machine methods, was usually performed by girls sitting at a revolving round table on which the piles of signatures were placed. It might be noted that if the gathering is done beginning at the last section and working back to signature A, time will be saved in the processes immediately following.

Folding

The sheets have now to be FOLDED, and great care ought to be exercised in order to get the margins equal and the lines of printed matter at right angles to the back fold of the sections. This is called 'getting a correct REGISTER', and no bound book can ever be good to look at unless this register is correct.

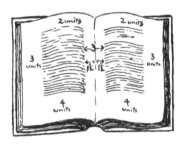

A word might be said here on the subject of margins. The ideal marginal proportions for a well-printed book are indicated in the diagram. Unfortunately many printers have often sacrificed the beauty of the margins at the altar of paper costs, and after the binder has cut the edges the appearance becomes even worse. The old-time printers nearly always made beautiful margins. The proportions need not conform exactly to those shown. So long as the head margin is the least, and the tail margins the greatest, with the dimensions of the side margins lying between, then a satisfactory appearance will be achieved.

An illustration of the terms used in describing the parts of a book will be of use here. These terms should be memorized and used freely while binding is in progress. For instance, it is a common mistake to speak of the 'sides' of a book as the 'backs'. A glance at the diagram will show where this is in error.

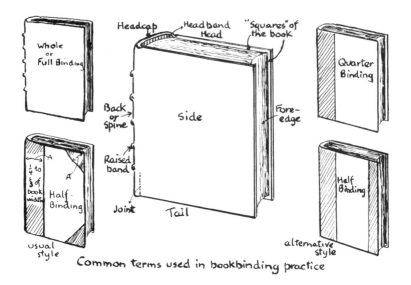

Common terms used in bookbinding practice

In order to fold a sheet correctly, it is placed on the table so that the SIGNATURE is facing downwards. The signature will be in the bottom left-hand corner, and can be seen by lifting that particular corner. The sheet is then folded RIGHT to LEFT, folded again HEAD to TAIL (i.e. top to base), and again RIGHT to LEFT, and so on. The example given is an OCTAVO folding, but the order is the same for the other foldings. It is useful to remember that the page containing the signature never moves from its original position on the bench during the whole of the folding. As the sheets are folded they should be held up to the light in order to check the register of the printing. This operation is called 'SHINING' them.

When a sheet has been folded it is then called a SECTION or QUIRE, and the book is built up from a number of such sections. Book sizes depend on the size of the sheets used by the printer, and the number of foldings of each sheet. The names given to the sizes of books indicate two things. One is the size of the sheet before folding, and the other the number of foldings required to make the book section.

An Octavo folding of a printed sheet.

FOLIO means 1 folding or 2 leaves or 4 pages—written Fo.

QUARTO means 2 foldings or 4 leaves or 8 pages—written 4to.

OCTAVO means 3 foldings or 8 leaves or 16 pages—written 8vo.

SIXTEENMO means 4 foldings or 16 leaves or 32 pages—written 16mo.

DUODECIMO—12mo—is a special folding, and needs further explanation. A sheet is printed 12 up on each side, and then the sheet is cut before folding so that 8 of the pages are on one piece and 4 on the other. The one with 8 up is then folded 8vo, and the other 4to. One is then inserted within the other to make up a complete section. The inserted one is provided with a SUB-SIGNATURE which takes various forms. The most usual appear to be either a small star with the appropriate letter, or a number following the letter, e.g. B* or B1. This must be specially noted when pulling a book.

The above terms are used in conjunction with the sizes of paper to give the book size. For example, if one speaks of a CROWN 8vo book it means that the printing has been done on a crown sheet (20″ by 15″), and then folded three times. This gives a measurement of 7½″ by 5″ for the book.

The text proper usually begins at section B. The section whose signature is A (seldom printed), usually contains all the preliminary matter, and is generally arranged in the following order:

> Half title
> Title
> Dedication

Preface
Contents
Lists of illustrations, etc.

The subject of plates and illustrations and their insertion in the sections will be dealt with under the section on guarding. All new books must be pressed after folding, but this will be described under the heading 'Pressing', as this also applies to books which are to be re-bound.

Collating a Book

The collating of a book is really the checking of all the sections to make sure they are in the proper order. To collate the pages about 50 are picked up in the left hand and fanned out a little at the head. It is then an easy matter to check off the page numbers, looking only at the odd numbers. To check the signatures of the sections fan the sections out at the tail, and run

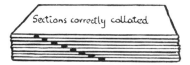

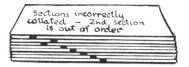

through them quickly. In modern editions a much quicker method has been adopted for section checking. When the sheets are printed a small black square is printed at the same time so that when the sheet is folded this mark will appear on the back of the section. By moving the position of the mark for each section a line of 'steps' will appear on the back of the collated book. If a section is out of place the continuous line is broken and the error is easily seen. Very valuable books must be collated with great care—even page by page rather than risk any mistake.

CHAPTER 2

First Stages in Re-binding

Pulling a Book

In re-binding a book the first process is 'PULLING'. This means taking the book to pieces, section by section. It is best to collate the book before pulling to make sure it is complete. With a sharp knife cut off the old covers down each joint, and the case should come clean away from the book. If the book has not been previously 'case-bound' rather more care will have to be taken. Throw back the boards, and cut the bands upon which the sewing has been done. The boards will then be detached from the book. A golden rule to remember in pulling is to do as little damage to the backs of the sections as possible.

Find the middle of the first section, and carefully cut the sewing thread seen down the fold. Go on turning the pages until the signature of the next section is seen. From the information already given on signatures, it should be clear that the beginning of the next section has been reached. Hold the book firmly on the bench with the right hand, and ease off the first section gently with the left. A thin folder inserted between the sections is often helpful in difficult cases. Remove all the sections in this way, and keep them in the right order by turning each one face down in a pile as they are detached. Break down the old glue and muslin with the left thumb as the sections are taken off. This helps the removal of the sections.

Great care must be observed in making sure that all the pieces of old glue and thread are removed from the backs of the sections, and none of this discarded material should be allowed to become lodged between the pages or the sections. Much damage would result when the book was pressed. All plates, maps, or single leaves which have been tipped into the book with paste must be removed carefully, and replaced loose. If they are left projecting a little at the head they will not be overlooked when the time comes to guard them back into the sections.

If an old leather binding is being dealt with, it may be that the leather is difficult to remove from the back. The book must be placed in a finishing press, and the whole of the back covered with thin paste, and allowed to stand until the leather has been soaked by the paste. Ten to fifteen minutes should be adequate, and it will then be possible to remove the leather. In the case of books—usually case-bindings—where the glue on the backs of the sections proves difficult to remove, i.e. if it is impossible to take the sections apart without considerable damage, then cover the spine with paste and allow to soak. Scrape off the surplus paste and pull the book immediately. In the cases outlined, it is very important that the pulling should be done while the book is damp, for if it is allowed to dry again it will be found that the glue has set even harder than before, and pulling would be all the more difficult. The greatest care must be exercised when pulling books dampened in this way as the backs of the sections become very weak when they are wet. No soaking of the above nature should be done at all if it can be avoided.

Books are often issued in parts, and such issues are frequently bound together by wire stitches or staples. For pulling, a knife and a pair of pincers are needed. The lifting of the staples should be done with great care, as the leaves can be badly damaged in the process. When the two ends of the wire have been lifted by the knife, they should be nipped off close to the book with the pincers, and a section or two detached. As the sections are taken off it is best to nip off more of the wire. Another method is used whereby the ends are first lifted, and then the whole of the staple withdrawn from the other side with the pincers. I prefer the first method, especially in the case of pupils in school. One other point arises with such books. It is usual to find that the sections have been stapled in such a way that the two ends of the wire are turned over at the end of the book, and not at the first section. This means that pulling begins with the last section.

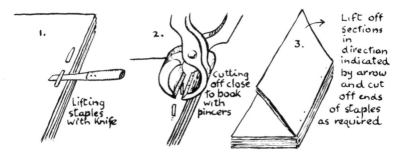

If the old glue on the backs of the sections cannot be removed by using the finger and thumb, lay the section down with its back along the edge of the bench. Then take a very sharp knife, and work it along the section behind the pieces of glue, keeping it as flat as possible on the paper. With care it will be possible to avoid cutting the paper.

The old endpapers need not be removed while pulling is in progress. They can be retained until the new endpapers are made as they help to keep the first and last sections clean.

If a valuable book has been pulled, and it is discovered that the sections have been badly folded so that the register is not correct, they must be re-folded, and given a new crease with a folder. In such books the edges are often left uncut, and the

C   33

leaves will need trimming, but details of this operation will be given in the section on gilding edges untrimmed.

Removing the Old Groove

The majority of books to be re-bound will have been given a groove or 'joint', that is to say they will have been backed. This groove must now be removed. A knocking-down iron is placed in the lying press, and covered with a piece of clean waste

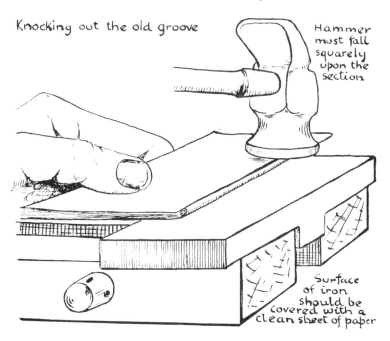

Knocking out the old groove

Hammer must fall squarely upon the section

Surface of iron should be covered with a clean sheet of paper

paper. This paper is there to keep the sections clean. The latter are now taken one at a time, and beaten upon the iron with a backing hammer all down the length of the groove on both sides. This should flatten out the old groove. The tapping must be done gently and, above all, the hammer face must fall squarely upon the groove. Careless hammering will cut the paper, and probably render the book useless. The face of the hammer must be thoroughly cleaned with emery paper before commencing the work. In the case of new books coming straight from the printer

in quires, or books which have never been backed, this operation is not necessary. It is possible in schools to carry out this
beating without a proper knocking-down iron. Old flat-irons
answer the purpose, and if the iron is placed between the knees
in the manner used by cobblers when beating leather, the noise
of the hammering is very much reduced.

Dry Cleaning

The book sections must now be examined for possible washing, mending, or guarding. Many marks found on books will
respond to treatment by dry cleaning, and these methods can be
considered first.

Hard and soft rubbers, paper cleaner, very fine sandpaper,
cuttlefish bone, ether, petrol, and similar materials are the
things needed for dry-cleaning soiled books. Many marks will be
removed with hard or soft rubber, and inkstains can be treated
carefully with the bone, provided they are only surface stains.
Where grease marks occur the sheet must be placed on a sheet of
clean blotting paper, and the marks washed with ether, petrol, or
benzine. The liquid should be poured in a small circle round the
spot, gradually lessening the circle until the mark is covered. A
heavy grease stain must be placed between two sheets of clean
blotting paper, and heat applied with a hot iron. The blotting
should absorb most of the grease, and the spot can then be
finished off by the ether method.

Before going on to describe the wet methods it will be necessary to say something about the sizing of paper because sheets
which have to be washed must be re-sized.

Sizing Paper

When book paper becomes soft and woolly it is a sign that it
has lost most of the original size, and where books are valuable
it will be necessary to re-size the pages. Prepare the size by
dissolving 1 ounce of isinglass or very good gelatine in 1 quart
of water. When warm, the size should be clear. It is now placed
in a size bath, and the diagram will give an idea of what is
needed. Bring up the temperature gradually to 120° Fahrenheit,

and at this heat it is ready for use, and during the whole of the process this temperature must be maintained. If the size does not become clear when warmed, it should be put through a piece of muslin to strain it.

Size Bath – shewing method of heating and maintaining temperature

The sheets to be sized must now be passed rapidly through the bath, and placed between clean sheets of blotting paper immediately they leave the bath. This only applies when a few sheets have to be done. If the whole of the book is going to be re-sized the sheets must be passed quickly through the bath, and placed in a pile. A sheet of clean blotting paper is placed at each end of the pile, and the whole placed between two pressing boards. Now place in a lying press, and have a dish under the press to catch the superfluous size. Tighten the press, and whilst the size is running from the sheets cover a large bench with clean paper, and spread out the sheets to dry. When they are sufficiently firm to handle with safety, hang them over clean strings to dry out. Then they must be re-folded into their appropriate sections and pressed well. A long light pressure is better than a quick heavy one. Mending and guarding will then follow in the usual way. If good gelatine be scalded with boiling water it should not give off any odour. If it does so, then it is not the best quality, and is not fit for the best work.

Washing

Many stains can be removed by merely passing the sheets through the size bath. Others will often yield to washing in hot water to which has been added a little alum. Again, some stains can be removed by brushing carefully with a soft brush dipped into a solution of good soap and water. Such sheets should be washed in plenty of clean warm water, and then re-sized. Ink and similar stains require rather more drastic treatment. There are two methods in common use, and the first one is the simpler.

A bath is prepared consisting of weak chlorine water, and through this the sheets are passed. They are then transferred to a second bath containing water to which has been added a little hydrochloric acid. Then they are dried and re-sized.

In the second method a permanganate bath is used. One ounce of permanganate of potash is dissolved in one quart of water. The water should be slightly warmed for this purpose. When the sheets are placed in this solution they will turn a dark brown colour, and they should remain in the bath for an hour. Then follows a thorough washing in running water until all trace of the purple stain disappears from the water as it runs away. The sheets are now transferred to another bath containing sulphurous acid and water in the proportion of one ounce of acid to one pint of water. Leave the sheets in this bath until they are white. If some stains still persist, wash in clean water and repeat the whole process, leaving the sheets for a longer period in the permanganate bath. When the stains have gone, wash the sheets in running water for an hour or two, dry between sheets of blotting paper by squeezing and hanging on lines, and then re-size them. Very often only a few sheets will have to be cleaned in this way, and it will be realized that the bleaching will cause these sheets to become whiter than the remaining pages of the book. It will be necessary in such a case to bring them back to the colour of the other sheets. This is done by adding the stain to the size when re-sizing. A very weak solution of permanganate will stain most papers to the correct colour. Tea, coffee, or liquorice will also answer quite well. There is some difficulty in getting the correct tone to match the uncleaned sheets, but this can be overcome by testing the stained size on a piece of absorbent paper and drying it quickly. If the colour is too strong water must be added.

If the sheets suffer from water stains and general dirt, the following method may be employed. After placing in a dish, sprinkle over them some soap flakes. Pour boiling water over the sheets, and agitate the solution in the manner adopted by photographers when developing plates. Gently brush the leaves with a soft brush whilst they are in the liquid, and if the dirt does not move readily add a little chlorine water. Take out the sheets, dry in the usual way and re-size them. This size should be made by pouring one pint of boiling water on to one ounce of isinglass and then adding a pinch of alum.

Sometimes old books show brownish spots on the leaves. These are called FOXMARKS, and they must be bleached out by placing the sheets in warm water and adding chlorine a little at a time. They must then be well washed in running water, dried and re-sized.

On occasion it may be necessary to restore faded writing. If the sheets are steeped in a solution of tannic acid the writing will be restored. Washing, drying, and re-sizing then follow in the usual way. If writing has been effaced by the chlorine method, it must be washed over with a weak solution of sulphide of ammonium.

Mending

Making repairs to torn or defective pages calls for care, time, and patience, and the damage falls roughly into two kinds, i.e. torn pages, and defective pages. The writer has been in the habit of keeping the materials and tools needed for this work in a drawer away from the general stock. A very sharp knife and a small piece of plate glass are essential. Japanese tissue paper, sulphite paper, and a collection of pieces of different kinds of paper, together with a small water-colour brush, complete the collection. The retention of the old endpapers from books that have come for re-binding is a useful habit to help in matching missing pieces of leaves. After several years of such collecting one drawer is by no means enough to house these papers, and an upright filing system is useful for classifying the different kinds and colours of such old papers. When repairing very good books use as white a paste as possible. Rice flour is one of the best.

Consider first the ordinary tear. It will be observed that paper usually tears in such a way as to give two frayed edges which overlap each other. Put a piece of tissue paper down on the plate glass, and over it place the torn portion of the page. Carefully paste the torn edges with the small brush, and lay down over the tear another piece of tissue paper. Turn all over carefully on the glass, and remove the first piece of tissue. Again paste along the torn edges, and replace the tissue, and rub down very gently with the finger. It must now be set aside until it is completely dry, when the superfluous tissue paper can be torn away and thus leave a good join which is practically invisible. A slight touch with very fine sandpaper or cuttle-fish bone will complete the operation.

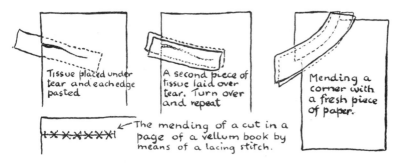

Tissue placed under tear and each edge pasted

A second piece of tissue laid over tear. Turn over and repeat

Mending a corner with a fresh piece of paper.

The mending of a cut in a page of a vellum book by means of a lacing stitch.

In the case of a page, the corner of which is missing, a piece of paper must be found to match the book-paper as nearly as possible. This must be placed underneath the torn edge of the leaf, and a folder point run carefully along to mark it on the new piece of paper. Carefully tear the latter about $\frac{1}{8}''$ away from the line. This should give a thin frayed edge, but it will be improved if it is pared down very slightly with a very sharp knife on the glass plate. It only remains now to treat the torn corner and the new pared piece of paper in the manner described above for a simple tear. The diagram will make the matter clear.

If a sheet of vellum has been cut, the best way to mend it is to use the lacing stitch as shown in the sketch. A very fine silk must be used to do this.

Sometimes old books have defects in the way of small holes made in the pages by bookworms. If they have to be made good, mix up a little clean white blotting paper with size until a pulp is obtained, and fill the holes with this mixture. Press it into the holes with a bone-folder. When dry it can be smoothed off with very fine sandpaper. If a page is very badly damaged it is often possible to try and obtain a second copy, and extract whole pages from it to insert in the book in process of being repaired. I mention this as sometimes I have had to repair large pulpit bibles, and a copy which has been discarded as beyond repair is often useful in the way of providing such pages.

Guarding

All sections of a book which are found to be damaged by pulling, and all loose pages and plates, must now be guarded. This means that the leaves damaged down the back fold must be strengthened with strips of paper called guards. The paper must be strong and thin, and for the best work Whatman's Bank Paper is used, but this is far too expensive for ordinary purposes, particularly in school. A good general-purpose paper is 11 lb. Large Post Bank. This indicates that the paper is large post in size and that a ream weighs 11 lb.

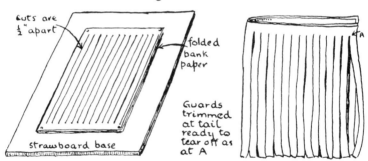

text on diagram:
cuts are ½" apart
folded bank paper
strawboard base
Guards trimmed at tail ready to tear off as at A
A

There are two methods of cutting the guards. Take one or two sheets of paper and fold them together until a size is obtained a little longer than the book from head to tail. Mark it across the top and bottom with the divider points so that the marks thus made are ½" apart. Place on the board cutter, and slice off the strips according to the marks made. These ½" strips are the guards. I have known students mark out the guards with pencilled lines. This must be avoided at all costs.

The alternative method is shown in the diagrams. I should use

40

the first method when it is known that a large number of guards are required to be used on an immediate piece of work. But it is not often that the guards cut are all used at once, and therefore the second method is to be preferred in that they are kept tidy and straight ready for the next book to be guarded. Fold the paper as before, and pin it down by the corners upon a sheet of strawboard and mark out at the head and tail in half-inches as in method 1. Using a steel straight-edge, and a very sharp knife, cut the strips so that a little margin at the head and tail is left uncut. Now cut off the tail margin so that the strips are only attached to each other at the head. They can then be torn off as required, leaving the remainder tidy. It is often useful to cut a number of guards in this way as it proves more economical in paper, and the process need not be repeated for each book as it is pulled. It is a good plan in schools to store such cut sheets in a large case cover so that they are kept flat. Guarding paper should be as near the colour of the pages as is possible, and it is sometimes necessary to stain the paper to the required shade. The method of staining has already been noted under 'Washing and Sizing'. In very large books the width of the guard can be increased up to $\frac{3}{4}''$, but for most ordinary work $\frac{1}{2}''$ should not be exceeded.

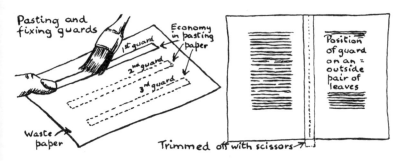

Some of the points arising when guarding is being done may be summarized in the following way:

1. Do not stretch the guards whilst pasting, or when placing them on the leaves. It will cause 'crinkling' of the pages due to contraction of the guard when drying.

2. Be very careful to see that the guard is pasted all over.

FIRST STAGES IN RE-BINDING

It is very troublesome to find guards which have not adhered properly, and a partially loose leaf will spoil the whole of the work when bound.

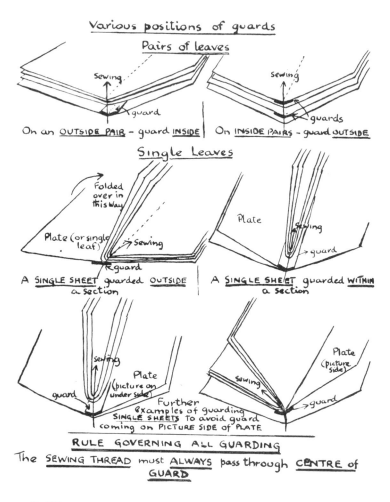

Various positions of guards

Pairs of leaves

sewing — guard

On an OUTSIDE PAIR – guard INSIDE

sewing — guards

On INSIDE PAIRS – guard OUTSIDE

Single Leaves

Folded over in this way

Plate (or single leaf) — Sewing — guard

A SINGLE SHEET guarded OUTSIDE a section

Plate — sewing — guard

A SINGLE SHEET guarded WITHIN a section

sewing — Plate (picture on under side) — guard

Plate (picture side) — sewing — guard

Further Examples of guarding SINGLE SHEETS To avoid guard coming on PICTURE SIDE of PLATE

RULE GOVERNING ALL GUARDING

The SEWING THREAD must ALWAYS pass through CENTRE of GUARD

3. The OUTSIDE PAIR of leaves in a section is guarded INSIDE.

4. The INSIDE PAIRS of leaves are guarded OUTSIDE.

5. SINGLE LEAVES outside a section must be guarded on the outside.

6. SINGLE LEAVES occurring inside a section must be guarded in such a way that the sewing will always pass through the middle of the guard. Plates usually come under this rule.

Rule 6 is a very good general rule to remember for all guarding. Guarding is of little use unless the actual sewing thread passes through the centre. If this rule is borne in mind, any individual problems can be easily solved. When plates are being guarded every endeavour should be made to have the guard on the back of the plate, but this is not always possible. No book should be guarded any more than is absolutely necessary, as this causes too much 'swell' in the back of the book. Some amount of 'swell' is necessary in binding a book, but when it is overdone nothing but trouble arises in the subsequent operations, and the result is most unsatisfactory. Guarding in the wrong way and guarding too many sections are very common faults amongst students, and such points need careful watching on the part of the teacher.

Sometimes one finds a section composed of only two leaves, i.e. four printed pages. These are called 'quarter sections' and they should ALWAYS be guarded as for an outside pair of leaves so as to give added strength to the back fold.

Students often ask why, in guarding PAIRS OF LEAVES, the OUTER PAIR is guarded INSIDE, while the INNER PAIRS are guarded OUTSIDE. The outer pair could be guarded outside and still obey the rule, but in doing so a new clean spine will be given to the section. If it is guarded inside, the roughness of the fold of the section, due to defects and its previous gluing, will give an added 'key' when re-gluing after sewing. In the case of the inner pairs, it will be found that guards placed on the outside are less obtrusive when the book is bound. In practice such guarding of the inner pairs is not often necessary, damage usually being confined to the outer pairs. When deciding whether a guard is necessary, hold the pairs of leaves up to the light and any 'splits' or very weak places in the fold of the leaves will readily be seen. If such are present, a guard is needed, but ignore the presence of the 'stitch-holes' caused by the previous sewing. These will be filled by the gluing-up after sewing.

The guarded work must not be allowed to dry out completely before being refolded and replaced in the sections. My own method is to place the guard in position and then refold the section immediately, but great care must be exercised in seeing that no paste is squeezed out from the guard. This will be avoided if, when pasting a guard, the paste is spread evenly but thinly, i.e. just sufficient to make the guard adhere and no more.

The Guarding of Plates

Some little guidance is needed for the guarding of plates into a book. Here is a summary of the chief points arising.

(*a*) If there are many plates to guard it will be wise to pare the back edges on a sheet of plate glass with a very sharp knife. This will reduce the swelling caused by the thickness of the guards. Time will be saved where a number of plates are to be guarded by pasting a few at a time together. This is made clear in the diagram. $\frac{1}{8}''$ of each plate should be showing and the pasting done in the direction shown. The remaining half of the guard must be bent round the back of the section, or the pair of leaves to which it belongs, and the sewing will complete the work of binding the plates into the book.

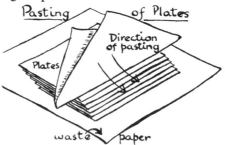

(*b*) A somewhat different method is employed in the case of thick plates. They require a hinge at the back. With a very sharp knife cut off $\frac{1}{4}''$ from the back edge, and cut also a wide guard of fine linen. Paste the plate and the $\frac{1}{4}''$ piece and place down on the guard as shown. The amount of space left between the strip and the plate should be equal to the thickness of the plate.

(*c*) Plates made of card need two linen guards, one on the front and one on the back.

(*d*) If a book is made entirely of plates a decision must be made as to how many plates are going to be taken to make up each section. This also applies to single sheets of printed matter. Each section must be arranged in the appropriate pairs of leaves and guarded in the usual way, but where the leaves are thick hinge them as in (*b*) above. In dealing with books of single leaves a little thought must be given to the nature and purpose of the

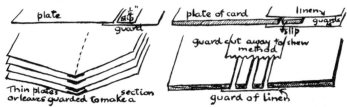

book. Guarding it may cause far too much swell in the back, and it may be better done by overcasting. This method will be described in the chapter on sewing.

The commercial method of tipping leaves into a book with paste is to be avoided. It is a method which can only be regarded by the craftsman as a temporary measure until a book is given a good binding. When a commercially bound book is pulled such tipped-in leaves should be carefully detached and then properly guarded back again.

Pressing must follow when the guards are almost dry, in order to reduce the swelling as much as possible, but this will be found in the section on pressing.

Throwing out Maps and Diagrams

Maps and diagrams are often referred to in the text of a book, and it is very convenient for the reader if these are 'thrown out'. This means that it is possible to bind the map into the book so that it can be opened out beyond the pages, and remain in constant view whilst the reading proceeds. The guard to which the diagram is attached must be as wide as the pages of the book, and when this is sewn in, the joint where the map is folded will then be somewhat inside the fore-edge. This will prevent the cutting of the map when the edge is trimmed. Usually such maps or diagrams are placed at the end of the book, as shown in the diagram.

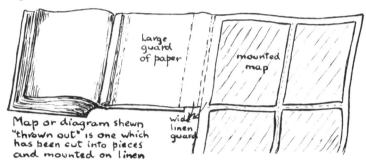

Large guard of paper

mounted map

Map or diagram shewn "thrown out" is one which has been cut into pieces and mounted on linen

wide linen guard

When the map is closed its total thickness must be noted, and sufficient ordinary folded guards placed inside each other to level up the thickness at the back of the book. If this is not properly done the book will not close satisfactorily. If the map or diagram is a large one with several folds it will be necessary to mount it on fine linen—generally called 'jaconet'. A piece large enough for the whole map is taken and damped slightly all over, and then placed on a flat table and pinned down all round the edges. Paste the map with thin paste, lay it on the linen and rub it well down under clean paper. Careless pasting will show all the brush marks through the linen when dry. If heavy pressure on the paste brush is used at first in order to spread the paste evenly, and then the pressure gradually lessened until the brush is merely running over the paper very lightly, the pasting should be evenly done. When dry, the map is folded and guarded to the whole page guard.

Guards are fastened by the sewing

Folded map or diagram

Sufficient guards are inserted to equal the thickness of the folded diagram.

A map or diagram made of thicker paper should be cut up into pieces a little less than the book size. These pieces are then pasted to the linen, leaving a small space between each piece and the next to allow for folding easily. It is important when pasting these pieces to spend approximately the same time on each. This will avoid uneven stretching of the pieces which makes it difficult to get the 'joints' straight all over the map.

It is often possible to attach the map to its wide guard AFTER the edges of the book have been cut and this would be very desirable indeed. If a map or diagram is folded in the book before cutting the edges, then there is a grave danger of pages being torn while ploughing. The reason will become obvious when it is realized that the folded map is less than the page size and therefore the edges of the pages nearest and beyond the map will not receive the pressure, necessary for a clean cut, from the jaws of the cutting press. In such a case it would be wise, before finally tightening the press, to insert narrow strips of card, such as manilla board, down to the edge of the map and of the same thickness as its folds. They can protrude a little above the level of the pages and be cut as the edge is trimmed, removing them of course after the cutting is done.

Inlaying

Occasionally it is necessary to place into a larger book a leaf or a plate which is smaller. A piece of paper is obtained to match the pages of the book, and trimmed to the size of the pages. The smaller sheet is then laid upon the larger one in such a position as will satisfy good taste. Mark the corners of the smaller sheet with a bone folder and remove it. Now mark again about $\frac{1}{8}''$ inside the first marks, and cut out the rectangle formed by these latter points. Turn the plate over on a sheet of glass, and very carefully pare the edges all round with a very sharp knife. Do the same with the upper edges of the 'frame'. Both pared edges should then be pasted and the leaf to be inlaid placed in position on the first folder marks. Rub gently down under a sheet of clean paper, and put under light pressure until dry. The new page is then guarded into the book in the usual way.

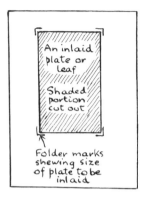

An inlaid plate or leaf

Shaded portion cut out

Folder marks shewing size of plate to be inlaid

The Straightening out of Vellum Leaves

In dealing with the general preparation of a book for sewing it is convenient to add here a few lines on the treatment of vellum leaves that have become 'cockled'. Vellum as a writing material is ideal, but it has one great fault. It is apt to cockle if exposed to dampness, and much difficulty is met with in putting it right again. The method is detailed under the following paragraphs:

(*a*) Take the book to pieces, and clean out the folds.

(*b*) Take a sufficient number of sheets of clean white paper, and double the number of sheets of clean blotting paper. The number of sheets of blotting paper required will be the same as the number of vellum sheets. Wet all the sheets of paper with a sponge and place a sheet of blotting on the bench. On this place a wet sheet of paper, then two pieces of blotting, another wetted paper, and so on until the whole of the blotting and wetted papers have been interleaved. Place the whole pile between clean pressing boards, and leave in a press for an hour or two. On removing from the press it will be found that the blotting paper is slightly but evenly dampened.

(*c*) On each of the vellum sheets place a piece of damp blotting paper so as to make a pile of vellum and blotting all interleaved. Put between boards and leave a light weight on top for an hour or two. This will dampen and soften the vellum, and in

48

this state the whole pile may be put into a press and left over-night.

(*d*) Next day all the pieces of blotting must be replaced by dry ones, and this process must be repeated at intervals of a day or two until the vellum is perfectly dry. No hard and fast rule can be laid down as to the time required to complete the work. Atmospheric conditions and the thickness of the vellum are two main factors, and experience will show that the time required may be anything from one to six weeks.

(*e*) It is important that any illuminated capitals, miniatures, and other forms of painted decoration found on the pages be carefully covered with waxed paper or cellophane to prevent damage from the damp blotting paper. The pressure on the vellum must never be great—just enough to keep the sheets flat.

More elaborate methods involving the use of weights to 'pull' the vellum are clearly described by Douglas Cockerell in *Bookbinding and the Care of Books*.

Pressing

Before a book comes to be sewn it is necessary to press the sections to make it 'solid'. The meaning of this term will be fully appreciated by anyone who handles a book before and after pressing. Two pressing boards a little larger than the book, several pressing tins, and some sheets of clean paper will be required. Duraluminium sheets, being rustless, are very useful for many purposes, but they are rather thin for use as pressing tins. The use of two together would help, but stouter tin plates would serve better, provided they are kept free from rust.

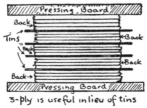

3-ply is useful in lieu of tins

Place one of the pressing boards on the bench, and pick up the first three or four sections. Knock them up square at the head and back, and place in the centre of the board. Over these place a tin round which has been folded a piece of the clean paper. Take the next few sections, knock them up and place in the middle of the tin, but this time the opposite way round, i.e. the backs of the sections facing in the opposite direction from the first lot.

The process is repeated until all the sections have been arranged in the above way, and the second pressing board placed on top. The whole must now be put carefully in the press so that the centre of the pile is directly under the centre screw of the press. This is simply achieved by looking both at the front and

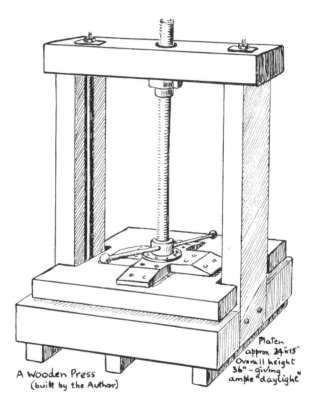

A Wooden Press
(built by the Author)

Platen
approx. 24"x15"
Overall height
36" - giving
ample "daylight"

the side of the press. A fairly heavy pressure must be applied, and the sections left for 24 hours. The reason for arranging the groups of sections first one way and then the other is to keep the whole pile perfectly level.

It must be remembered that before any pressing takes place all guarding, interleaving, and repairing must be thoroughly dry. When plates are present it may be necessary to cover them with tissue paper—especially if they are newly printed. Folded plates should have tins placed on either side to prevent an impression of the folds being transferred to the pages next to them.

Great difficulty is met with in schools in this important business of pressing, usually owing to lack of proper presses. The common type of 'nipping press' seldom has enough 'day-light' between the platen and the bed, and is constantly in use for other purposes. If a handicraft department is available it is possible to have one made like that in the diagram, but it would be necessary to obtain the centre screw and its base fitting from an engineer. If a cutting press is worn out as far as the cutting of books is concerned, it may well be that one of its large wooden screws is sufficiently good to be used as the centre screw for a standing press.

Pressing is an important operation, and when it is well done many difficulties are avoided in the processes which follow. It is often indifferently done in schools, with disastrous results when the sewing, rounding, and backing come to be done. When young pupils 'pull' a book their inexperience causes rather more work in 'guarding' and efficient pressing relieves this difficulty to a moderate extent.

CHAPTER 3

Endpapers

In the past great difficulty was experienced in preventing the first and last sections of a book from 'dragging away' as a result of constant use. This was one reason for the introduction of endpapers. Various methods were tried in attaching endpapers to the book, but the one which has been most successful in the light of long experience is the one in which the endpapers are sewn on. It should be obvious that any endpaper, which is merely pasted on after the book has been sewn, is useless when a good and lasting binding is contemplated. In this class stand the cheap publishers' bindings of today, but such bindings are not intended to be permanent, and therefore such a temporary end-paper is quite legitimate. If these bindings come to be put into more permanent form then fresh endpapers must be made and sewn in. In constructing an endpaper the second condition of sound binding must be satisfied in that it must allow the book to open easily. The modern practice of overcasting the first and last sections is not satisfactory as it merely transfers the strain of opening to the next section, and causes the book to open stiffly. This practice seems to imply an admission that the endpapers will not bear any wear and tear. In addition to giving strength and protection to the book, endpapers should show good taste, and add neatness and beauty to the binding.

ENDPAPERS

The paper used should be tough and durable, and a cartridge paper between 40 and 50 lb. to the ream gives about the right thickness. 'Offset cartridge' used in lithography is a most satisfying paper to have, as it is usually 'double-faced', i.e. both sides are alike in appearance and texture. A bone folder must always be at hand in the construction of endpapers in order that good sharp creases may be the rule.

The 'W' or 'Zig-zag' Endpaper for books bound 'Out-of-boards'

This is one of the most useful and efficient endpapers used in letterpress binding, and fulfils all the conditions outlined above. The method of construction is as follows:

Cut out two coloured sheets and two white ones, and fold them neatly in such a manner that when folded they are a little larger than the book. Crease the folds well with a folder. Now take the folded sheets and with a pair of dividers mark a point at each end ⅛" away from the fold (henceforward known as the back of the sheet). On the WHITE SHEETS ONLY place a straight-edge along the marked points, and run a thin folder lightly down the paper so that a crease is made passing through the points. Turn the two sheets over and repeat on the other side.

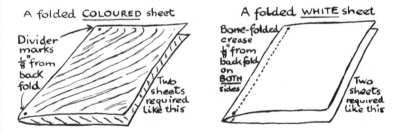

A folded COLOURED sheet — Divider marks ⅛" from back fold — Two sheets required like this

A folded WHITE sheet — Bone-folded crease ⅛" from back fold on BOTH sides — Two sheets required like this

Before proceeding any further obtain four slips of clean white bank paper, one to two inches wide, and a little longer than the endpapers, and place them in a handy position on the bench. If a box is kept containing all waste slips of clean bank paper which accumulate during the binding of books, it will be a useful collection from which such slips can be drawn. Alongside the four slips place three pressing boards, and it is essential that

53

these things should be ready in this way before any pasting is attempted.

Now place the two WHITE sheets upon a sheet of clean waste, in such a manner that the topmost sheet is lying with its back fold along the creased line of the lower one. Lay down over the upper sheet another piece of clean waste folded to give a straight edge so that the fold runs along the crease of the upper sheet. Paste the two portions of the endpapers left exposed, being exceedingly careful to move the paste-brush in an outward direction, and holding all down firmly with the left hand. It is necessary to say here that the pasting must be thoroughly done. Take away the top sheet of waste paper, and gently lift both endpapers to remove the lower pasted waste. Dispose of these at once to avoid any accidents which may happen in the way of getting paste on a clean endpaper.

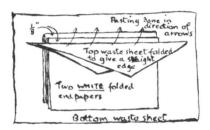

Take one of the pressing boards and on it place one of the clean slips. Over this put one of the COLOURED sheets with its back fold midway along the slip, and with the divider marks upward.

Place one of the pasted white sheets—the pasted side facing downwards—along the divider marks on the coloured sheet and run the finger lightly along the back fold. Over the whole gently place another clean slip and then another pressing board. Upon this board repeat the whole process for the remaining two folded sheets, and thus find the pasted endpapers completely enclosed between the three pressing boards. These can now be carried carefully to the press and allowed to remain under a moderate pressure for no more than half a minute. On removal from the

54

press the slips are stripped off and the endpapers laid out on the bench to dry.

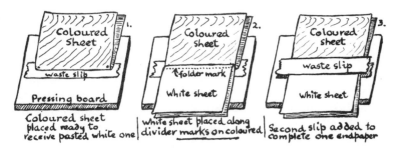

Coloured sheet placed ready to receive pasted white one | White sheet placed along divider marks on coloured | Second slip added to complete one endpaper

The writer has evolved the above method to reduce the risks of error in the case of beginners, but it is essential that in following such a method the paste on the white sheets should be thoroughly brushed out. The slips of paper will take any small amount of paste which may be squeezed out in the pressing, and it will be found that if any is left on the endpaper itself it will only occur on the board paper, and so will not be visible when the endpapers are finally pasted down. It is this slight spreading of the paste which gives the reason for leaving the papers in the press no longer than half a minute. This short time is sufficient to ensure that the coloured and the white sheets adhere to each other, but not so long as to allow the clean slips to become so attached that they cannot be stripped off cleanly.

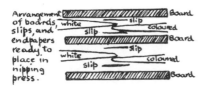

Arrangement of boards, slips, and endpapers ready to place in nipping press.

When the joints are dry the endpapers are now ready for folding, and they should be laid down on a flat board or slab, so that the coloured sheet is over the white at the joint, and the white sheet on the right-hand side. These and the following instructions may seem childish to the expert, but they are of great assistance to the beginner, and create a habit of systematic and accurate working.

Take a thin straight-edge and place it, with the left hand, along the back edge of the coloured sheet. The rule is actually lying on the coloured sheet. Pick up one white sheet lying on the right, and fold it over the straight-edge. It will tend to spring back again, but if a folder is picked up in the right hand and run gently down the fold it will crease the white sheet enough to make it lie flat. It should be noted that during this operation the straight-edge must be firmly held down. Now take out the straight-edge, and complete the folding of the white sheet over the coloured with a folder until a sharp knife-edge crease is made. It will save a lot of confusion if at this stage the white sheet, which has just been folded, is marked in the centre with a large 'O' to indicate that this is the outer (or waste) sheet of the endpaper. Experience proves that for most beginners identification of the outer sheet of an endpaper is a stumbling-block, and it is lessened to a great extent by marking it while the endpaper is actually being made. Later on, when a more complete understanding of the principles governing the use of endpapers comes to the student, he will continue to mark his endpapers in the above way through sheer force of habit.

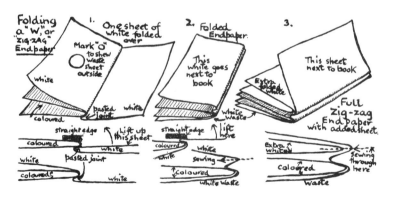

Next, pick up the whole endpaper at the HEAD, and turn it completely over from HEAD to TAIL so that there is still a white sheet on the right-hand side. The bone-folder mark is visible along this white sheet, and along this line place the rule, again allowing the body of the latter to rest upon the coloured sheet. Pick up the white sheet in the right hand, bend it over the rule, crease it, take out the rule, and complete the creasing with a folder.

This last creasing gives the 'zig-zag' or 'W' joint, which allows a little play in the endpaper when a book is opened. Repeat the process with the other endpaper.

If it is desired that a book shall have white endpapers then two of the four white sheets required must be treated as though they were coloured ones. A faint pencil mark in a corner of each will serve to identify them until the endpapers are completed.

It is often desirable to have extra folded sheets placed in the endpapers. These both add to the beauty of the book, and also give more strength at the point where it is most needed. They are sewn into the endpaper when the book comes to be stitched. An extra folded white sheet is added to each endpaper in the position shown in the diagram. If more blank sheets were required they would have to be made up into sections, and sewn in the ordinary way like printed sections.

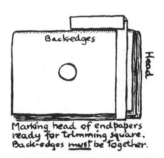

Marking head of endpapers ready for trimming square. Back-edges must be together.

There remains now the 'squaring of the head' of the endpapers in order to prepare them for marking up for sewing. Place both with the back edges together and showing the O's outward. Square them at the HEAD with a trysquare and a pencil. Replace the trysquare with a straight-edge, and trim along the line with a sharp knife. In doing this see that as little as possible is taken off, and that both the white and coloured sheets are trimmed. This operation can be done on a board cutter provided care is exercised in keeping the back edges together and at right angles to the blade. The trimming must be done only at the head—it is not necessary anywhere else. For books cut at the head only, the tail of the endpapers must be trimmed instead of the head.

The position of the sewing in these endpapers must be carefully noted. It is a common fault to put the sewing through the wrong fold, and so defeat the whole object for which the endpaper is made.

Sometimes fancy or patterned endpapers have to be used, and they present some difficulty for two reasons. The first is due to the fact that most of these papers are thin and need to be mounted on a thin cartridge paper before the endpapers are made. The patterned paper is pasted carefully all over, and laid down on the cartridge, and rubbed down under a sheet of clean waste paper. A quick nip in the press between clean sheets will help, and then the pasted sheets should be hung in a warm room until they are nearly dry. If they are left until the drying is complete they curl badly, and are difficult to fold. It is necessary therefore to place them under a light weight until the drying is complete. An alternative way of backing thin papers is to use them as they are in the endpaper, and then to paste down the inner coloured one to the white sheet next to it just before the

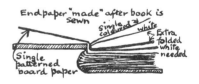

book is cut. This leaves the 'board paper', i.e. the one pasted down to the book board, rather weak.

The second difficulty arises when using papers with a definite repeating pattern. It is quite common with beginners to find one of the endpapers has its pattern wrong side up. This can be easily avoided, for it is only necessary, when marking the folded pattern papers $\frac{1}{8}''$ from the fold with the dividers, to see that one paper has its pattern right way up and the other one the wrong way up, and while they are in this position, make a small pencilled cross near the back fold to indicate that this is the side to which the white sheet must be pasted. If the instructions for making the endpapers are then correctly followed the problem will solve itself. It is one of those small things which can easily ruin a book.

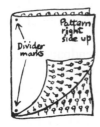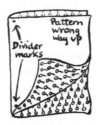

The 'W' or 'Zig-zag' endpaper for books bound 'In-boards'

Although the form of 'W' endpaper already described is adequate for all books bound 'out-of-boards', I have found much advantage in an alternative modification when binding books 'in-boards'. A reference to the table of styles at the end of the book will show that the particular types I have in mind are styles D and G. The reasons for the use of this variation will become clear to the student as the description proceeds.

Take TWO COLOURED SHEETS, fold them and mark with the dividers in the manner already detailed for the normal 'W' endpaper. Then take TWO WHITE SHEETS of such a size that when folded ONE SIDE ONLY is a little larger than the book, but the other side only about 1½" to 2" wide, so that the appearance is as shown in the diagram. Mark these in the usual way with dividers and crease both sides, as before, with a folder. Then prepare the usual four slips of bank paper and place three pressing boards to hand.

In the pasting of the WHITE SHEETS the point to be stressed here is that the side to which the paste is applied is the SHORT ONE. If this is overlooked and a full-sized side is pasted, the endpaper cannot be made properly. The pasting is done as in the diagram on p. 54 and the making of the endpaper as on p. 55. The folding follows the same procedure, observing, of course, that the 'outside' is now the short flap, instead of a full sheet.

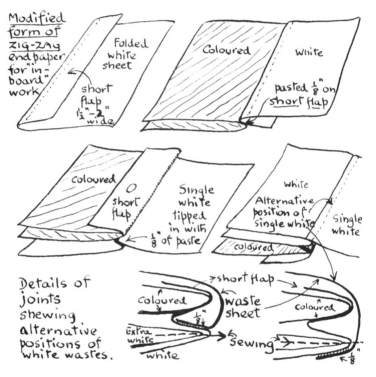

From this point the method departs still further from that of of the ordinary 'zig-zag' endpaper. Take two pieces of white cartridge paper, approximately the same size as the folded end-paper and each piece having one long edge cut straight. This paper is a 'waste' and a common cartridge, in weight not more than 40 lb. to the ream (Imperial), should be used. Again pre-pare four slips and three pressing boards and paste $\frac{1}{8}''$ of each sheet down the straight edge. Take these sheets and place them in the position indicated in the diagrams. They may be placed either outside or inside the joint. It does not matter which posi-tion is used, but for ease of working the former is to be preferred. Place in a press for half a minute: then strip off the slips and set aside the endpapers until dry. When dry, fold the single sheets over the short flaps and mark them with an 'O'. After this is done, the extra folded sheet is added, if desired, and the endpapers squared at the head in the usual manner.

Students will surely ask why this alternative method should be employed for 'in-board' bindings. The reason lies in the final pasting down of the board papers. Hitherto it has been the practice to do this pasting down of the board paper OPEN, but with the above method it is possible to paste down SHUT and produce a more satisfactory joint. In my opinion, pasting down open requires experience and skill, far beyond that of the average student, in assessing exactly how much 'opening' of the zig-zag is necessary to give a perfect closure of the joint when the book is closed. If the endpaper is 'pulled' too much over the board it will tend to split down the joint when dry; if it is not pulled over enough, an ugly crease will form down the back-edge of the boards. By pasting down SHUT, it is possible to have a perfect closure practically automatically. To achieve such a result, it is necessary to have a joint completely free of glue and this is attained by the addition of the single sheet, which 'covers' the joint completely when gluing up the back. The reason for the presence of the 'short flap' is one of economy. It would be very extravagant in paper to have two full-sized wastes. Indeed, one could even do without this short flap, but for the difficulty of making a 'W' with only $\frac{1}{8}''$ of paper to work on at one side when folding the zig-zag.

The 'V' Endpaper with Leather Joint

This is the type of endpaper used in full leather bindings done in the best style; it adds to the beauty of the book as well as giving a small amount of extra strength to the joints.

The construction in the initial stages is not unlike that of the 'W' endpaper. Two folded sheets of good cartridge paper, corresponding to the two white sheets of the zig-zag endpaper, are marked $\frac{1}{8}''$ from the back and a bone-folded line run down both sides. With the assistance of a thin straight-edge, crease them in the manner shown in the diagram on page 64. Let the creases be clean and sharp and lying directly over each other, giving a V-shaped fold. A common fault lies in making the creases more than $\frac{1}{8}''$ in width. Each sheet is now opened out on the bench, when it will be seen that there are now three parallel creases running down the middle of each sheet.

Attention must now be given to the coloured sheets for the endpaper. One of the best papers for this kind of work is 'Michallet' or 'Ingres'. It is thin and strong, easy to paste, and is supplied in a range of delicate colours admirably suited to use with leather. It has a delightful texture, and can be hand-painted or printed with design if desired. Messrs. Reeves & Sons Ltd. have a good range under the name 'Charcoal Papers'. Russell Bookcrafts of Hitchin also stock them. Other coloured papers may be used, but the important thing to remember is the avoidance of thick papers. A large range of marbled papers is available from Sydney Cockerell of Letchworth. The reason will become obvious as the construction is described. Take two folded sheets of this coloured paper a little larger than the book, and place one of them in a safe place, as it will not be needed until the binding is practically finished. One way of doing this is to have a set of large envelopes or thin folders into which such sheets can be placed and labelled until they are required. Most beginners have a habit of mislaying these sheets, and it is very annoying, and sometimes disastrous, to find them gone by the time they are needed.

Now take the coloured sheet which has been retained and, having made sure that the right side of the paper is folded inside, mark both outer sides near the fold with a pencil to identify both the wrong side of the paper and the straight edge about to be made. With a sharp knife and a straight-edge—or the board cutter—cut off the fold of the paper no more than $\frac{1}{16}''$ from the crease. This will produce two single sheets each having one edge perfectly straight.

These coloured sheets must now be pasted all over. Careless pasting will ruin the whole work, so that the student must see that not only the whole surface is covered, but that too much paste can be just as detrimental as too little. It must be well and evenly brushed out, and sufficient time spent on it to allow the moisture to soak the paper evenly too. Have the opened-out white sheets ready, pick up a pasted coloured sheet and place its straight edge exactly along the middle crease of the white. Stretch the coloured sheet very slightly over the white, and then rub it down thoroughly under a clean sheet of waste. A nip in the press between clean sheets and pressing boards is given, and the endpaper is hung over a line to dry. Leave both sheets there until only a slight dampness is perceptible, when they should be taken down and placed under a light weight until drying is complete. When this has taken place the sheets must be placed on the bench, and re-creased as they were before the folded white sheets were opened out to receive the pasted coloured ones. Replace under a light weight until they are required for the next operation.

Now comes the question of the leather joint. The paring of leather will be described fully in its appropriate place, but it would be well to include a paragraph here with special reference to these joints. The width of a piece of leather for joints depends on the size of the book, and on the available leather. For most books in the commoner sizes a piece 2″ to 3″ wide, and a little longer than the length of the book, is adequate for two joints. Sufficient leather should be put on one side at this stage to provide for the cover and the joints. It is much easier to pare one piece of leather before cutting it to make two joints, but it is not always possible to do this when selecting the leather from the skins. The piece for the joints should be pared carefully all over until it is a little less than half its original thickness. There must be no uneven places when the work is done, and only by feeling over the whole surface carefully with the thumb at one side and the fingers on the other, can such uneven paring be detected. When the whole surface has been completed place the leather upon a piece of plate glass, or a paring stone, and with a straight-edge and a very sharp knife, cut it down the centre, thus making two joints. Each of these cut edges must now be very carefully pared down to a very thin edge, sloping back into the leather no more than $\frac{1}{8}''$, and still retaining a clean edge. If this edge is destroyed by a false cut it must be re-cut, and the paring begun again. The width of the leather joint will not allow many errors of this nature to be made. These joints are now ready to be attached to the endpapers.

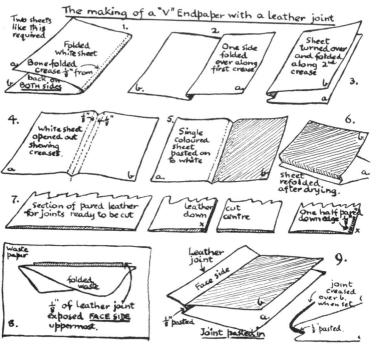

Only one joint should be pasted at a time, and it should be laid down on a piece of waste *right side of the leather uppermost.* Cover it with a folded waste within $\frac{1}{8}''$ of the straight pared edge, and paste it thoroughly, allowing the paste to soak into the leather for a few minutes. Place this pasted edge in the 'V' so that it will be attached to the coloured side, and make sure that the leather goes right down to the base of this 'V' all along the length of the endpaper. When it has adhered sufficiently to be handled gently, place it between slips and boards, as in the case of the 'W' endpaper, leave in a press for half a minute, and then lay aside to dry. It is wise to open the 'V' under the joint by running a fine folder gently down it. This frees it from sticking together where a little paste may have been squeezed out in the pressing. When dry the leather joint should be creased over the coloured sheet as shown in the diagram.

At this point it is necessary to sew in the leather joint. Take one section of the book, for which the endpapers are being made, and place it *inside* the folded white, in such a position as to ensure that the head and tail of the section lie WITHIN the extremities of the leather joint and the coloured part of the endpaper. With a pencil, mark the position of the head and tail of the section upon the endpaper, near to the fold. With a very fine needle make holes down the whole length of the 'V' holding the leather joint, at intervals of $\frac{3}{8}''$ to $\frac{1}{2}''$. These holes must begin and finish NO LESS than $\frac{1}{2}''$ inside the pencilled marks mentioned above. It is also very essential that the holes be placed the slightest amount short of the actual crease of the 'V', otherwise the sewing thread is apt to be seen on the face-side of the leather joint. It only remains now to take a fine needle and thin white silk—or silk to match the colour of the leather if this be preferred—and sew through the holes in a continuous figure-of-eight stitch. Tie off on the *outside* with a double knot and cut off the loose ends $\frac{1}{8}''$ from the knot and gently fray the two small ends, left on the knot, with the needle. The leather joint is now, not only fixed securely with paste, but firmly sewn in too. The most convenient method of doing this sewing is shewn in the diagram.

Now take two SINGLE sheets of white paper, each a little larger than the book, and trim one edge of each with a sharp knife or the board cutter. Paste $\frac{1}{8}''$ of the paper along these edges in exactly the same manner as the leather joints were pasted. Each sheet must now be inserted into the 'V' of the endpaper, but on the opposite side to that on which the leather is fixed. Rub down gently until it adheres sufficiently to place between slips and boards in the press for a minute, and then leave out on the bench until dry. This single sheet is known as the 'waste', and it must be creased over the leather joint and the coloured endpaper in the manner shown. Then it can be marked

E   65

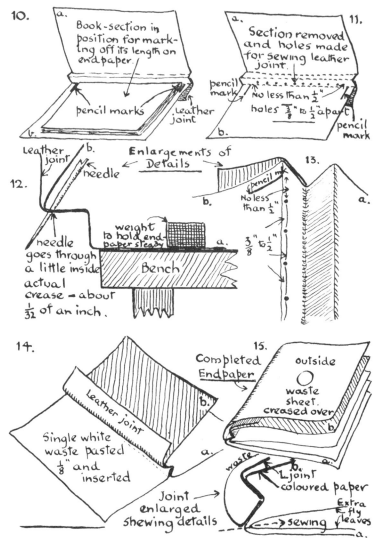

10. a. Book-section in position for marking off its length on endpaper.

pencil marks

Leather joint

11. a. Section removed and holes made for sewing leather joint.

pencil mark No less than ½"

holes ⅜" to ½" apart

pencil mark

b.

b. Leather joint

needle

Enlargements of Details

13.

pencil mark

b. No less than ½"

a.

12. needle goes through a little inside actual crease – about $\frac{1}{32}$ of an inch.

weight to hold endpaper steady

Bench

a.

$\frac{3}{8}$" to $\frac{1}{2}$"

14.

Leather joint

Single white waste pasted ⅛" and inserted

15. Completed Endpaper

outside

waste sheet. creased over

b.

b.

a.

Joint enlarged shewing details

waste

L.joint coloured paper

Extra fly leaves

sewing

a.

b.

a.

with an 'O' to indicate that it is the outside of the endpaper. To complete the work another folded white sheet should be inserted loose in the position shown in the diagram, and be allowed to remain so until the sewing is begun, when it will be stitched in as the endpaper is sewn, but first see below.

When both endpapers are complete they should be placed face to face with the 'O's showing outside. Inside the head of each endpaper—inside the tail in the case of books remaining uncut and therefore sewn straight at the tail—there remains the pencilled mark defining the head of the book section, while sewing in the leather joint.

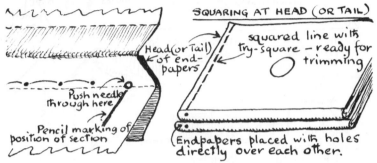

In the crease, exactly in line with this mark, make a hole with a needle so that this hole is visible on the outside of the endpaper. Now insert the extra folded sheet and place both endpapers together, each being flush with the other down the back fold and having *the two needle holes coinciding perpendicularly*. Square and trim them, in line with these holes, as in the case of the zig-zag endpapers.

If a coloured paper having a pattern upon it is used, then the rule observed in the making of the 'W' endpaper also applies here. One sheet is pasted to the white sheet right side up, and the other one upside down. Alternatively they can both be pasted on the right way up, provided they are pasted on opposite sides of the folded white sheets. The illustration will make this clear.

Two methods of pasting patterned endpapers on to whites.

Before leaving this type of endpaper one important item should be noted. It is often found that the leather joint, whose face side is in contact with the coloured endpaper, tends to impart a stain to that paper—especially in the case of Michallet or Ingres papers. This occurs during the operations involving the presence of moisture, e.g. covering, and it must be prevented, although even when dry the leather tends to give this stain, owing to the presence of natural oils in the skin. Place a sheet of clean white blotting or cartridge paper, the same size as the book, between the leather joint and the coloured paper. Tip the edge of the leather joint lightly with paste so that it adheres to the blotting or cartridge paper, and this will hold it in position until it is detached at the time the joint is finally pasted down. The spare folded sheet of coloured paper, which has already been carefully put away, is of course the piece from which eventually two single sheets will be cut to form the 'board papers', i.e. the sheets which are pasted to the inside of the boards in the final stages.

Before leaving the subject of the above type of endpaper, some explanation is needed to account for my departure from the hitherto orthodox 'V' endpaper. I have always been troubled in my teaching by the difficulty most students experience in pasting down the leather joint 'OPEN'. The assessment of the exact position of the joint requires much skill, for, if it is not pulled over the board sufficiently, the closing of the book produces an ugly crease in the leather down the edge of the board. On the other hand, I have known many students pull it over too far and even pull the joint away from the endpaper. If the drawing over has been overdone in this way, and allowed to dry, it is quite likely that the joint will come away from the endpaper when the book is first opened, or the leather will tear at the stitch-holes. In trying to surmount these difficulties I have added somewhat to the making of these endpapers, but I consider the small amount of extra work involved well worth it.

The orthodox method, in which I was first trained, requires a DOUBLE sewing of the endpaper, up one 'V' and down the other. Now the whole purpose of these 'V's is to provide a 'joint' which would give free play to the endpaper when opening or closing a book and to do away with 'drag' on the book sections. The double sewing seemed to me to defeat this principle, as it fastened the two 'V's together at each kettle-stitch and tended to do so at each raised band, so that free opening and closing of the joint was thereby prevented. Unfortunately the first edition of this book was printed before I had tested a method of surmounting the difficulty. Since introducing it to students, I have had complete success in pasting down the joints SHUT, thereby placing them in the exact position required for the opening and closing of the boards and giving the correct amount of free play to this 'gusset' in the endpaper. The same principle was applied to the 'zig-zag' endpapers, as has already been described, with equal success.

A Library-style Endpaper with a Cloth Joint

This is an important endpaper, and is used in books bound in what is known as 'library style', i.e. in books which have to stand a considerable amount of wear and tear, such as those to be found in our public libraries.

The materials required for this type are as follows:

(a) Four folded sheets of white cartridge paper a little larger than the book.

(b) Two strips of linen or cloth about 1″ to 1½″ wide, and a little longer than the book.

(c) Four single sheets of thin coloured or fancy paper, each a little larger than the book.

Take the cloth joints and fold them with the RIGHT SIDE INWARDS so that the crease is approximately one-third of the width across the joint, and then open them out again flat. Glue them all over. Place a folded white sheet on the glued joint so that its folded edge is lying along the crease in the cloth. Take another folded white, and place it on the remainder of the joint so that its fold is no more than $\frac{1}{32}$″ away from the fold of the first sheet put down. Turn the whole over and rub the cloth down thoroughly under a sheet of clean waste until the glue is set. Fold the two sides over so that the cloth is inside, and crease the cloth well with a folder. It will be seen that the cloth joint is wider on one white sheet than it is on the other, and this wider side is the outside of the endpaper, and must be marked in the usual way with an 'O'.

When the joints are dry, open out the endpapers again so that they are flat on the bench having the cloth joints upwards. For each endpaper take two of the thin coloured sheets, and trim one edge of each perfectly straight. Paste them thoroughly all over. Lay each piece down on the white sides of the endpapers with the straight edges lying over the cloth, and rub them well down. A slight nip in the press between clean sheets will help. There will be a strip of cloth now showing on each side of the middle crease, and it is a matter of individual taste as to how

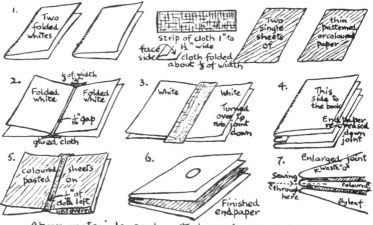

Above materials and method are for ONE endpaper only. Two such ends will be required.

much cloth is allowed to show in this way. The writer prefers a width of cloth visible which is twice the amount which is to be seen around the inside edges of the boards when the endpapers are pasted down. This is usually approximately $\frac{1}{8}''$, so that $\frac{1}{4}''$ of cloth joint would be showing. In practice this means that when one is putting down the coloured papers the straight edges should come within $\frac{1}{8}''$ of the middle crease in the cloth. Allow the endpapers to lie flat on a bench until they are NEARLY DRY.

Then place them between boards under a light weight until completely dry. It should be particularly noted that the sewing in such an endpaper should go through the middle of the cloth joint.

A Second Type of Endpaper having a Cloth Joint

This endpaper is slightly different from the library style in that it has a separate board paper. It can be used in cloth-bound books, and is sewn on. It is a cheaper version of the one with a leather joint, and the materials required for two ends are as under:

(*a*) Four single sheets of fancy or coloured paper, a little larger than the book. It should be thin paper as it will be pasted to another sheet.

(*b*) Four folded sheets of white paper—thin cartridge is best.

(*c*) Two cloth joints about $1\frac{1}{2}''$ wide and as long as the book. Place a folded white sheet on a piece of clean waste, and a cloth joint, face-side down, on another piece of clean waste. See that the joint has a clean-cut edge, and cover it with a folded waste to

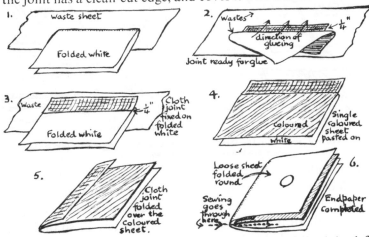

within $\frac{1}{4}''$ of this edge. Glue carefully this portion of the joint left showing. Place it along the folded edge of the white sheet, as shown in the diagram. Rub the cloth down thoroughly, and take one of the single coloured sheets. One of its long edges must be trimmed straight, and the sheet pasted all over. Place it so that the trimmed edge is $\frac{1}{4}''$ over the cloth joint, i.e. directly over the fold of the white sheet. Nip in the press, and hang it up to dry. It will now be seen that the cloth is partly enclosed between the coloured and white sheets.

The remaining portion of the cloth joint which projects beyond the back of the endpaper is now folded neatly over the coloured side, giving it a clean sharp crease. The whole endpaper is then enclosed in another folded white sheet, which remains loose until the sewing is done. When the other endpaper has been made in the same way, both must be marked with an 'O' on the white leaf which goes over the joint and the coloured paper, and placed face to face. Square and trim the head as for the endpapers already described, and the sewing will pass through the place indicated in the diagram. The pasting down of the two remaining pieces of coloured paper will be dealt with later in the section on 'Pasting-down', and they must be put away until this needs to be done.

So far all the endpapers described have been of the 'sewn-on' type, and these are most desirable from the point of view of 'bookbinding by hand'. The advent of machinery, making possible the mass production of books, has brought with it endpapers which are edged on with paste after the book has been sewn; the parents of this method are cost and speed. From this point of view they are adequate for the purpose, but in any book where hard wear and a reasonably long life are desired, such endpapers are totally inadequate. There are occasions, however, when the hand-binder has some case-binding to do, and at such times he may have to compromise and use a modified endpaper. The ones which follow are of this type.

A 'Made' Endpaper

This name is given to endpapers which are 'made' by pasting two sheets together, and there is a definite reason for such a method. Many of the fancy papers supplied for cheap bindings are too thin for use in the ordinary way as flysheets, but thick enough for the board paper which must have only a little thickness down the joint. Added to this, many of these papers show the pattern through the under side, and present an untidy appearance. This made endpaper surmounts these problems, and for two such ends the following materials will be required.

(*a*) Four folded sheets of white paper a little larger than the book.

(*b*) Two folded coloured sheets of the same size.

Place one of the folded white sheets on a piece of clean waste, fold away from you, and paste thoroughly all over. Lay over this one of the coloured sheets so that its back fold is lying along the back fold of the white sheet. Over this place the other coloured sheet but this time *unpasted*. Paste the other white sheet and lay it down over the last coloured sheet, place the whole between clean sheets of paper, and give a nip in the press. Now hang them out separately to dry. It should be noted that a number of

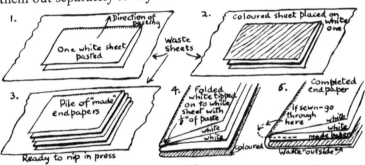

these endpapers could be made at the same time in one pile, but care must be taken to see that the back folds are lying over each other. If a number are being made it would save time if a folded white is placed over the coloured one, and actually pasted in that position to receive the next coloured. The thing to bear in mind is that it is better to paste the white sheets rather than the coloured ones to prevent the flysheets curling the wrong way when the book is opened.

Now take another of the folded white sheets, and tip it along its back edge with paste to a depth of $\frac{1}{8}''$. Place this sheet over the white side of one of the sheets already made, rub it down, and place under light pressure until it is dry. Do the same with the other endpaper. This white sheet which has just been attached is opened out so that one leaf of it goes right round the coloured side, and so forms a 'waste' sheet. This is marked 'O' and both ends trimmed square at the head, as usual. This end-paper can be tipped on to the book with paste, or sewn. If sewing is desired, then the stitching goes through in the place indicated.

Another 'Made' Endpaper—Edged on with Paste only

This endpaper is edged on with paste after the book has been sewn, and is very similar to the one just described. For two such ends the following materials are needed:

Two folded coloured sheets.
Two folded white sheets.
Two single white sheets.

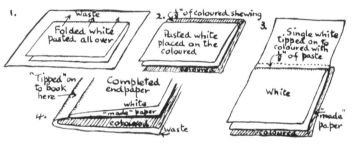

Take a folded white sheet and place it on a clean waste sheet. Paste it all over, working towards the back fold, and lay out the folded coloured sheet on the bench. Place the pasted white sheet upon it in such a way that the back edge comes within $\frac{1}{8}''$ of the back fold of the coloured sheet. Rub it well down, nip in the press, and hang up to dry. Repeat with the other endpaper. Take a single sheet of white paper, trim one edge straight, and run paste along this edge to a depth of $\frac{1}{8}''$. Lay this pasted portion along the $\frac{1}{8}''$ of coloured sheet that was left protruding beyond the white one. Rub it down and allow to dry under a weight. This single sheet is then folded round the coloured side and forms the waste sheet. Mark with an 'O', and when the remaining endpaper has been made put them together and trim square at the head, fore-edge, and tail to the exact size of the book. They are 'edged' on to the book by $\frac{1}{8}''$ of paste.

A Folded-sheet Endpaper for Cloth-cased Books

This type of endpaper is the simplest of all, and consists of just one folded sheet of white or coloured paper—cartridge is best—cut to the size of the book. An $\frac{1}{8}''$ of paste is run down the back edge, and then the endpaper is placed in position on the book. A variation of the above is to place a single waste sheet $\frac{1}{8}''$ on to the folded sheet with paste, and use it as a means of attaching the boards when casing the book. This alternative is

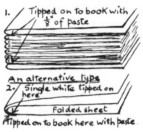

shown in the diagram. These endpapers cannot withstand much wear and tear, and should be used by the hand-binder in cases where little value is attached to the book, and where a volume is going to be used for reference only.

Leather Doublures and Fly-leaves

Of great interest and even greater satisfaction to the real craftsman is the use of leather doublures and fly-leaves. If reference is made to the making of the 'V' endpaper it will be remembered that a coloured sheet was pasted on to the folded white sheet to give the fly-leaf, and that coloured sheets were put away to provide the paper for the board when the pasting down comes to be done. If leather is used in place of these pieces of coloured paper then we have doublures and fly-leaves

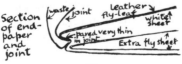

of leather. The leather may be used in two ways. The joints, doublures, and fly-leaves may be cut out of the same skin of leather, or the doublures and fly-leaves may be of another colour, but it should tone well with the colour of the cover and the joints. All the leather must be cut out together, and the cover placed safely away until it is required. The pieces used for the fly-leaves must be pared, but not excessively as the weight of the leather will help the leaf to lie flat in the book. Particular attention must be paid to the paring of the edge of this leaf where it enters the gusset of the endpaper. It must be pared down very thin for a distance of $\frac{1}{4}''$ from the edge, otherwise the joint would be far too thick to allow the board to close properly. When the leather is pasted on to the endpapers it must be placed between sheets of clean blotting paper, and left under a weight to dry. The doublure, i.e. the leather that goes on the board, must be pared all over down to at least half its original thickness. Such endpapers look exceedingly rich, especially so when beautifully tooled, but the craftsman must be prepared to do a large amount of very careful work, and only the very best books are worthy of such an ambition.

A variation of the above is very satisfying, where leather is used for the board doublure only and the flyleaves given a good plain or patterned paper in keeping with the rest of the binding.

Design applied to Endpapers

It will be convenient at this point to describe some of the methods in use for the making of hand-made endpapers. There is always an additional interest given to a book when the endpapers have been designed and decorated by the binder himself, and this principle applies even more in the case of bindings done by pupils in school. There is a freshness and charm about such endpapers which can never be attained by the machine-made product, and many examples of this type of work can be found in books of the past. Miss Prideaux has some good examples in one of her publications.

ENDPAPERS

Marbling

In some ways this is the most mechanical way of producing designed endpapers, but Mr. S. Cockerell has experimented with much success in this line during the last few years, and has produced some striking examples of good patterns. A treatise on marbling was published in 1881 by a craftsman named Woolnough, and this seems to be the only authoritative work on the subject to date. His methods were those used in the trade, and require specially prepared colours and size, but I will summarize the main points in his methods, and mention other ways which are rather more suited for use in schools, and which can produce quite pleasing results. The art of marbling seems to have come originally from Holland, and the whole process depends on the fact that of two liquids the lighter one can be floated as an extremely thin film upon the surface of the heavier one, provided they are of a different nature, e.g. oil and water.

The colours are fairly expensive, and can be obtained from most firms who supply bookbinders' requirements. Messrs. Dane & Co., of London, specialize in such colours. If one has the time and patience, they can be obtained in powder form, and ground and mixed by hand as required. They must be ground very finely, and this is done on a smooth stone with the aid of a 'muller' (another smooth stone, conical in shape), or in a mortar, using a pestle to do the grinding. The colours are classified as follows:

Reds: Carmine, drop lake, peach wood lake, vermilion, rose pink, burnt ochre.

Blues: Indigo, Chinese blue, Prussian blue, ultramarine.

Yellows: Chrome, Dutch pink, raw Oxford ochre, English pink, yellow lake (in pulp form).

Greens: Chrome green, green lake, emerald green, Brunswick green.

Blacks: Vegetable lamp black, common lamp black, drop ivory black, blue black.

Browns: Burnt Turkey umber, burnt sienna.

Whites: China clay, pipe clay, flake white, Paris white.

They are prepared in the following way. Grind them in beeswax in the proportion of 1 oz. of prepared wax to 1 lb. of colour. The preparation of the wax is done by taking 2 lb. of the best beeswax and putting it into an earthen vessel. Add to this $\frac{1}{4}$ lb. of the very best white curd soap which has been cut into very small pieces. Gently heat the mixture until both are dissolved, but on no account allow it to boil. Pour into it cold water, a very little at a time, whilst continually stirring the mixture. If the water is added too rapidly it will hiss and splutter, and become dangerous to the person doing the mixing. It will thicken as the water is added until it is hardly possible to stir at all. When this happens set the mixture aside to cool, and after it has cooled, take it out and pulverize it between the finger and thumb. It is now ready to be ground into the colours in the proportion already mentioned.

Now for the size. There are various sizes upon which marbling can be done, but the best, without doubt, are obtained from gum tragacanth or carragheen moss. Mr. S. Cockerell has written a small pamphlet on simple marbling, published by Messrs. Russell Bookcrafts, Hitchin, who will also supply the necessary materials. The pamphlet is a good little treatise from the school point of view, and the reader would be well advised to add it to his craft library.

Consider first the size from gum tragacanth. It has other names such as gum dragon, or gum elect, and to be of good quality it should be large, white, flaky, and hard. Into a large glazed earthenware vessel put 1 lb. of the gum, and pour over it 2 gallons of soft rain water, allowing it to soak all night. Next day stir it with a birch broom for about five minutes, and repeat this operation at intervals of three to four hours during the day, adding more water as it thickens and absorbs the original water. After seventy-two hours it is ready for use. It should be diluted until a proper consistency is obtained, and then strained through fine muslin. Some papers need the size to be thicker than others, and only by actual experiment can the proper mixture be arrived at.

Another size can be obtained by boiling linseed, but the great drawback in this case is that it soon goes bad. Another can be got from flea seed (plantago). The seed is saturated in boiling water and well stirred. It will keep longer than linseed, and it can be mixed with gum tragacanth. It makes very good Spanish or French marbling, but it cannot be combed very well.

The size which is made from carragheen moss is a very convenient one, and the one most generally used. Take 4 oz. of the moss and place it in a bucket, pouring on to it 5 to 6 quarts of rain-water. Bring this very slowly to the boil and simmer and stir for a while. Put it aside to cool, and then add another 4 quarts of rain-water, stir again, and leave it for a day or two. It should be strained through muslin and reduced again with rain-water to the proper consistency required for use. This should be about that of milk. It was possible at one time to obtain this size ready made in a concentrated form, and this was very convenient for use in schools.

Oxgall is used in marbling, and it is best purchased ready for use. If obtained from an abattoir it soon goes bad, and gives off a most offensive smell.

Turpentine is used occasionally to get a kind of 'bubbly' effect, and paraffin gives a similar result.

Alum is very necessary in marbling, and is used to counter the effect of too much oxgall in the colours. When colours run too much on the size, a few drops of alum water will check them. Alum water is also used to sponge over the paper before marbling.

A marbling trough must be obtained, or made. It is better to have one of metal which can be thoroughly cleaned after use. If made of wood, the joints should be perfectly watertight. It will be seen from the diagram that there is a small partition at one end. The smaller compartment receives the used colour when the skimming is done. It would be a big advantage to have a slope at one end, as it is so much easier to skim the size. The size of the trough is rather an important point, especially when the marbling of endpapers and cover papers is intended. It is difficult for the amateur to produce two papers alike when they are marbled separately. If a single sheet can be printed of sufficient size to produce both endpapers of a book it will be a great advantage. For instance, a crown octavo book would require two sheets a little larger than $7\frac{1}{2}''$ by 10", so that a suitable trough size would be 16" by 12". No one need be deterred by the lack of a trough. Quite successful marbling can be done in old metal tea-trays.

A wood or metal skimmer is a useful thing to have, but skimming can be done just as efficiently with slips of waste paper cut a little longer than the width of the trough.

Colour troughs are helpful to good results. Three or four could be made from tinplate as shown in the diagram. The ends serve the double purpose of being both ends and feet on which to stand. They are best made the length of the marbling trough. Where the application of colour is done by brush, no such troughs are needed.

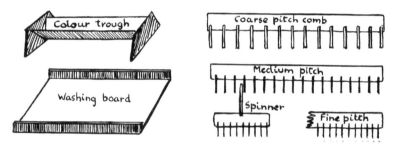

Various combs will be needed for the work, and these can be made from brass strips and brass wire. The wire is cut into lengths of $1\frac{1}{2}''$ and soldered in the required manner to a brass strip $\frac{1}{4}''$ wide and a little less than the length of the trough. The comb pitches are varied, and the most useful sizes are $1\frac{1}{2}''$, 1", and $\frac{1}{2}''$ pitch. These give coarse, medium, and fine patterns. Two spinners would be useful. These are combs with a small handle attached, so that they can be twirled round between the fingers.

One about 6″ wide and one about 3″ are useful, and the pitch should be a fine one. An effective type of comb can be made by gluing pieces of brass wire, or needles, between strips of cardboard. The needles have, however, a drawback in that they readily rust.

To complete the equipment there remain a washing-board, a number of glass jars, and some thin sticks. The washing-board, which is similar in construction to the domestic drainer-board, should have two sides but no ends. The glass pots can be those in which meat pastes are sold, and the thin sticks are provided from a length or two of thin basketry cane.

The actual process of marbling can be divided into two sections. The first method may be cleaner and more economical in school, but the equipment is more elaborate. It is the method in which the colour troughs are used. The making of the size has been described, and this should now be ready in the trough to a depth of about one inch. The temperature is important. It should be as near the heat of the room as possible, but no warmer. Adjustments may be made with hot or cold water, using a thermometer, but by far the better method is to allow the size to stand in the room for some hours before use. The paper must be prepared, also any book edges which are to be done. A solution of alum is made by adding 2 oz. of alum to 1 pint of warm water. Allow it to stand until the alum is dissolved and then sponge the sheets to be marbled, in an even manner, with the solution. No portion of the paper must be missed as the alum acts as a mordant, i.e. a fixative, and the colour will not adhere properly to any portions of the paper which have not received a coat of the solution. The best way to ensure a complete covering is to run the sponge across the paper in one direction until the whole surface has been wetted, and then run across again at right angles to the first direction. Place a clean board on the bench, and as the sheets are treated lay them down one on top of the other. When a sufficient number have been done, place another clean board on top, and this will keep them flat and slightly moist. All kinds of paper may be used in this work,

but one of the best is known as Kraft paper. There are two kinds
—glazed and unglazed—and to most people this paper is
familiar as brown wrapping-paper. I prefer the unglazed kind
myself. It is a durable, strong paper suitable for endpapers,
covers, and other processes in bookbinding, and can be damped
very evenly. It also provides in its colour a very suitable background not only for marbling, but for other forms of pattern.
It is indeed one of the most useful papers for the bookbinder. If
the edges of a book are to be marbled they too must be sponged
with the alum solution.

Whether the colours are to be used in the colour troughs or
put on with sticks or brushes, it is best to mix them first in the
pots. Pour the colours into the pots, and if they are too thick,
thin them with a little soft water. Always shake the bottles
thoroughly before pouring colours out. They can be mixed in the
usual way, e.g. red and yellow to make orange. The addition of
more water will produce paler colours.

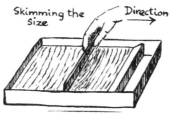

When they have been properly mixed they are ready to be
'adjusted'. This is done by adding oxgall. If this were not done
the colours would not spread on the size. The order in which the
colours are to be used must be decided, and a drop or two of
oxgall added to the first colour, being mixed well in. Use a drop
bottle for this purpose, counting the number of drops added.
Skim the size with a skimmer, or with slips of paper cut for the
purpose, and immediately afterwards drop a little colour on the
size. If it tends to sink, the size is too thick, and must be thinned
with a little warm water, stirring very carefully. Skim and test
the colour again. Over-thinning will destroy the power of the
combing to produce a definite pattern, as the size will follow the
comb, but will not cease moving when the comb is withdrawn.

If the spots of colour spread, and immediately contract slightly, the size is too cold and must be raised in temperature by adding a little warm water. From the foregoing it will be realized that at this stage the whole process is one of trial and error, and considerable patience must be exercised in order to ensure that everything is fulfilling the required conditions. If the right amount of oxgall has been added each spot of colour will spread out about an inch in diameter. If this does not happen, add a few more drops of oxgall and test again. If no difference is noted, then some of the other factors may be the cause, and tests must be made to put them right. If too much oxgall is added the colour spreads too fast and too far. This is remedied by the addition of a few drops of the alum solution. Always remember to skim the size after each experiment, and after any addition of water to the size, or oxgall to the colours, the mixing must be thorough. Try to avoid the creation of bubbles when stirring the size.

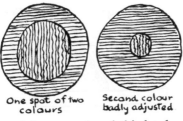

One spot of two colours   Second colour badly adjusted

The adjustment of the second and third colours must now be done. It is very unwise for any beginner to attempt to work more than one or two colours at first. Add to the second colour a drop or two more oxgall than was added to the first colour. Skim the size and drop on the first colour. After it has spread allow a drop of the second colour to fall in the middle of the first colour. It will not spread as far as the first colour, but should appear somewhat similar to the diagram above, if it has been properly adjusted. If it is not correct, the addition of more oxgall may put it right if the spread is not enough, and drops of alum if the spread is too much. The same procedure should be followed with the third colour, but it is wise to practise with two colours until some experience has been gained.

After all this experimenting it is now time to try on a sheet of the paper. Two or three methods may be used to place the colour on the size. When the combs and colour troughs are used, the teeth of the comb are dipped into the colour, and then allowed just to touch the surface of the size. This method is clean, and does not waste colour, and owing to the fact that the spots are evenly distributed, some very beautiful pattern designs can be formed. It also means much more control of the colour on the size. Put on a row or two of drops in this way, and draw a comb very slowly through the spots. Take one of the sheets of paper, hold it alum-side downwards so that the left hand is near the top left-hand corner, and the right hand near the bottom right-hand corner. Lower the left-hand edge towards the size, and immediately this edge touches the size begin to lower the right hand so that the paper is gradually brought into contact with the size. On no account must the paper be released by either hand. As soon as all the surface of the paper has come into contact, begin to raise the left hand, and so strip the paper from the size. After practice, the whole operation will be done in a kind of rocking motion, and the colour is thus transferred to the paper. If the sheet is not laid evenly on the size air bubbles will be trapped between the size and the paper, and where these occur large patches of unmarbled paper will be the result. Only confidence born of practice can perform this operation in a satisfactory manner. Immediately the sheet is taken off the size it should be placed on the washing board, and water poured over it to rinse away any size or colour which is loose; then the sheet should be hung over a line to dry. Skim the size for every fresh sheet to be marbled.

Mention was made of other methods of applying the colour to the size. If the brush method be used the colour is placed in small pots and thoroughly mixed. The surplus colour is taken out of the brush by wiping it on the edge of the pot, and then it is tapped on a stick over the size. This sharp tap shakes the colour from the brush on to the size, but it is easily seen that there is not the control over the spots of colour as in the comb method, and it would be very difficult indeed to attempt to make a regular pattern. When the spots have spread combs can be used to make a variety of effects in the same fashion as the first method. The brushes should always be washed after using.

Marbling can also be done by using thin sticks to drop on the colour, but again it is far more difficult to obtain regularity of pattern compared with the dipping of combs into colour. These methods are useful when no colour troughs are available.

Certain effects can be obtained by just dropping on the colour and transferring it to the paper without any combing at all. Again oxgall can be used unmixed with colour. When dropped on the colour already on the size it spreads the spots out more, and gives an open effect to the pattern. There are many rakings that can be tried for different patterns, and the student should experiment for himself in these combings.

To complete the process it is best to size the sheets. When dry they must be passed through a warm bath of size. One quart of water to 1 oz. of glue size is the consistency required, but it must be a good quality size that is used. A better size can be made by using one part glue, one part soap, and thirty parts of water. It is hardly worth while mixing and warming such a quantity of size if only a few sheets are to be done. In such a case put a little of the marbling size into a trough, and thin it down considerably with warm water, and run the sheets through this. The sheets are hung up to dry and then glazed. The latter process is done by rubbing beeswax on a clean cloth, and then rubbing the sheets all over with the waxed cloth. A warm iron is then passed over the surface to polish them. This polishing helps to prevent any rubbing of the colours. Colourless shoe-polish, or furniture cream will answer the same purpose as the wax. Book-edge marbling will be described in the chapter on the treatment of edges.

Marbling with other Media

There are other ways of marbling apart from the use of Carragheen or Gum Tragacanth sizes. It is possible to produce pleasing effects by using oil colours instead of water colours. In such a case the size must be thinner, and although the sizes already mentioned may be used, yet it will be quite sufficient to use ordinary glue size. It must be made by scalding ½ oz. of good glue size in a pint of water. The process of marbling is then carried forward in a similar fashion to that already described. It is a useful and simple method for secondary schools. The colours used may be ordinary artist's oil colours, or printer's inks, and they must be thinned with turpentine only. Tests have to be made in the usual way until the proper consistencies are arrived at. Oxgall can be used as before. There is no need to wash the paper with alum before use, but it would be of value if it were done. After the marbling has been done there is no need to size the paper as oil colours are fast to water and will not rub. They can be glazed and polished in the same way as the water colours. There is a certain difficulty arising out of this method, due to the oil in the colours. It stains through the paper and appears as dark patches on the back. Sponging with alum before marbling helps a little, and running the sheets through very thin size will also help. A more definite way of surmounting this difficulty is to paste the sheets after they are dry, and mount them on clean sheets of white paper. This will mean that a very thin paper must be used for the marbling, otherwise the two sheets pasted together will be too thick. In the case of such endpapers as those made in the library style this difficulty is obviated by the very construction of the endpaper itself, wherein the coloured sheets are pasted on to the white sheets at the very outset. The same remarks apply to endpapers made with a leather joint.

Mention must also be made of Linmarblin. The colours sold under this name are quite useful for various purposes, but they do not take the place of Carragheen marbling. As far as being very convenient for quick work without much preparation, they are excellent, but there is little or no control over the spreading of the colours. Some control may be obtained by using the medium called Lintrole, sold by the same makers. This corresponds in this method to oxgall in the other methods. The simplest way in which these colours can be used, lies in the substitution of water for the size. The trough is filled with water, and allowed to stand until it acquires the same temperature as the room. The colours are stirred and dropped on in the usual way. A good deal of adjustment can be tried, and the behaviour of the colours when dropped upon each other must be noted and kept for future reference, as they vary widely in the way they react to each other. The colours are fast, and the marbled sheets can be used as soon as they are dry. No sizing is necessary, but they may be polished, if desired. If only two cover- or endpapers are needed, and no definite pattern desired, then this method is very convenient indeed. A remarkable thing about these colours is the way in which more than one printing can be taken from one dropping of colour upon the water. I have taken as many as eight prints from one application of colour. Of course the prints become paler as one proceeds, and the design changes, but some very attractive pale marbled effects can be obtained. More control is obtained by using glue size instead of water, and more still by using Carragheen size itself.

In actual practice much depends on the student's power to make experiments both in methods and materials, and I am convinced that a large field of new effects and patterns is awaiting the enthusiastic investigator. To break away entirely from the conventional marblings to which bookbinders have been wedded for so long, would be a step forward in both art and craft. School-children, almost without exception, thoroughly enjoy this experimental side of marbling.

Paste-graining

Most interesting work can be done in paste-graining. Any type of water colour can be used, and ordinary paste is the medium. A great improvement is effected by the addition of a little soap to the paste, which should be mixed to the consistency of thick cream. Starch can be substituted for paste, and is very clean to use. A tablespoonful of starch is mixed in a basin with enough cold water to make it into a smooth cream. Add boiling water, and stir well until the mixture clears, and allow to cool. 'Gloy' is an excellent medium for use by the individual, but too expensive for class-work.

The paper used for graining should be damped between sheets of wet blotting paper and squeezed in the press. When used like this, the paste will remain workable for a longer period. Many methods of treating the pasted paper may be tried. One popular one is that of brushing the paste all over the sheet, applying the colour with brushes, and running the colours into each other as desired. Again, powder colour may be dropped upon the paste, and treated in any manner that occurs to the student. Some like to have several pots of paste already coloured, and applied direct to the paper. Two sheets can be treated and placed face to face. Novel effects can be produced by the separation of these sheets, as they can be pulled apart in various ways. The above results are chiefly obtained by the use of brushes.

When graining-combs are introduced another large range of patterns can be made. Combs can be made of celluloid, wood or metal. Rubber and lino are excellent, and strawboard can be used, but only for a short time, as the paste reduces it to a pulp. A set of decorator's metal graining-combs is excellent, but in some cases they must have a few teeth removed in order to get more open effects in the designs. Pictorial effects can be produced by the thumb nail or a bone-folder. Almost anything may be used to make markings in the paste, and there appears to be no limit to the different kinds of design that can be carried out by an enthusiastic student. Personally I incline to the use of the fingers in conjunction with other tools as more imaginative feeling is put into the work, and the freedom of design is very evident. When graining is done, it is necessary to work rapidly, as the paste must be wet to obtain a successful design. If the paste is too thick the combing will cause it to go into ridges, which are inconvenient when the pattern dries. If the paste is too thin the pattern lines will not stay clear, but will 'run out'. Even when the paste is adjusted it is possible to produce ridging by applying it too thickly to the paper. The brushes used for obtaining brush-grained effects should vary in texture. A decorator's brush grainer will give coarse lines, and ordinary flat brushes produce fine lines. Such brushes soon become wet and clogged with paste, so that after every stroke it is advisable to wipe them on a large piece of dry rag. All brushes should be washed thoroughly after using, and the sheets can be waxed and ironed in the usual way when dry.

Dyeing and Staining

Dyes and inks can be dropped on wetted paper and allowed to run together. When the desired effect is obtained wash the surplus colour off under running water, and hang up to dry.

Waterproofing

An important point arises when endpapers are made by paste-combing. It will be impossible to paste down such end-papers 'shut' without some precautions against their sticking together when put into the press. Polishing the sheets with wax will waterproof them to some extent, and the addition of a little waterglass to the paste will help, but even then the wetness of the paste on the back of such papers will re-wet the paste-grained side, and make it difficult to handle. The use of water-proof colours is an improvement, but expensive. A way out of this difficulty is to be found in the manner of putting the book into the press. If after pasting down, a thin bright tin is inserted between the two coloured endpapers, they should not give any trouble. If the tin appears to be too thick, use an oiled paper instead.

Hand-drawn End- and Cover Papers

This type of decorative paper is the finest of all, as it allows complete freedom and originality in design, and gives indivi-duality to the book. The design can be an integral part of the binding itself in every sense, and can be carried out in all kinds of media. Included under this type are lino and wood-cut end-papers and covers. These can be carried out with small units making repeat pattern designs, or with blocks to print the whole cover or endpaper at one impression.

CHAPTER 4

Preparation for Sewing

The object in view when sewing a book is to fasten the sections together in such a manner as to ensure a secure and permanent piece of work. At the same time the book must open freely when bound. Therefore the method of sewing any book will depend on the covering material. A book bound in morocco will not be sewn in the same way as a book bound in vellum, or again a calf binding will have one kind of sewing, and a library binding a different type. The value of the binding, the quality of its paper, and the use to which the book is going to be put will determine the style in which the book is to be bound. This problem is solved by the craftsman before beginning work on the book, and this will decide the style of the sewing.

Trimming before Sewing

It is necessary here to deal with the question of books whose edges have to remain uncut. In the case of very valuable books such as ancient manuscripts, and books dating back to the early days of printing, and also good first editions of more modern works, it is bad craftsmanship to cut the edges. I have seen books treated in this way chiefly by nineteenth-century binders, who were so wedded to the use of the guillotine that all books which came into their hands had of necessity to be executed (in

90

more than one sense) in this way. Such books are thereby reduced to a mere fraction of their original value.

The binder must choose whether a book is to be left entirely uncut, or whether some amount of trimming of the pages is to be done at this stage. It is this latter case which demands attention now; in all other cases the marking up for sewing can be carried out.

Pricking off margins at the Head

The sheets of the book to be trimmed must be held up to the light—'shining them' is the correct term—and the register of the printing inspected. If the sheet has been correctly folded, the type on each page should 'register' over the type on the page behind it. If it is not true the sheet must be carefully refolded. Glance through the pages now, to find out which one has the narrowest margin at the head, and measure this exactly with a pair of dividers. Going through all the sheets of the book, any variations from this measurement must be pricked off at the head with the point of the dividers, thus making sure that all the head margins are equal. Through these points draw light pencil lines with a try-square, so that the lines will be at right angles to the back fold of the sheet. The sheets are now trimmed. With a sharp knife and a straight-edge, trim off the sheets at the head along the pencil lines. If a board cutter is available it may be used to do the trimming. A piece of millboard or similar hard board is now cut out square and true to the exact size to which the sheets are going to be trimmed. Good taste and judgement are needed in this matter. It is usual to choose for the purpose a page of average size, so that only the larger ones will be trimmed, and the smaller pages left untouched. The latter are known as proof pages, and present evidence to the owner or the purchaser that a book has not been unduly cut after leaving the hands of the printer.

Method of trimming sheets

Obtain a flat piece of board—an old drawing-board will do—and this can be kept specially for the trimming of sheets. Take three good-sized tacks and a piece of strawboard larger than the sheets to be trimmed. Place the strawboard centrally on the board, and drive the tacks through it into the board just enough to make them firm. The positions for the tacks are determined by placing the cut millboard in the middle of the strawboard, and arranging them in the positions indicated in the diagram by A, B, and C. Take a sheet to be trimmed, and place its head and back fold up to the tacks, laying over it the millboard, also up to the tacks. The trimming is then performed with a sharp knife along the edges of the millboard at the fore-edge and tail. When the under strawboard becomes scored by the cutting, the moving of nail C a little to the right or left will bring a fresh surface into operation for the cutting. When all the sheets have been trimmed they are often 'rough gilt'. This is done next, but the method will be found in the section describing the gilding of edges in general.

Marking up for Sewing

This process is one in which the positions of the bands or tapes, upon which the sections are to be sewn, are marked across the backs of the sections. These lines indicate to the person sewing the places where the needle passes in and out of the section. In all cases, whether the book be sewn on bands or tapes, the following procedure must be observed. A slight variation occurs in the case of books of single sheets. This will be mentioned when single-sheet binding is described.

Books Cut on all Three Edges

Take first the case of those books which are going to be cut on three edges. Place the endpapers, already squared at the head, in position on the book, i.e. with the squared heads at the head of the book and the 'O's showing outwards on each side. Place the whole between two pressing boards which are about the same size as the book, but no less. Grip all in both hands, and knock up boards and book together on a solid

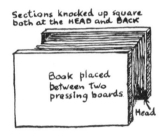

surface until they are flat both at the head and the back. Do not be satisfied until the back and the head are true and straight, as much trouble will be avoided later if this is done with care. Lower the whole into a lying press, the backs of the sections uppermost, gripping firmly and allowing nothing to slip. When the book and boards project above the press an inch or so, gently tighten the press until it grips the book firmly. There is no need to use the press pin for tightening, as it is sufficient for the operation if only hand-screwing is done. The book is now in position for marking up. Have to hand a pair of dividers, a soft pencil, an old tenon saw and a try-square.

Books Cut only at the Head, left just Trimmed, or entirely Uncut

The procedure for marking up books which are only going to be cut at the head, books which are trimmed only, or left entirely uncut, needs mentioning. In the latter two cases the method

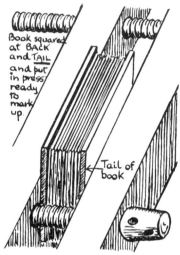

Book squared at BACK and TAIL and put in press ready to mark up

Tail of book

used is the same as that already outlined, but where the head only is to be cut, an important variation occurs. The square edges of the endpapers must be placed this time at the tail of the book, and the whole knocked up square at the tail and back. It is then lowered into the press for marking up. The importance of this variation lies in the fact that in such cases the head is often cut and gilt, and headbands sewn on. If the book had been knocked up square at the head, the tail would not be even enough, either for headbanding or for fitting the boards. Knocking-up square at the tail obviates this difficulty and, of course, the cutting of the head solves it for the headband. I have known students fail in bookbinding examinations on this very point. They have only discovered their error when the tailband came to be sewn, and it is there too late to remedy the fault.

Marking up for all types is dependent on the kind of sewing to be done, and such types divide themselves into three natural classes:

(*a*) Books sewn on tapes or vellum strips.

(*b*) Ordinary sewing on sawn-in bands.

(*c*) Flexible sewing on raised bands.

Marking up for Three Tapes

The number of tapes required depends entirely on the size of the book to be sewn, but the number used in hand binding should never be less than three. Only on very small books do I ever use three tapes, but I have seen people sewing books on two, and even on one solitary tape. It is a lazy and degenerate form of work, and should not be countenanced. Such a sewing is hardly likely to withstand much wear and tear, and reducing the number of tapes in this fashion is simply 'spoiling the ship for a ha'porth of tar'. Mary Collet, in the seventeenth century, was so well drilled by her tutor, Thomas Buck, a Cambridge binder, in the importance of having sufficient cords for strength, that she went to the opposite extreme, and sewed some very large books on no fewer than sixteen bands. This would seem to be overdoing matters, but the fact remains on record that after a lapse of three hundred years the leaves of such of her bindings that still remain have never come loose. Ordinary books should always have four tapes, and as the size increases so must the number of tapes. The decision is very much a matter of common sense, bearing in mind all the time that the chief object in sewing any good book is to give strength and durability, and this cannot be achieved if the number of tapes or cords is insufficient for the size and weight of the book.

Again the width of the tape used claims consideration. I am of the opinion that a larger number of narrower tapes is better craftsmanship than a few wide ones. It has been my practice to obtain a roll of the best stiffened unbleached linen tape $1''$ wide. If this cannot be obtained, ordinary tape will serve provided it is stiffened by dipping it in size or starch, and ironing it when dry. Bookbinder's cloth can be used also. When tape is $1''$ wide it can be cut along its length as required, into widths of $\frac{1}{4}''$, $\frac{1}{3}''$, or $\frac{1}{2}''$. One-third of an inch will be found to be a most convenient and neat tape for most work. For a large book the width could be $\frac{1}{2}''$, but again I should prefer to increase the number of tapes rather than the actual tape width. This tape width must be known before any marking up is done. I like to see a neatly marked-up book, as marking up and sewing should always be done as though they would always be open to view, and not done in a slipshod manner with the idea that the cover will hide the careless work. In the case of three tapes there is a slight variation in the method of marking up, and this will be taken first. The instructions given here in the use of the try-square and dividers are applicable to the other cases of marking up, and will not be repeated.

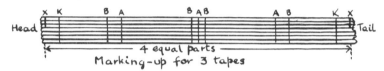

Marking-up for 3 tapes

Here is a diagram of the back of a book marked up for three tapes, and it is done in the following way.

First mark two points with a pencil, one at the head and one at the tail, as at X, X. The distance of these points from the head and tail should show the amount that is going to be cut off the book in the cutting press. These amounts should only be sufficient to allow for a clean trim of all the pages. If the book

Position of try-square for marking-up for sewing.

has been knocked up square at the head, the amount to be trimmed off will be less than at the tail, where the sections are apt to be more uneven. Take the dividers, and by the method of trial and error, divide the distance between X and X (which is now known as the 'length of the book') into four equal parts. Mark the points of division by small dots shown at A, A, A.

Place the try-square in position, and draw clearly marked lines through these points across the backs of the sections. Be careful to see that the back edges of the endpapers receive a clear mark when these lines are drawn. Then mark the points B. It will be seen that these points are distant from the points A by an amount equal to the width of the tape to be used, except in the case of the centre tape. In this case half the width of the tape is measured on each side of A. It will be seen that the outer tapes are shown by placing B outside A in each case. This spacing of the tapes rather nearer the head and tail gives added strength where weakness is likely, but this is only done when three tapes are used. The final markings are for the 'kettle-stitches', and are shown at K, K. These should be placed no less than $\frac{1}{4}''$ from X, X, but this distance is a matter of good judgement. If the book is a small one, i.e. less than crown octavo, $\frac{1}{4}''$ should be right; with larger books this distance may be increased, but let $\frac{1}{2}''$ be the maximum.

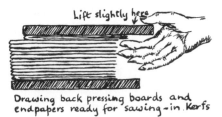

Drawing back pressing boards and endpapers ready for sawing-in Kerfs

The next operation often gives difficulty to the beginner, but by dint of practice the knack can be acquired. Grip the boards and the book firmly in the left hand, and with the right gently unscrew the press until the book and boards are free. Lay all flat on the press cheeks, and place the thumb on top of the upper pressing board, the first finger under the board, catching at the same time the small portion of endpaper projecting beyond the fore-edge of the book. It is for this reason that it is wise when making endpapers to have them a little larger than the book. The remaining fingers can rest gently against the book sections, and so prevent any movement. Now draw back the pressing board and the endpaper, very gently, a matter of $\frac{1}{4}''$

away from the back edge. Deftly turn the boards and book right over, gripping firmly, and repeat the process for the other board and endpaper. Replace in the press in the same manner as before. Grip the sections at points X, X with the thumb and first finger, and with a worn saw make two clean grooves at K, K. These cuts are known as the 'kettle-stitch kerfs', and the

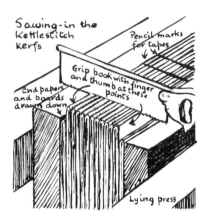

saw must not go too deeply into the backs of the sections; just enough to receive the loop stitches when sewing. On no account must the endpapers be left standing with the sections when drawing back the pressing boards, as the saw would make holes in them, and this cannot be remedied. I have seen careless students forget to do any drawing back at all, with the result that not only are the endpapers spoiled, but the pressing boards damaged too. Some binders prefer to leave the endpapers out of this process, or to use strawboards instead of pressing boards. This no doubt does away with the difficulty of drawing back, but I prefer the first method, as the presence of the boards gives rigidity to the sections whilst marking up, and if the endpapers are not included they will have to be marked separately before the sewing is done. The book is now ready to be sewn, and it makes for neater workmanship if it is kept between the boards until ready to commence the sewing.

A small historical note may be of interest here in connection with the terms 'kettle' and 'kerf'. The Oxford English dictionary has the word 'kettel' as derived from the German, and meaning a small chain or loop; there does not appear to be any written evidence of its use previous to 1880, but as a term passed on orally from craftsman to apprentice it might well have a much longer history. This might be assumed in view of the fact that its companion word 'kerf' is a modified form of the Old English 'cyrf', whose meaning is given as an incision or slit made by cutting, especially in the sense of sawing.

Marking up for Four or more Tapes

The diagram illustrates the completion of the marking up for four tapes.

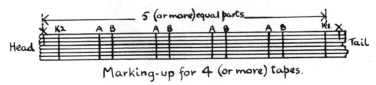

Marking-up for 4 (or more) tapes.

The process is slightly different from the case of three tapes, and one which is the outcome of experience gained in trying to simplify the method as far as is possible for pupils between 11 and 15 years of age. Its value lies in the fact that its main principles hold good even for flexible styles of binding, and there is nothing later to confuse the pupil, or for him to 'unlearn'. If the book is going to be cut on all three edges mark X, X, as the trimming marks. Then mark K1, the TAIL kettle-stitch, first. Its distance inside X has already been discussed. Then, with the dividers, mark off in five equal parts the space between K1 and X at the head. Draw across with the try-square at these points, marked in the diagram at A, A, etc. Now mark the kettle-kerf K2 at the head, and continue down the book marking all the points B the width of the tape away from A in each case. Note that B is on the TAIL SIDE of A. Draw back the endpapers and boards, and saw in the kettle-kerfs. Never be tempted to make saw cuts at the tape marks. The only time one would consider this would be in the case of a series of magazines having very thick single-sections. A little judicious sawing of the tape marks nearly half-way through the thickness will help in getting the needle through, in such cases.

Exactly the same method is followed if more than four tapes are required. The only variation lies in the number of divisions needed between K1 and X at the head. If five tapes are used, the number of parts will be six, and so on.

Two more points remain before leaving the sewing of books on tapes. Mention has been made of uncut books and books cut at the head only. In the case of an uncut book there will be no need to indicate the points X, X. The division distance must be the whole length of the sections. Where a book is cut only at the head, it has been pointed out that for marking up it is knocked up square at the tail. There will be therefore no X mark at the tail, but one will be placed at the head, and the length for division will then lie between this point and the tail itself.

In the true library-style binding the leather is placed directly upon the backs of the sections, making a FAST BACK. It will then be possible to see slight ridges under the leather, indicating where the tapes are raised a little. These are often emphasized on the leather by some tooling, but the point to remember is that if the tapes have not been evenly spaced the fault will be visible when the book is finished. The methods of marking up already outlined will obviate this difficulty, and at the same time give a longer panel at the tail of the book. This longer panel will be considered in the section on flexible binding.

Ordinary Sewing—Marking up for Sawn-in Bands

Four, five, or even six cords may be used for this sewing according to the size of the book, but the only difference lies in the number of divisions needed when marking up the book. A combination of circumstances may have conspired to produce this type of binding. Two main causes can be mentioned. When calf began to be used for books it was found that any glue which came into contact with the back of the skin stained the leather on its face side, and so some method had to be found of preventing the calf from coming into contact with the glue used in gluing up the back of the book. This led to the introduction of the hollow back, and as such a back cannot be placed over a set of raised bands, the idea arose of making a saw cut in the backs of the sections to allow the cords to sink into the back of the book, and so give a level surface. Another factor may have been a desire to have the books 'throw up' more in the centre when opening them. This method of sawing-in the cords is considered by many of the older craftsmen to be a degenerate form of binding, and apt to damage the backs of the sections. This may be so if the 'sawing-in' is carelessly done and the grooves cut too deeply. If neatly carried out, I see no objection to it. Very valuable books should not be bound in this manner, and in such cases, where it is desired that the bands should not be raised, it is better to sew on tapes. On the other hand from the point of view of design, it can be said in favour of this type of binding that far more freedom is given in the conception of design for the covers, as a study of modern bindings will show.

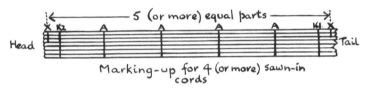

Marking-up for 4 (or more) sawn-in cords

The above diagram sets out the marking up for four sawn-in cords. The usual knocking-up between boards is done, and the whole placed in the lying press. Mark off first X, X, the points where the book is to be cut, and then divide the distance between these points into five equal parts, and mark lines across the back. Note here that in this style no allowance is made for a larger base panel, but the whole available length of the book is used for division. The position of the cord is shown at each A. Next mark the kettle-kerfs at K1 and K2. Draw back the end-papers and boards, and then saw-in the whole of the markings, i.e. all the A's and K1 and K2. The saw cuts at A should be just sufficiently deep and wide to allow the cord used to sink into the groove comfortably. Barbour's Hemp cord No. 8—4 cord soft finish 'Netting twine' is excellent for this work. The book is now ready for the sewing press.

Marking up for a Flexible Binding

By far the most ancient and the finest method for the sewing of a good book is without doubt the 'flexible binding', or, as it is sometimes called, 'sewing on raised bands'. Here the marking up must be done most carefully, as the bands will show under the leather when the book is covered. Most books look best when done on the traditional five bands, but this rule is not rigid, as large but thin books would look better with six bands, whereas a small but thick book has a better appearance if done on four bands.

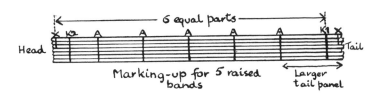

Knock up the book and endpapers square and true as before, and place in a lying press. There will be the usual difference in the method of determining the X positions when dealing with books cut on all the edges, books left uncut, and books cut at the head only. The rules have already been noted. Mark off K1 at the tail first. This position will vary according to the size of the book, and much depends upon it, as this is the amount by which the tail panel will be greater than the other panels. The increase in the size of the tail panel is needed owing to an optical illusion. If it were made equal to the others, it would actually appear to be a little less, and this would destroy the decorative balance of the spine, and cause the appearance to be top-heavy. In addition to this, a book placed on a shelf above the eye-level has its tail panel shortened by the projection of the shelf. Now divide between X at the head and K1 into six equal parts, and mark across the back the lines A. Mark the kettle-kerf K2, draw back the endpapers and the boards, and saw K1 and K2 *only*.

PREPARATION FOR SEWING

Many good books are sewn on double bands, and it is advisable in such cases to draw two lines across the book at points A. They should be a distance apart equal to the thickness of the cord it is intended to use.

CHAPTER 5

Sewing

The objects in view in the sewing of a book have already been detailed in the previous chapter, and the various methods of carrying out this process must now be described.

One type of sewing press has stood the test of centuries. It is shown in the diagram, and the main principle is the movable crossbar. It can be raised or lowered by moving the nuts which support it on the uprights. As these sewing presses are fairly expensive, many ideas have been tried in schools with the idea of reducing the expense, and at the same time giving a press that is equal in performance. There have been many failures from the craftsman's point of view, and one reason lies in the ignoring of the principle of the movable crossbar. Without this movement the cords or tapes cannot be tightened satisfactorily. Another reason arises from the mistaken notion that books sewn on tapes must always be done on a press. It is possible to work with a simple solid bridge provided a wedge is placed under the lay cords, but this is very unsatisfactory. A better idea is shown in the diagram whereby wedges are used to raise a loose bar. Such wedges are apt to slip a little as sewing proceeds, and they must be attended to at frequent intervals. It is necessary to attach these wedges to the press by pieces of string, otherwise they are usually missing when required. Still another and better idea is to build the base and uprights in the usual way, the latter being 1½" to 2" square, and about 8" high. These can be bored at the top to take a piece of round iron rod ½" thick, and about 6" long. The rod need not sink into the wooden upright much more than an inch, but it should be a good fit. The other end is threaded with a coarse thread down to ½" from the top of the upright. It should be furnished with a winged nut and a large washer. The crossbar, although round in the middle, should be square at the ends, and bored ⅝" to fit loosely on the

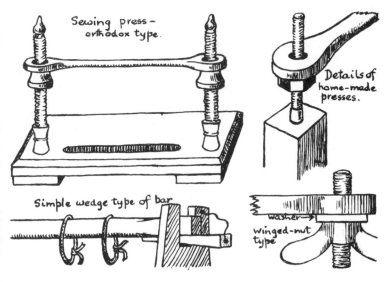

Sewing press – orthodox type.

Details of home-made presses.

Simple wedge type of bar

washer→
winged-nut type

iron rods. In an old print of a bookbinder's shop in the seventeenth century, it is curious to note how little the equipment has changed in character since that day. The sewing press is hardly distinguishable from that of today.

Thread will be required, and this should be the best unbleached linen type. It is made in various thicknesses, but for most work only two kinds need to be kept in stock; 2 cord 16 is a good general-purpose thread, and the second one is 2 cord 25. The first one is thicker than the second. Occasionally there may arise a need for other varieties, but it is not necessary to keep them in stock. Thread is best bought in the hank, and to buy cheaper substitutes is false economy, as the work will not be durable, and the total amount of thread used in the work is small indeed in comparison with the amount done. Hanks should be opened carefully, cut with the scissors through the whole of the threads, and then plaited. As lengths are needed they are pulled by the looped end from the plait. This plait is usually hung over one of the uprights of the press whilst sewing.

Tape should be of unbleached linen stiffened, and I have noted in the last chapter that a roll 1″ wide is an economical way of buying it. Such a roll usually contains 36 yards, and when cut into three will give over 100 yards $\frac{1}{3}$″ wide. This will last a considerable time, even when classes are using it every day. If in an extreme case it is necessary to sew with tapes on a sewing press, the tape left over from this operation should be used to sew books in the usual way without a press.

The bands, or cords, should always be made of hemp, and for ordinary work this should be unsized; 5 cord is the best size for most work, but No. 8—4 cord is best for sawn-in work (see p. 101). Hemp is necessary because it is of such a nature that it will fray out in a fine and silky manner without losing too much strength, and being unsized, this facilitates the fraying. With reference to finer bindings on raised bands, considerable judgement is required in choosing a suitable cord. A thick band on a small book would look very clumsy, and thin bands on a large book would give an appearance of weakness. If a book be sewn on single cords then a thicker cord can be used, but double cords would call for something thinner. For very good bindings the best cord is Italian line, and a small stock of this cord is useful if kept in a number of thicknesses. It is more difficult to fray as it is sized. Each problem should be judged as it arises, and the only hard and fast rule is that the cord should be hempen twine.

A well-sewn book is one wherein all the stitches are of equal tension. If the sewing is done too tightly the book will be 'nipped in' at the kettle-stitches, and when the book comes to be backed the hammering will most likely cause the loops to break. If the sewing is done in a loose fashion, the inner leaves of the sections will work away from the outer leaves along the back, and eventually fall out. Loose sewing is also very difficult to deal with in the ensuing processes.

Sewing on Tapes

Sewing on tapes is the first method to be considered. On occasion it can be done on a sewing press, but for the great majority of books no press is needed. The work is quite as well done, and with much less trouble, especially in schools; it is far more economical in tape. Two or three small books can be sewn on the tape that is wasted if presses are used. It must of course be stiffened tape.

Cut off the number of tapes required $\frac{1}{3}''$ wide, and in length equal to the width of the book back, plus 2″ to 3″, so that a book 1″ thick would have tapes approximately 3″ to 4″ long. Crease each tape about 1″ from one end, so that the shorter end remains roughly at right angles to the longer portion. The stiffening will cause it to retain this position. Thread a needle with a length of thread, and place the book about to be sewn on the bench. In teaching pupils in school, it is wise to insist on things being done in an orderly manner; it saves much confusion. Even the placing of the book upon the bench is of

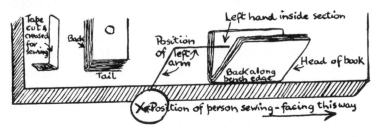

importance, and I have indicated in the diagram the relative positions of the book, bench, and pupil. The book is now on the bench right side up, as though it were about to be read. Many binders work in different ways, but in the case of young pupils, much confusion and error is avoided by having the book placed in the above way. The sewing is best done when the worker is sitting sideways, i.e. with his left side next to the bench, and his left elbow actually resting on it. Left-handed people are a continual thorn in the flesh to the teacher of bookbinding, especially when leather paring comes along. All I need say here concerning sewing is that left-handers must reverse all these instructions, or learn to use the right hand!

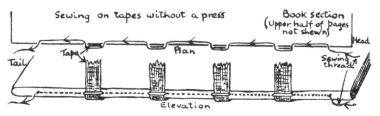

Now take the endpaper in the left hand, and place it with its back edge along the edge of the bench in such a way that its head is away from the worker, and its outer face (the face with the 'O' upon it) downwards on the bench. The position of the sewing in the endpaper has already been detailed in the chapter on endpapers, and this should be referred to. It varies with the different types. In the case of the zig-zag endpaper—for this is the commonest type in this kind of sewing—one sheet must be lifted, or if the endpaper is provided with an extra folded white sheet, then lift up two sheets. Place the left hand inside the endpaper, and insert the threaded needle into the head kettle-kerf with the

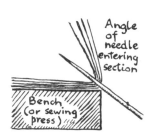

right hand *from outside*. The needle should be pushed in at such an angle as will bisect, in an approximate fashion, the angle formed by the portion of the endpaper lying on the bench and the part lifted up. The needle is received by the first finger and thumb of the left hand, immediately turned round and pushed back through the first tape mark, when the thread is then drawn through with the *right hand*. It is most important to remember that the thread is never drawn through by the left hand. This is not one of the duties of that hand. There is a two-fold purpose in having the left hand inside the book, namely to keep the book in position on the edge of the bench whilst sewing, and to turn the needle round and push it back through the next point. It is therefore wise to adhere to the rule that the left hand must not leave the book whilst any section is being sewn on. It is a very common fault to try and pull the remaining thread through from the inside of the section. All the actual sewing is therefore done by the hand outside the book. This point may seem to have been overstressed, but a little teaching experience will compel agreement on this point. Another very important

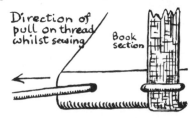

thing to note here is the method of pulling the thread through. Always pull it along the length of the section, either to right or left, whichever way the sewing is going in that particular section. Never pull at right angles to the back of the book, as this action would tear the fold of the section. This is especially important when sewing the endpapers, and failure to remember this point may mean the making of a new set of endpapers. It eases sewing greatly if the thread be pulled across a piece of beeswax, or wax candle, before commencing.

Having emerged at the first tape mark, return through the second mark, and out again at the third, and so on until the

tail kettle-kerf is reached. Gently pull the thread along the length of the endpaper until 3″ to 4″ is left hanging out at the head. There will now be a series of thread loops along the back of the endpaper, corresponding to the position and number of tapes to be used. Lift the first of these loops slightly with the

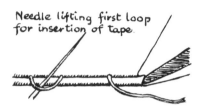

Needle lifting first loop
for insertion of tape.

needle, and insert the shorter end of one of the tapes. Lifting the next loop will tighten the first one, and the second tape is inserted. Continue until all the tapes are in position. Pull the thread tight all along the book and see that the shorter ends of the tapes are all neatly tucked in between the endpaper and the bench, and the longer ends all standing up straight, and parallel to each other.

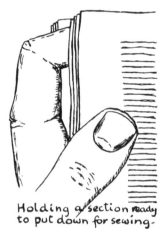

Holding a section ready
to put down for sewing.

Take the first section of the book in the left hand, and with the right hand open it at the centre of the section. Make quite sure that the centre has been found, especially so in the case of books composed of very thin paper. Place the first finger of the left hand in the centre leaves just found, and carry it thus, placing it down on the endpaper, head to coincide exactly with the head of the endpaper, and with its first page face downwards. Push the back fold close to the tapes, and slide the left hand inside the section to hold it in position. If these apparently trivial details are carried out, it should be nearly impossible to place a section upside down. It is very important indeed that during the whole of the sewing the head and back of the book are kept very square and true. Endless trouble will come later if these details are not observed all the time.

Go in with the needle at the tail kettle-kerf, come out again just clear of the first tape. On no account catch the tape with the needle; then in again at the other side of the same tape, and so on until finally coming out at the head-kettle kerf. The piece of thread left hanging out at the head of the endpaper is now tied in a simple knot to the thread in use, and the spare end of thread cut off ¼″ away from the knot.

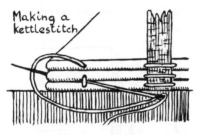

Making a kettlestitch

Take the next section, placing it down in the manner already described, go in at the head, and sew as before, coming out at the tail. At this point the kettle-stitch must be made. Including the section just sewn, count a couple of sections down the book, and push the needle with a sideways motion, underneath the second section down, in the space between the first tape and the kettle-kerf. Then push the needle further so that it comes out at the tail of the book. The first sideways motion prevents the needle from piercing any pages. Pull the needle out at the tail, and thread it upwards through the loop which has just been formed, until it is tight. This stitch will then fit snugly into the kettle-kerf, and it is known as the 'kettle-stitch'. When the thread is being pulled tight through the loop, let it be done in an outward direction at an angle of 30° to 45° from the perpendicular. This tends to keep the kettle-stitch neatly fitted into the kerf all the way up the sections as they are sewn. Some binders do this operation twice at the end of each section, so making a double stitch. Greater safety is achieved by this, but where thicker thread is being used, once will be enough.

The remaining sections are sewn on in the same way, the kettle-stitch coming alternately at the head and tail as the sewing proceeds. The last endpaper will be sewn on in the reverse position, i.e. if one sheet was lifted up in the first one, then three will be lifted up in the last, or if an extra folded white sheet is inserted, then two for the first one and four up for the last. Keep the sewing at an equal tension all through the book, and as each section is sewn on keep it pushed well down on the tapes. Give an eye to the tapes during the sewing to keep them straight and upright. The last endpaper is finished off with a double kettle-stitch, and the remaining thread cut off $\frac{1}{4}''$ from the knot.

1st stage

Dark thread
is attached
to book.

2nd stage —
made by pulling
on C.

Light thread
is the new
piece.

Reference must be made to the joining on of a fresh piece of thread when the one in use is exhausted. A knot is required which will not slip, and yet be flat, and the best type is the 'weaver's knot'. It will hold and yet is not bulky. Reference to the diagram will make this clear. The advantage of such a knot is to be found in the way in which it can be tied quite close to the back of the book. If some distance is left between the knot and the back of the book, there arises the inconvenience of pulling the knot through the section in several places. It is understood, of course, that the knot is tied OUTSIDE the book, and not inside. Any knot which has to pass through the section should be carefully eased through, with both hands, at *right angles to the back*. The knot must also occur somewhere between the kettle-stitches, as it is impossible to make this loop stitch when a knot is present on the thread. Always test the knot after tying it, and cut off the loose ends $\frac{1}{4}''$ from the knot. Inspect the inside of each section before making a kettle-stitch, in order to make sure that the thread has been properly pulled through all the length of the book. It is most annoying to find a large loop of loose thread inside the book after it has been sewn. The above type of work is known as 'sewing all-along'. A reef knot will serve instead of the weaver's knot.

Before leaving the subject of sewing on tapes, mention must be made of the same type of sewing done on a sewing press. A piece of round rod about $\frac{3}{4}''$ thick is slung through the lay cords which hang from the crossbar of the press. The tapes will go round this rod without having any twist put into them, whereas if the lay-cords are used an awkward twist in the tape will result; there is also a saving in tape. Place a pressing board on the base of the press. This raises the book, while sewing is in progress, away from the front edge of the base board. The latter is apt to interfere with the free movement of the needle when the first few sections of the book are being sewn. Put the book face down on the pressing board, with its head to the right. Take a piece of tape round the rod and pin it, as shown in the diagram. Cut off a length sufficient to go an inch under the press, and fasten it securely with a drawing pin. There are special keys made for tapes to avoid the necessity of fastening with pins, but ordinary sewing keys may be used if care is taken not to put a twist in the tape. In using such keys, allow more tape below the press. Bring the appropriate tape mark on the book into line with the tape, and fit the remaining tapes to coincide with the other tape marks. After the tapes have been tightened a little by the screwing up of the nuts on the press uprights, the sewing proceeds in exactly the same manner as already outlined. When the book is finished it is taken out of the press, and the tapes are cut down to leave about one inch on either side of the book. The pieces thus cut off should be put aside for use when sewing books without a press.

Tape-sewing on a press.

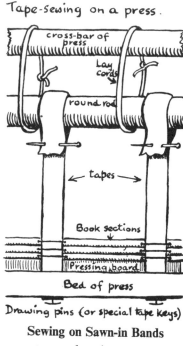

Sewing on Sawn-in Bands

Consideration must now be given to the method of 'sewing all-along' on sawn-in bands. This is done on a sewing press, and loops of string must be placed round the crossbar and securely tied. These are the 'lay-cords', and once they are on the bar there is no need to take them off, as they will serve for the sewing of book after book. It is usual to have five lay-cords slung on the bar. They may not all be required, as in the case of a small book sewn on four bands, but the spare one can be pushed to the end out of the way. Lengths of hemp cord are now tied to the lay-cords, according to the number required. A simple knot, or one as shown in the diagram, is all that is necessary, and there should be enough cord left hanging below the base of the press for attachment to the sewing keys. Three to four inches is sufficient. Sewing keys are made of brass, and can be purchased by the dozen. A good substitute is $\frac{1}{8}''$ galvanized wire. The wire is cut into lengths about $8''$ long and bent round into the form of a narrow 'U', leaving about $\frac{1}{2}''$ between the legs. Take one of the cords in the left hand, and a sewing key in the right, its legs pointing away from the body. Place the neck of the key on top of the cord, both being laid against the front edge of the press. The key

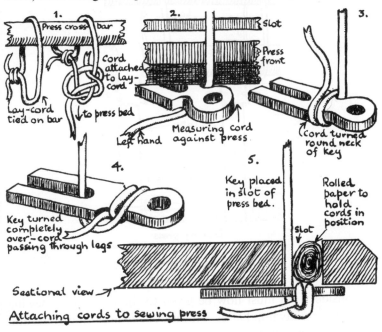

1. Press cross-bar
Cord attached to lay-cord
Lay-cord tied on bar
to press bed

2. Slot
Press front
Measuring cord against press
Left hand

3. Cord turned round neck of key

4. Key turned completely over—cord passing through legs
Sectional view →

5. Key placed in slot of press bed.
Rolled paper to hold cords in position
Slot

Attaching cords to sewing press

should be $\frac{1}{4}''$ clear of the press when the cord is held taut. Hold this position with the first finger of the right hand, and take two turns of the cord round the neck of the key. Then turn the key right over, so that the cord comes up through the legs, and holding it in this position carefully put it through the slot in the press, and turn the key at right angles to the slot. The head of the key should face the front when correctly placed. Do this with the remaining cords. I have a sewing press which has a board screwed down permanently to the base. It has the advantage of not being liable to move whilst the sewing is going on, and, if pressing boards are not too plentiful, it does not withdraw them from other uses. A sewing block can also be fixed to help keep the sections straight at the head. If this block is made so that it can move along a slot it will cater for all sizes of books.

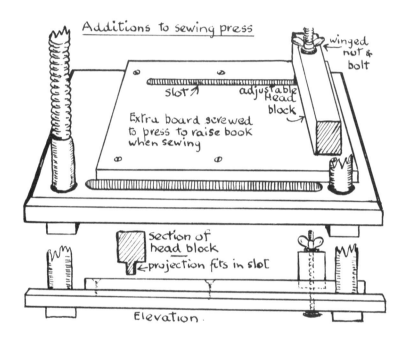

Now take the book and place it on the press, with its head to the right hand, and its face down, as in sewing on tapes. Set all the cords opposite the sawn kerfs in the back, being careful to keep them parallel and upright. When this has been done, the cords must be tightened by turning the nuts, thus raising the crossbar. A piece of paper, tightly rolled, should be pushed into the slot in order to keep the cords pressed against the inner side, and to prevent them moving. The book is then taken off the press, and placed on the bench right side up, and rather to the left, as in the case of tape sewing.

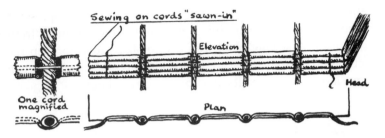

There is little difference in the method of sewing from that used with tapes. Take the endpaper, and place it on the press with its head to the right, and its outside sheet down on the board. Go in with the needle at the head kettle-kerf, and come out at the next saw-cut on the right-hand side of the cord. On no account allow the needle to catch or go through the cord. Go in with the needle again on the left-hand side of this band through the same saw-cut, so that the stitch will go right across the back of the cord. Continue down the length of the endpaper as shown in the diagram. Proceed with the sections in the same manner, being careful to see that the bands rest in the saw-cuts as each fresh section is added to the book. Tap down the sections as the sewing proceeds. The method is described on p. 118.

Flexible Sewing

The next type of sewing to consider is known as flexible sewing, or sewing on raised bands. There are two varieties, namely, that sewn on single cords, and a second one sewn on double cords. Flexible binding is the most ancient method of sewing; it is the strongest form, and the one often used by the binder of very good books, although many such books are now sewn on sawn-in cords and given a hollow back; this gives much more freedom in designing the covers. The sewing press is fitted up with cords in the same manner as was done in sawn-in work. In very good work the best Italian line is a good cord to use, especially when single bands are being considered, and the thickness of the cord chosen depends on the size of the volume to be bound. Many beginners err on the side of choosing bands which are too thick. Great care should be exercised in getting the cords perfectly parallel and upright in the press. The sewing is carried

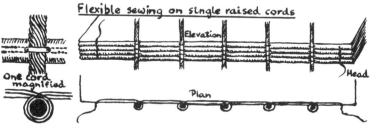

forward in the usual way, the variation in this style being the way in which the sewing thread is carried right round each cord. The diagram will make this clear. The strength of this sewing will be seen when it is realized that every stitch is locked round each cord, and if any breakage of thread occurred later, it would be confined to the piece of thread between the two cords, and would extend no further.

It is very important in flexible sewing that the sections be knocked down as they are sewn on. This is done by holding the book firmly with the left hand, and tapping the backs of the sections between the cords with a loaded stick. This prevents too much 'swell' in the back of the book when sewn. Care must be taken, while sewing, to see that every stitch is properly pulled through. It is quite easy to forget this point, and later to find loose loops of thread in the sections.

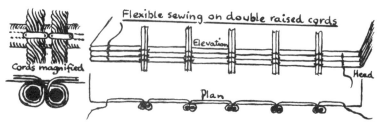

Sewing on double cords is the strongest method of all, and was adopted by medieval binders when dealing with large vellum books. Where we use cord, they used leather or vellum strips. Very often the headbands were sewn on at the same time by placing an extra cord at each end of the press to form the foundations for the head- and tailbands. It is a very strong method of sewing headbands, but difficulties arise later when the leather cover is turned in, thus offsetting to some extent the strength gained.

The method of sewing is indicated in the diagram, and the rules previously outlined must be followed. In stringing the cords on the press, each piece must be threaded through the lay-cords, and pulled through sufficiently to allow of two equal lengths hanging below the baseboard. A single tie made on these two cords round the lay-cord will prevent any movement when attaching them to the sewing keys. In doing this they are treated as one cord, and no twist should be given to them in the process. It will be obvious that thinner cord must be used for double cords than that used for single bands. Care must be exercised when pushing the needle between the bands to avoid catching them; taking the needle and thread round the back of the bands in one movement of the sewing hand is a knack that is easily acquired.

Sewing Two Sheets on

This style of sewing is a variation of sewing 'all-along', and is so named because two sections are sewn on at the same time. If a book is composed of a large number of very thin sections, it must not be sewn in the ordinary manner as this would cause too much swell in the back, due of course to the abnormal amount of thread used. Sewing 'two sheets on' reduces the amount by half. Naturally, the strength of the binding is reduced, but an ugly swell in the back is the greater evil to overcome.

Set up the press with cords in the same way as for sewing 'all-along' on sawn-in cords and sew the endpaper and the first two sections in the normal way. Take a piece of clean waste paper, about 6″ wide and a little less than the length of the book, and fold it down the centre, so that it is now about 3″ wide. Cartridge paper is suitable as it is fairly stiff. Put the next section down on the press, and insert the needle as usual, at the tail kettle-kerf, and come out at the first band. Insert one half of the cartridge paper in the middle of this section. Pick up the next section, find the centre, and lay it down, inserting the other half of the cartridge paper in this centre. Now go in with the needle at the other side of the first band, and on coming out of this last section at the next band, proceed into the lower section, and so on from section to section. For the kettle-stitch let the needle be inserted under the last of the sections caught up by the previous stitch. This will be obviously more than two sections down. The insertion of the folded sheet facilitates the transfer of the left hand from the centre of one section to that of the other whilst sewing. Finish off the last two or three sections and the endpaper sewn 'all-along', as for the first endpaper and the first two sections. This type of sewing may also be done on tapes if required, and this is one of the few cases better carried out on a sewing press. There are variants of the method of sewing, just described, and one alternative is shown in fig. 2 of the diagram.

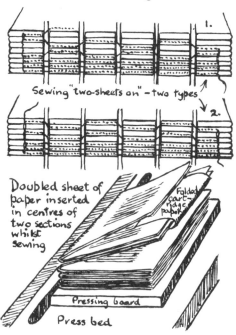

SEWING

Fraying out the Slips

When books sewn on cords have been completed, they should be 'cut out'. The cords are cut with a pair of scissors just below the lay-cord loops, and the keys removed. The cords are then trimmed to leave about 3″ on each side of the book. These portions of the cords left projecting from the book are called the 'slips', and they have now to be 'frayed out'. Bearing in mind that beginners may easily ruin the slips in this process, either of the following methods should be adopted.

Take the cord in the finger and thumb of the left hand, and untwist the strands by revolving it in the opposite direction from that used when the cord was originally twisted. At the same time insert a needle between the strands at a point near the book, and separate them. Take each one of these separated strands, and untwist them in the same way as was done with the original cord. It will be found that the twist in this case is always in the opposite direction to the first twist. The insertion of the needle near the base of these strands, and the drawing upwards of the needle so as to 'comb' it along its entire length, should be sufficient to straighten out all the fibres and make them fine and silky. No coarse fibres should be left in the finished slip, and a final combing through the slip as a whole should complete the fraying out. The diagrams will make this clear, and the further

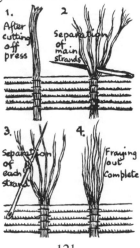

1. After cutting off press
2. Separation of main strands
3. Separation of each strand
4. Fraying out complete

work to be carried out on the slips will be described in its appropriate place. A warning is necessary in the case of cords sewn sawn-in. When drawing the needle through it is quite easy to draw the whole slip right out of the book back, and replacing it is not an enviable task. If the slip is held near the book whilst being combed, the risk will be reduced, but the root of the trouble lies in failure to untwist the fibres enough before applying the needle.

A quicker and more efficient method is found in the use of a small wire teazle brush, such as is used in brushing up suede leather. An alternative to this is a piece of file card tacked on to a small wooden block.

Proceed with the needle as shown at Nos. 1 and 2 in the preceding diagram. Then place a piece of tin plate on the book and comb the slips, one at a time, with the teazle; the combing is done upon the plate until all the slips are fine and silky throughout.

It makes for easier working in the subsequent operations if, after fraying out, the slips are given a little touch of paste on the EXTREME TIPS. This keeps the fibres neatly together, but on no account paste the whole slip.

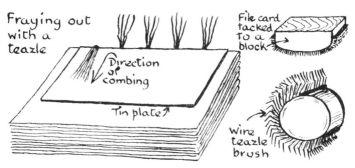

The Sewing of Books Cut only at the Head

Where a book is to be cut only at the head, it is essential that the sewing be done in such a way that the sections are kept square and true at the tail.

Books composed of Plates

Plates should not be overcast in the manner used for single sheets, but should be carefully guarded together in pairs. A decision must be made regarding the number of such pairs to be used in the making up of a section. They are then sewn in the ordinary way. The thickening of the back due to the presence of so many guards may mean that the book will have to be 'packed' for subsequent operations. Reference to guarded albums, described on p. 276, will clarify this point.

CHAPTER 6

Pasting-up and Gluing-up

Pasting up the First and Last Sections

There seems to be some divergence of opinion amongst binders concerning this operation as to whether it should be done or not. All case bindings having stationery endpapers are automatically pasted up, but books with sewn-on endpapers may or may not be done. The decision depends on the judgement of the craftsman, who will take into consideration the type of book, quality of paper, and the possible usage the volume will have to undergo. I should invariably paste-up all books bound 'out-of-boards', as the endpapers are apt to 'start' forward when rounding and backing after the fore-edge has been cut. This would necessitate re-trimming of the endpapers at the fore-edge. Pasting-up does away with this difficulty.

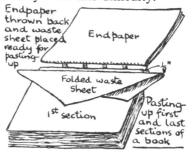

Place the book to be pasted up on the bench, and throw back the endpaper. Take a piece of clean waste paper, and fold it to obtain a straight edge. Place it on the book so that this straight edge is $\frac{1}{8}''$ away from the back edge of the first section, and parallel to it. Paste along this $\frac{1}{8}''$ of the section left uncovered, remove the waste sheet, and bring over the endpaper on to the book. Repeat the operation for the other endpaper, and immediately knock up the back of the book on the bench until it is square, and the back edge of each endpaper flush with the backs of the sections. Then set the whole under a weight until dry.

Knocking out the Swell

The 'swell' in the back of a book is due to the addition of the thread to the sections when sewing, and also to the presence of any guarding that may have been done. It is necessary that some amount of swelling be present in a newly sewn book, in order to be able to round and back it properly, but too much will produce very undesirable results at a later stage. If the book is found to have more swell in the back than is necessary, steps must be taken to reduce it to reasonable proportions. Knock up the back

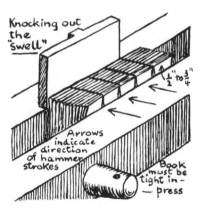

Knocking out the "swell"

$\frac{1}{2}''$ to $\frac{3}{4}''$

Arrows indicate direction of hammer strokes

Book must be tight in press

on the bench until it is square, and carefully lower the book into a lying press until only $\frac{1}{2}''$ to $\frac{3}{4}''$ is left projecting above the press cheeks. Some binders prefer to put a piece of strawboard on each side of the book, but such pieces should not project above the

125

jaws of the press. Tighten the press until the book is firmly held, but still square along the back. It is not advisable to screw up the press too tightly because this will prevent the glue going in between the sections. Take a knocking-down iron, and place it in the position indicated in the diagram. Then holding it upright and firmly against the book, gently tap the other side of the book with a backing hammer until the swelling has been suitably reduced. Then change the position of the iron to the side already tapped and repeat the hammering at the other side. The slips or tapes may have a crumpled appearance, except in the case of flexible sewing, and will need to be pulled out a little. Great care must be exercised in performing this operation, or they may be pulled clean out of the back. If one end is held firmly whilst the pulling is done at the other end, this danger will be avoided.

Gluing up the Back

The back is now ready to be glued up, and this is a process often indifferently done by the beginner. The glue itself must be hot and thin; thick glue must be avoided at all costs. Apply the glue to the back evenly, working it well into the spaces between the sections until no part remains uncovered. Then work it in thoroughly with the finger. The importance of rubbing the glue well in cannot be overstressed. It is not the quantity of glue that is applied which counts, so much as the amount that can be rubbed in between the sections, that makes for good craftsmanship. The whole purpose in gluing up is to hold the sections in position during the operations to follow, and unless this is achieved, rounding, backing, and cutting cannot be successfully accomplished. One more point deserves mention. If the book is not held square in the press whilst the glue is applied, it is difficult to right it afterwards.

Some small books may be placed flat on the bench with the back projecting slightly over the edge. If a knocking-down iron is put on top of the book, and the whole held firmly whilst the gluing is done, it should be adequate in such cases. This method is an asset under the conditions obtaining in many schools, where lack of apparatus is the rule rather than the exception.

After gluing up, the book must remain undisturbed until the glue has set, but not until it has dried. A word of explanation is necessary here upon the setting and drying of glue. After it has been applied to the back of a book it begins to set, and in doing so loses its stickiness, but not its elasticity. It is therefore important that the operations of rounding and backing shall be performed whilst the elasticity is present. The glue does not retain sufficient of this elasticity when it has dried. There is not the same urgency when prepared elastic glues are used, but in the majority of schools ordinary cake glue is used, and where a pupil has finished sewing towards the end of a period, it is inadvisable to go on with the gluing up. If, however, this is done it will be necessary to soften the glue when the work is taken up again. This is done by applying paste to the back with the finger, and allowing it to stand for a few minutes. Then sponge off this paste, and allow the book to stand aside until the stickiness has gone.

Thick glue applied to the back of a book is utterly useless, and in cases where this has been done—it often occurs with the beginner—it must be washed off before proceeding any further. To do this the inner portion of the glue pot must be lifted out and the brush rinsed in the hot water of the outer pot. Use the brush right away on the book, rubbing the back vigorously until most of the glue has been cleaned off. Repeat the rinsing of the brush if necessary, but do not overdo this washing off as damage may be done to the backs of the sections by too much moisture. Alternatively, paste the spine; allow it to 'soak' a few minutes; then scrape off with a stick or folder and sponge all clean.

Avoid getting glue on the tapes or slips projecting outside the endpapers. With glue that is fairly brittle there is a danger that they may actually break off when the glue is dry, if this small point is ignored. The gluing up of a book back seems at the first glance to be quite a simple operation, but it is far from being so, and much depends on its being done in a careful manner.

127

Prepared Glues

If specially prepared glue can be obtained it has many advantages. It is most economical in use, and can be diluted to an astonishing degree, and yet at the same time retain its adhesive quality. I have used this glue for many years, and find that a 14 lb. tin will cover a period of about a year with adult classes meeting two sessions per week.

Since the first edition of this book was published, the problem of glue coming to the binder in metal containers has been eliminated with the advent of plastic bags. Provided the mouth of such a bag is kept closed, the glue will remain soft and pieces may be cut from it as required.

Books left Uncut—Trimming Endpapers

Where books are to have their edges left uncut it is advisable, at this point, to trim the endpapers down to the book size. It will be remembered that when the endpapers were made, the folded sheets were cut a little larger than the book. This surplus must now be trimmed off.

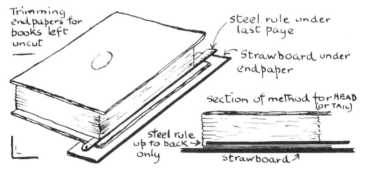

Take a piece of waste board, a little longer than the edges to be cut and place it underneath one of them. Insert a thin steel rule between the last page of the book and the endpaper, in such a manner that its edge lies exactly along the edge of the page. Hold the book down with a very firm pressure and run a sharp knife along the edge of the steel rule, thus cutting off the surplus endpaper. Repeat this for the other edges.

128

CHAPTER 7

Cutting Fore-edge 'Out-of-boards'

The method of cutting a book 'out-of-boards' applies to all books whose boards are eventually attached to the book by gluing, i.e. all books whose boards are not 'laced-in'. The boards are actually used on the book as guides when cutting the head and tail, so that the term 'out-of-boards' really means 'cutting the book with the boards loose'. Such a method has been adapted from the more ancient way of cutting the edges after the boards have been attached, i.e. cutting 'in-boards'.

In cutting 'out-of-boards' the fore-edge must be cut before the rounding and backing is done. It must also be clearly understood that after the back has been glued up, the fore-edge is cut, and the rounding and backing done before the glue is dry. The reason for this is to be found under 'Gluing up the back' in the previous chapter.

In preparing to cut the fore-edge, lay the book down on the bench and open it slightly with the left hand. If the pages vary in width, open at the point where they are narrowest. With the right hand insert a slip of paper right up to the back of the section. This slip should be about ¾″ wide, a little longer than the width of the book, and having one end square. My own habit is to make the endpapers somewhat larger than the book, and at this stage this extra piece of paper can be used to provide the

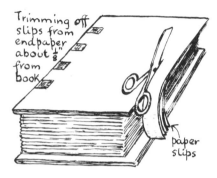

slip. Run up the fore-edge with scissors, cutting off the over-hanging pieces of endpaper. One of these will serve the purpose in view, and it will also have a square end, as the head of the endpapers was trimmed square before sewing.

Do not open the book too wide when inserting the slip, as damage would be done to the back whilst the glue is still soft. The slip now lies across the width of the page, and if the pages in the left hand are lowered a little, the pressure of the hand

upon the book will retain the slip in position without fear of movement. Make a pencil mark on the slip at the exact point where it crosses the fore-edge of the page. Take out the slip and close the book.

The slip is now used as a measure to determine where the book is to be cut. Place the slip with its square end on the back edge of the endpaper, a little below the head of the book, and mark a point on the book to coincide with the mark on the slip. Before moving the slip make another mark on both the endpaper and the slip $\frac{1}{16}''$ 'inside' the first mark. The term 'inside' here means between the first mark and the back of the book. There are now two marks on both the book and the slip; the outer one represents the approximate width of the book before cutting, and the inner one the width after cutting. Transfer the slip to the tail of the book, and mark *both* widths here too. Rule lines through both sets of marks with a straight-edge. Turn the book over, and on this side mark only the outer points on the slip. There are now two parallel lines on one side of the book, and a single line on the other.

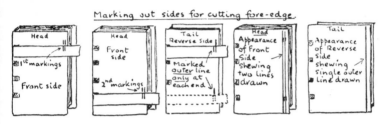

Marking out sides for cutting fore-edge.

A few words are necessary concerning the distance of the inner line from the outer line on the front of the book. No more should be cut off a book than is absolutely necessary, and the less one can take off effectively the better. Considerable judgement is required in deciding how far the inner line should come inside the outer one. Experience will show that, although the slip is placed as far as it will go into the section, yet it will never give the actual width of the pages accurately. There is the thickness of the paper in the back folds of the sections to account for, and in practice it will be found that the measurement on the slip gives a line on the endpaper slightly less than the actual width of the page. The inner line can usually be drawn about $\frac{1}{16}''$ inside this line if the above details are borne in mind, but the student must use common sense in this matter, keeping in mind the nature of the book to be cut, the width of its margins, and the reducing to a minimum of the amount cut off.

Now take two pieces of waste board—strawboard will serve, but a harder board is much better—about 3″ wide and a little longer than the length of the book from head to tail. Each piece must have one of its edges cut perfectly straight. Put two small

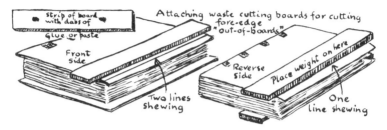

spots of glue (or paste) on each board, and place the straight-edges along the lines drawn on the book. In the case of the side having the two lines, the board should lie along the INSIDE line. Place a weight on the book until the glue has set.

Pick up the book, and examine the back in order to make sure that it is perfectly square. If by any chance it shows any twist, knock it up gently on the bench. It is a most important matter to make certain of this point. Grasp the middle of the fore-edge firmly between the fingers and thumb of the left hand, and lower

the whole carefully into the cutting press until the fingers come into contact with the cheeks of the press. Do not attempt to lower the book any further at this stage, but with the right hand turn the press screws gently until the book is nipped enough to hold it without any slipping, but no tighter. The double line should now be showing at the front, and the single one at the back of the press. It is quite a common occurrence to find pupils trying to put the book into the press in the reverse manner, and it is wise to check the work before any cutting is done.

Place both hands underneath the press, and holding the book firmly, draw it gently down until the edge of the strawboard is level with the cheek of the press. The position of the board on the reverse side must now be inspected—an important matter

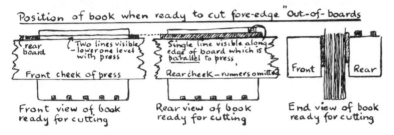

Position of book when ready to cut fore-edge "Out-of-boards"

Front view of book ready for cutting

Rear view of book ready for cutting

End view of book ready for cutting

very often forgotten. It should be quite obvious that if the book is square, the edge of this rear board will be as much above the cheek of the press as the distance between the two lines drawn on the front side of the book, and, withal, perfectly parallel to that cheek. If this is not the case the book is not square in the press, and a gentle twisting by the hands underneath is required. If the alignment is very far out it is better to take all out of the press, knock up the back square and reset. Even when both boards are true, it is still wise to glance under the press to see that the back is perfectly square. Ploughing a book before all these details are correct is quite fatal. The press is now screwed up tightly, care being taken to keep the cheeks perfectly parallel in doing so. It is a very common fault to screw up one end of the press more than the other, and the rule to remember is that of turning each screw alternately a little at a time.

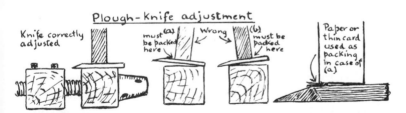

Plough-knife adjustment

Cutting may now be proceeded with, and the plough knife must be very sharp, being adjusted so that it runs flush along the front cheek of the press. Knife adjustment is a matter needing care, and the diagrams will give guidance in the principles to be followed. In course of time the cheeks of the press wear a little hollow in the middle, and this causes much trouble. They should be tested at intervals with a long steel straight-edge, and planed up true again if necessary. Several things combine to ensure a clean, smooth cut, viz.,

(*a*) A very sharp knife, correctly adjusted.

(*b*) Pressure on the plough downwards to prevent 'kicking'.

(*c*) Pressure of each hand towards the other, thus holding the plough firmly.

(*d*) A free swinging movement of the plough from end to end without hesitation.

(*e*) The turning of the screw only a very small amount at a time, and that only when nearest the body.

(*f*) Pressure of the whole plough consistently against one or other of the runners. Wobbling between these wood strips is a fatal error.

The whole movement needs experience to carry it out success-fully, and the student should endeavour to achieve what is known as 'the feel of the plough'.

Knives may be ground pointed as at A, or round as at B. I prefer the B type, but both cut well. The B type is rather more difficult for the beginner to sharpen. To keep such tools in good order oilstones must be at hand, an India type for quick grind-ing and a smooth one of the Washita variety for finishing off the edges.

A note is necessary here on the use of strips of strawboard on each side of the book while the fore-edge is being cut. The orthodox method uses only the rear strip plus a wooden cutting board, but the method already outlined is an adaptation to meet the difficulties arising in schools and other institutions. One of the chief problems in such classes is the condition of the cutting presses. So many people use them (often ill-use them) that the inner edges of the jaws become dinted and damaged, and this always prevents good clean cutting. The placing of the strips along each side of the book is tantamount to providing the cutting press with two new temporary jaws each time a book is cut. Millboard strips are much better than strawboard, as they are harder, and such strips should not be too narrow. Narrow strips will tend to leave a mark on the book, and this is the only danger to avoid in this method. On a book 5″ wide it is possible to have the boards up to 4″ wide. When the cutting has been done, a quick pull under the edges of the strips nearest the back of the book will detach them. If the wastes are damaged it is of little consequence, and the book can now be rounded and backed.

Notes on the Sharpening of Knives

Some general observations on the sharpening of knives will be appropriate at this point, as many students have little idea of the principles underlying the achievement of a razor-like edge on a knife.

In bookbinding, five types of such tools are in general use, viz.: (a) ordinary knives for general work; (b) ordinary paring knives; (c) French paring knives; (d) spokeshave blades, and (e) plough knives. The first grinding must be done upon a coarse stone and must be continued until a 'burr' is achieved. In the case of (a) both bevels on the knife must be ground alternately until the 'burr' appears as a very thin sliver of metal hanging on the edge. In cases (b), (c), (d) and (e) the 'burr' can be felt along the flat side of the blade and, when this appears, the knife must be placed flat side down and ground until the 'burr' is turned back and, again as in (a), hanging on the edge.

Then transfer to a finer stone where the rubbing strokes must be much lighter and the change from bevel to bevel, or bevel to flat side, much more frequent and getting lighter. During this process a very sharp watch must be kept on the tiny sliver of metal on the edge. When this drops off, grinding must immediately cease, as the razor-edge required is now present on the knife. Further work on paring knives will be dealt with at a later stage.

CHAPTER 8

Rounding and Backing

Rounding

If a book were not rounded, the tendency after a little use would be for the back of the book to 'fall in' and assume a concave shape. This is both ugly and inconvenient, and it was discovered at a very early date that the difficulty could be surmounted by giving the back a convex curve. Indeed, many books assume this roundness in a natural manner, and this may

A rounded back

have led to the introduction of the process itself. Rounding gets rid of a certain amount of the 'swelling' in the back caused by the presence of the sewing threads in each section, and this swell is given a more even distribution. Even though a book is intended to have a flat back, it should be rounded very slightly to prevent the fore-edge 'flying out'. Flat backs certainly open better than round backs, but it would be a mistake to allow this fact to overrule the necessity for a little rounding. The determination of the amount of roundness to be given is not entirely under the craftsman's control. It is governed by the appearance of the book after sewing, the amount of swell caused by sewing threads, together with any guards inserted, and the purpose of the book when bound. A book of thick sections has very little thread in the back and will therefore tend to have a flat back; whereas a book of thin sections will have a larger quantity of thread, and so develop a much rounder back. Large numbers of guards will also produce the latter result. It should be clear now to the students why books of thick sections must have thicker thread, and those composed of thin sections, thinner thread. Do not, when rounding, use force to defeat that which is natural to the book. A book of thick sections is bound to have a flattish back, and it would be a great mistake to try and force it very round. It is also difficult to obtain a well-shaped back where the sections are of unequal thickness, or where they have been overcast.

In order to carry out the rounding, place the book upon a firm bench, or thick litho stone. Its fore-edge should be towards the worker, and, as previously mentioned, the glue on the back no longer tacky, but not yet set. With the left hand draw the upper portion of the book forward gently with the fingers, and at the

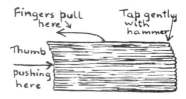

same time place the thumb along the fore-edge, and press against that edge to balance the drawing motion of the fingers. Tap the book with a backing hammer very lightly down the back edge of the endpaper throughout its whole length. Turn the book over and repeat the operation on the other side in the same manner. This is a kind of preliminary to the actual rounding, and I have found it to be very effective. Combined with the pull of the fingers, this gentle tapping of the back edge of the endpapers definitely starts the rounding of the back in a most natural manner, and prevents damage to the endpapers.

To carry out the rounding proper the left hand is again placed in the position already noted. By pulling with the fingers and pushing with the thumb, the hammer is brought down along the backs of the sections in the upper half of the book. They will begin to slide slightly over each other, and this produces the rounding. Turn the book over and repeat, and continue turning over in this way until a fully rounded back has been achieved,

making sure that both sides are evenly balanced. Great force must never be used, as damage can be easily done to the backs of the sections by heavy hammer strokes. Practice is needed to enable the student to assess the weight of the stroke required for any particular book. In dealing with a book sewn flexibly on raised cords the hammer must not fall on these cords, and it is necessary to use a much smaller-headed hammer. Fortunately nearly every such binding needs only a little rounding, and a lot of hammering is not called for. A flexible binding with a very round back would look dreadful, even if it were possible to achieve such a roundness in this style of sewing.

Backing

After long experience in the teaching of bookbinding, I regard the process of 'backing' a book as the most important of all the operations involved in this craft. Failure in backing spells failure in the remainder of the work, and it is vital that the student should thoroughly understand what he is doing, and why he is doing it.

During the sewing of the book, every time a fresh section is added there is also added another thickness of sewing thread to the total thickness of the back. When the sewing is finished, it will be obvious that the book will be thicker at the back, by the number of threads in the sections, than it is at the fore-edge. This extra thickness must be disposed of if the book is to have an even and square appearance throughout. Two things will accomplish this. The process of rounding, in itself, will distribute a portion of the 'swell' by the slight sliding of the sections over each other. The backing will dispose of the remainder, and leave the book equal in thickness from the back to the fore-edge. The operation of 'backing a book' indicates the method by which the backs of the sections are bent over from the centre towards the right and the left until a groove is formed into which the boards will fit comfortably. This groove also acts as a hinge for the boards when opening or shutting the book; unnecessary strain is removed from the joint, preventing the latter breaking away, and its presence gives an assurance that the back will return to its proper shape every time it has been opened.

Two most important points arise here; they are seldom given the care and attention needed. The depth of the groove is governed by the thickness of the boards to be used for the book. A large heavy book will need heavier boards, and therefore a deeper groove, whereas a small book, having thinner boards, will have a correspondingly smaller groove. The appearance of many books bound by students is ruined by failure to observe this simple rule.

Boards correctly fitted

Boards too thin or groove too deep

Boards too thick or groove not deep enough

There are two alternatives. Either the boards are chosen first, and the groove made to fit them, or the groove may be made first, and boards chosen to fit the groove. If the boards are selected first, it is wise to draw a line on each side of the book indicating the thickness of the boards. This measurement can be marked by standing the board on its edge, as shown in the diagram, and then a line drawn through this point parallel to the back

140

edge of the endpaper. It will be found in practice that the groove should be very slightly larger than the thickness of the boards, but the marking of the point by the pencil will give the necessary addition, for the pencil mark itself will be slightly inside the board thickness. The second method calls for more experience in estimating the thickness of the groove required for that particular book, and knowledge of the thicknesses of the

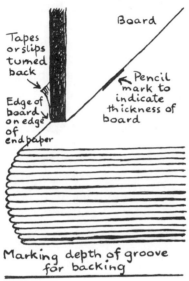

Board

Tapes
or slips
turned
back

Edge of
board
on edge
of
endpaper

Pencil
mark to
indicate
thickness of
board

Marking depth of groove
for backing

boards in stock. It often involves making boards by gluing different thicknesses together. Years of experience in the backing of books are needed to be able to assess with complete accuracy the exact thickness of the groove in relation to the boards the craftsman has in mind for any particular book, and the beginner would do well to adhere to the first method until confidence and experience have been gained.

The second point concerns the assessment of the depth of the groove in relation to the amount of swell present. If a book is given a deeper groove than the swell will allow, it will never shut properly when bound. This becomes clear to the student when it is realized that such a groove has made the book thickness at the spine less than it is at the fore-edge. It is quite a common, but disastrous, error with students to give too much groove when backing.

The backing is carried out in the following manner, presuming that the glue on the back is still soft, but not tacky. Take two backing boards a little longer than the book. Even this small point needs stressing in the case of many students, as one often finds 13″ backing boards being selected to back a book 7½″ long. The shape of the boards is indicated in the diagrams, and they should have a straight sharp edge. To retain this edge it is necessary to trim them up with a sharp plane at fairly frequent intervals. They should be made of beech, and a convenient dimension, when new, is 4″ wide by ¾″ thick at the top, tapering to ½″ at the base. Taken in pairs, the most convenient lengths are 8″, 11″, and 13″.

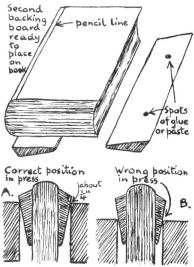

Place the book flat on the bench, and having put two very small spots of glue or paste on the inside of a backing board, lay it down exactly along the pencil line already marked. This line gives an added advantage in that any slipping of the board is immediately detected. Carefully turn book and board over, and fix the second board. If at this point, the whole is placed in a press, as at B, and nipped *very slightly* for a few minutes the backing boards will have adhered to the book. Tapes or slips should remain outside the boards, and the whole is picked up, and lowered gently into a backing press, gripping all in the left hand very firmly all the time. Go on lowering into the press until the outer corners of the boards project only $\frac{1}{4}''$ above the press, as at A, and nip up just enough to hold all in position. If the boards are not lowered as far as possible but left half-way, the subsequent tightening of the press will split the backing boards lengthwise. The position of the book should be very carefully inspected to ensure that no slipping has taken place. If anything like this has occurred, it is far better to take all out of the press and reset. Screw up the press very tightly, and commence to back the book with a backing hammer. The hammer strokes should not fall directly upon the backs of the sections, but a glancing blow is used. The hammer should fall first at the points marked 1, and gradually work down both sides of the back as shown by 2, 3, and 4, until the backing boards are reached, and the book takes on the appearance shown above. The sections should lie straight

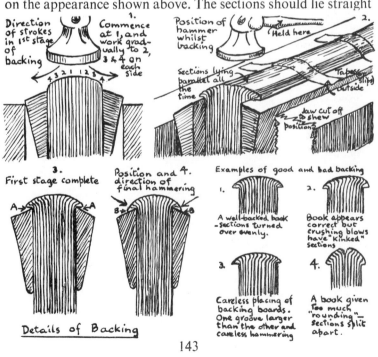

Details of Backing

and parallel as they were before the backing was commenced. It will be found that when the hammering is done, there will still be a small space between the edge of the endpapers and the backing boards, as at A, A. To leave it in this condition is to leave the backing incomplete; to finish off the work satisfactorily, the hammer must be used in a different way. A direct blow must be employed along the whole length of the endpapers until this small aperture is closed, and the outer sections lie snugly on the backing boards, as at B, B. This last process is one which is often neglected, but it makes all the difference between an indifferent piece of work and that done in a craftsmanlike fashion. The reason is not far to seek, and an understanding of this reason will prevent its omission.

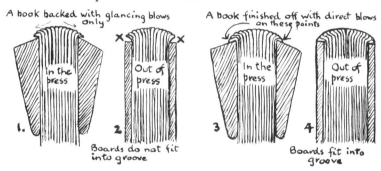

When a book has been backed, and is taken out of the press, the groove springs back a little, as at 2. The boards will not fit neatly into such a groove, and gaps are observed at X, X. If, however, the backing has been completed, as in 3, and on taking out of the press the springing takes place, it will assume the appearance shown in 4, and the boards will fit properly into the groove. Another error often committed lies in giving heavy blows with the hammer. This crushes the sections, and spoils the shape of the back. The blows should be light when backing begins, and should be increasing a little in weight as the backing boards are approached. Any departure from an even appearance of the backing spells failure, and brings in its wake difficulties in subsequent operations.

The above applies to all books sewn on tapes or sawn-in

cords, but in the case of books with raised bands there is more difficulty. Mention has already been made of the use of a smaller hammer for the rounding of such books, and now, for the backing, a special hammer is needed. The diagram shows the type required, and is drawn nearly actual size.

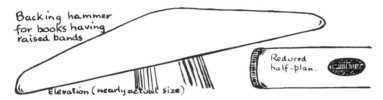

Backing hammer for books having raised bands

Elevation (nearly actual size)

Reduced half-plan.

Begin the backing in the usual way from the centre outwards, carefully avoiding the bands. It will be found that the hammer will go right up to the band immediately under its head, but not right up to the band above its head. It is necessary to reverse one's position frequently, first standing at one end of the book and then at the other. This will keep the sections parallel. The finishing-off process with the direct blows must be gently and carefully done. Above all, the backing of any book must never be hurried, and especially is this the case with flexible bindings. It cannot be adequately done in less than 15 to 20 minutes per book. Note also should be made of the manner in which the hammer is held for all types of book. The hand is quite near the head, and the handle always lies over the back of the book parallel to the sections, i.e. from head to tail or tail to head.

First position →

Second position

Method of going right up to bands with hammer by changing position

Backing Board

CHAPTER 9

Boards

Before the advent of elaborate machinery, bookbinders made their own boards by pasting waste sheets of printed matter together until the required thickness was obtained. These were known as 'pasteboards'. Today, many varieties of boards are produced, and, of these, three kinds are in common use for books:

(*a*) *Strawboards.* The best kind is of Dutch manufacture, and is useful for bookbinding in schools. It is yellow in colour, and is not suitable for very good work, being of too soft a nature to withstand long wear. The size of these boards varies, but the majority are 30″ by 25″. The thickness is calculated by the weight of one board, e.g. a 2 lb. board is of such a thickness that it weighs approximately 2 lb. The most useful thicknesses for bookbinding are 8 oz., 1 lb., 1½ lb., and 2 lb., and a 2 lb. board is about $\frac{1}{10}$″ thick.

(*b*) *Greyboard.* This board is harder than strawboard, and is light grey in colour. It is often used by box-makers, and can be employed for all types of books as it will withstand considerable wear and tear. Each full board usually measures 40″ by 30″, and the thickness is indicated by the number of boards to the cwt., e.g. '30's greyboard' means 30 boards to the cwt., and this particular weight is approximately the thickness of a 2 lb. straw-

146

board. The higher the number, the thinner is the board. Some box-makers are willing to sell offcuts from such boards and these can often be used for small books, and for cutting boards.

In recent years the makers of greyboards have adopted a different system of classification, wherein thicknesses are indicated in thousandths of an inch. For the bindery, ·048″, ·064″, ·080/ ·090″ and ·116″ are needed, and the usual dimensions are $25\frac{1}{2}″$ by $19\frac{1}{2}″$.

(*c*) *Millboards*. These are very strong and durable, and should only be used for the very best work as they are very expensive. They vary in colour from dark brown to black, and are made from old rope. The thickness is indicated by names which used to indicate the price. These are sixpenny, sevenpenny, eightpenny, eightpenny cross, eightpenny double cross, and tenpenny. Some idea of the thickness can be realized by remembering that 8d.X is roughly equal to a 2 lb. strawboard. Seldom are millboards needed in school, for apart from the expense, they are too tough for pupils to cope with.

Preparation of Boards

Single boards

Whether boards are to be used for ordinary tape-sewn books or for flexibly bound ones, they must always be cut a little larger than the book. This is known as 'rough cutting', and for this purpose the board-cutter is usually used. Such a cutter should never be used to cut boards to their finished size, as this machine gives a bevel rather than a square edge to the boards.

On one of the boards place two very small spots of glue or paste, lay the other board squarely upon it, and place in the press for a few minutes. In this matter many students fall into error by overdoing the quantity of glue or paste required. Only the slightest smear is needed, and any more than that is disastrous, as it spreads out under pressure, and causes damage to the boards on taking them apart. It is only intended that the boards should hold together in a very temporary fashion while they are being cut to size.

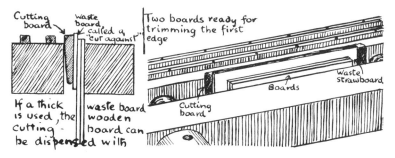

Place both boards in the cutting press ready to trim a small amount from one long edge. They should have behind them a piece of waste strawboard and a cutting board, in the manner shown in the diagram; $\frac{1}{8}''$ is a sufficient trim. This operation applies to boards for all types of binding, but where they are going to be lined for leather covers, it is not necessary at this stage to stick them together for this first trimming. I often dispense with the cutting board and retain only a thick 'cut-against'.

Lining single boards for full leather bindings

It is necessary to put 'liners' on boards when full leather is intended, and after the initial trimming of one edge has been carried out, rub down with fine sandpaper any burr left on these

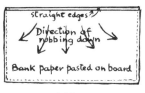

edges by the plough knife. Cut out two single sheets of a thin strong bank paper, the same size as the boards, and having one long edge perfectly straight. Paste them thoroughly, and place the straight edge of the paper $\frac{1}{16}''$ away from the trimmed edge of the board. Rub the paper down, working outwards as shown in the diagram. Give a quick nip in the press, and lean the board against a wall, papered side outwards, to dry. Then cut out two more pieces of bank paper large enough to cover both sides of each board. Each sheet is then creased down the centre, opened out, and pasted all over. Place the straight edge of the board along the crease and draw the sheet over from A to A1, rubbing down in the directions indicated. Turn the board over, lift the

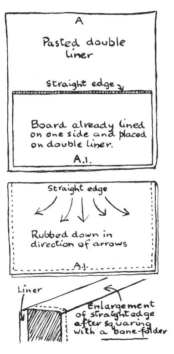

pasted paper and draw down again, as for the first side. Rub down the paper round the straight edge of the board, with a bone-folder to make it square. Nip in the press and stand up until nearly dry, leaving the double-lined side outwards. Then place under a weight to dry out completely. The presence of two thicknesses of lining paper on one side of the board causes it to curve, and this concave double-lined side becomes the inside and goes next to the book. This curvature is required to counteract the pull of the leather covering. Upon drying, the leather will actually curve the board in the opposite direction, leaving it to be finally straightened by the drying of the endpapers. After some experience, the student will be able to assess the amount of curvature required in order to produce a straight board when the book is complete. The lined boards are now tipped together with tiny spots of paste, care being taken to have the two straight edges coinciding with each other exactly. Leave them in the press until they need trimming to the finished size.

Split boards

These are used for books bound in a library style, and are made by gluing two thicknesses together. There are two methods:

(*a*) Two boards are required, one about 8 oz. and the other 1 to $1\frac{1}{2}$ lb. in thickness. The latter board will vary according to the depth of the groove made by backing. This board, plus the 8 oz. one, should fit the depth in such a way that the surface of the combined boards is level with the top of the groove. A piece is roughly cut from each board a little larger than twice the size

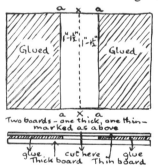

Two boards – one thick, one thin – marked as above

of the book. Both boards are marked with a line XX down the centre, and two parallel lines, aa and aa, 1″ to $1\frac{1}{2}$″ on each side of this centre line. Apply glue to the shaded portions on BOTH boards and place them squarely over each other. Leave them under heavy pressure between pressing boards for at least 12 hours. Cut them down the centre, apply two small spots of glue as described in the case of single boards, and place the boards together so that the unglued 'split' edges coincide. This edge is then trimmed in the cutting press in the usual way.

(*b*) Split boards may be made separately. In this case cut out two boards from the 8 oz. sheet, and two from the thicker board, each piece being a little larger than the book. Draw lines parallel to one edge at a distance of 1″ to 1½″ from it, on each

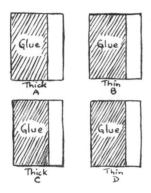

board. Glue all the shaded portions and apply A to B and C to D, so that the unglued parts are together in each case. Place in a press between boards, and treat them as described in (*a*) above.

'*Made*' boards

These are used chiefly for the best bindings, more particularly for large heavy books, and are made by gluing boards together until the necessary thickness has been obtained. It is usual to select two thicknesses for each complete board—one thin and one thicker. Both the thin and the thick are glued all over, and

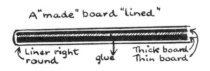

151

pressed as long as possible. One of the long edges on each board is trimmed in the cutting press, and a single liner pasted right round each board. There is no need to have a single sheet as a liner first, as in the case of single boards, because the presence of a thin board in the made board ensures the same curving effect as the single liner would produce. The side having the thinner board is the 'inside' and goes next to the book. Stick the boards together with spots of paste after the lining paper is dry, making sure that the straight edges coincide exactly, and the thinner boards face to face.

Cutting Boards to Size

Whatever the type of board, cutting them to size is the next operation. In all cases the boards have been trimmed along one edge, and this is the edge which fits into the groove of the book. Two main divisions must be considered, namely, boards for books 'cut out-of-boards', and those for books 'cut in-boards'.

1. Boards for Books 'Cut out-of-boards'

(a) *For books with a 'close joint'*, i.e. books where the boards fit close up in the grooves.

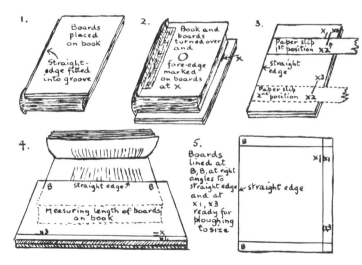

Place the straight edges of the boards close up in the groove, as in Fig. 1, and holding it firmly in this position turn the book over, and mark the position of the fore-edge on the board, as at X in Fig. 2. Take the boards away from the book and place a slip of paper across the width, having its square end on the the straight edge, as in Fig. 3. Make a second mark, X1, on the board $\frac{1}{8}''$ OUTSIDE X. This amount is called the 'square of the boards', and is usually about $\frac{1}{8}''$, but varies a little according to the size of the book. Large books would need more than $\frac{1}{8}''$, and smaller ones rather less. Transfer X1 to the paper slip at X2, and move the slip down towards the bottom of the boards and mark X3 from X2 on the slip. Join X1 and X3 by a pencil line. Open the book, as in Fig. 4, place the boards a little way inside a page, and allow them to extend about an equal distance beyond the head and tail. Mark the exact length of the page at B, B on the boards. Take out and square both ends as in Fig. 5. Plough along the marked lines, cutting the head and tail first, and the fore-edge last. Spring the boards apart, and glasspaper any burrs on the edges and any roughness where the paste spots held them together.

(*b*) *For books having a 'French joint'*. These are books whose boards do not fit into the groove, but leave a small gap known as a French joint. All split boards come under this heading. The only difference in the cutting of such boards lies in the marking

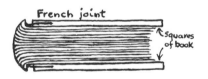

of the fore-edge. No square is added to the point X, i.e. these boards, when cut, are exactly the width of the book from the groove to the fore-edge, and as long as the pages measured from head to tail. The square of the board on the fore-edge is obtained later by drawing the board forward on the book and this automatically leaves the small gap at the joint.

2. For Books 'Cut in-boards'

All such books have boards which are 'laced-in', i.e. the boards are attached to the book before any edges are cut by means of the cords on which they are sewn. Take a pair of dividers and place one point in the groove near the head of the book. Turn over the endpaper at the corner and adjust the dividers until the other point is on the fore-edge of the first page, as in the diagram. Transfer this measurement to the boards, making one mark near the head and the other near the tail. Join these two points and then measure for the length of the boards in the same way as shown in Section 1 (*a*) above. Square at these points, and proceed with the cutting in the manner outlined for other types of boards.

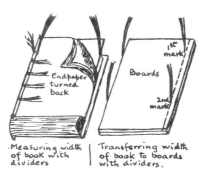

.Measuring width of book with dividers | Transferring width of book to boards with dividers.

In all cases, the boards must now be placed in position on the books to which they belong, and kept there as much as possible until they are finally attached to the book. This procedure protects the grooves and keeps the book tidy and craftsmanlike while the work proceeds.

Boards for books left uncut, or only cut at the head. If a book is to be left uncut, on measuring the length of the boards for such a book two 'squares' must be added to this length. Where a book is to be cut at the head only, the addition of one 'square' to the normal length of the boards is required. It will also be seen that small adjustments can be made in a similar fashion in the case of books cut on all three edges, where some allowance has to be made for very narrow margins.

BOARDS

Bevelling Boards

Where it is desired that the boards be bevelled, it is possible to do this at this stage or, alternatively, carry it out immediately after cutting the edges of the book.

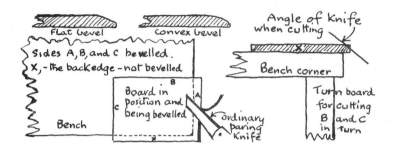

Take one of the boards and place it, outer side upwards, on the corner of the bench. Take the ordinary leather paring knife and, in a firm and steady manner, run it along the edges to be bevelled. Then smooth off all irregularities on the bevels with a coarse glasspaper block. The bevels may be made flat or a little convex, according to personal preference.

CHAPTER 10

Cutting Books 'Out-of-boards'

All books whose boards are not 'laced-in' are cut 'out-of-boards', i.e. the boards are actually used during the cutting, but they are not yet attached to the book permanently. Such books have already been cut on the fore-edge, and this chapter therefore describes the cutting of the head and tail.

Cutting the Head

Place the front board squarely in position on the book, i.e. in the position it will occupy when finally attached to the book.

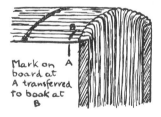

Make a mark, A, approximately $\frac{1}{8}''$ from the head of the board to indicate the 'square' of the book, and transfer this mark to the back of the book, as shown at B. Slide the board down the groove until its head is level with the line B. Cast an eye down the fore-edge to ensure that the edge of the board is parallel to

the pages, and then draw a line on the endpaper along the head
of the board. Now place the rear board level with the head of
the book, square with the fore-edge, and while it is in this

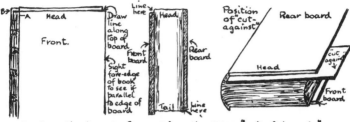

Setting the boards for cutting the HEAD "out-of-boards"

position run a pencil line along the bottom edge of this rear
board, as shown above. At the head of the book slide a piece of
thin waste board between the rear board and the endpaper, as
far as the groove but no farther. Let it project a little above the
head of the book. This slip is used to protect the board while the
cutting is carried out, and is known as the 'cut against'. Lower
the book into the cutting press, and nip up evenly but only
enough to hold the book lightly without slipping. Grip the book
in both hands, below the press, and draw it down until the edge
of the front board is level with the front cheek of the press. Pass
round the back of the press and inspect the pencil line underneath the rear board. If this board edge does not coincide with
the line some movement has taken place when the book was
placed in the press, and it must be rectified by taking the book

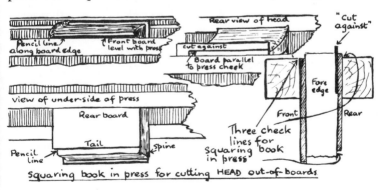

Squaring book in press for cutting HEAD out-of-boards

out and resetting the boards. Then look at the head of the rear board. If the book is square in the cutting press, the edge of this board will be a little above the cheek, but parallel to it. If this is not so, the book is twisted, and it must be gripped under the press, and by a turning movement of the hands the fault corrected. No attempt to cut the head must be made until all the three points have been carefully checked, and when all are correct the press may be tightened, and the cutting carried out. It should be noted that the cutting is always done from the spine to the fore-edge, and as the ploughing proceeds paper shavings will gather at the back of the book, but these should never be pulled off. Leave them until the book is taken out, and then nip them off smartly with a pair of scissors. As soon as the cutting knife reaches the rear endpaper take careful strokes, looking between each cut to ascertain when the knife has cut the last leaf. If cutting proceeds further, there is grave risk of the knife going through the 'cut against' and damaging the rear board. Take the book out of the press, remove the cut against, and nip off the shavings, as already directed.

Cutting the Tail

Turn the book over so that it is gripped in the left hand round the spine, the tail now being uppermost. Rotate the book to the left until the view in Fig. 1 is seen. While it is in this position,

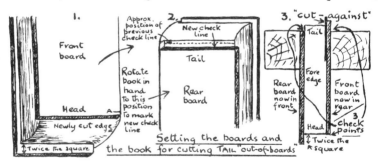

pull down the rear board until an amount equal to two 'squares' is visible below the newly cut edge of the book. Turn all back again in the hand to position in Fig. 2, and mark a line along the

158

top edge of the rear board which is now uppermost. Adjust the other board until its bottom edge is level with the cut edge of the book. Insert the cut against, and lower into the press. The final position is shown in Fig. 3, and the three check points are indicated. It should be noted that the rear check line used for cutting the head must be entirely ignored during the setting of the boards for cutting the tail. When all the points have been checked and found correct, the tail may be cut.

Books with Split Boards

In the case of books having split boards, there will be no 'square' of the boards visible along the fore-edge during the cutting of the head and tail. The fore-edge of each board should lie along the edge of the endpapers.

General Note on Cutting

Very often when a book has been backed, it will be found that the fore-edges of the endpapers project a little beyond the pages of the book. This projection should be trimmed off with a knife and straight-edge. A thin steel rule is placed between the last page and the endpaper, and a cutting card put under the latter. If this is not done it may be a little difficult to square the boards on the book whilst cutting the head and tail. This trimming operation is described on pp. 128 and 225.

In order to prevent damage to the sections at the spine by the return stroke of the plough knife, it is wise to practise cutting on the FORWARD STROKE ONLY. For the return stroke, the plough is lifted a little at the right-hand side, allowing the knife to pass just clear of the book, while the left-hand side remains between the runners.

The method outlined in this chapter may appear rather elaborate, but it was introduced to avoid much error in cutting, and it has been found very effective for pupils in school. It is an adaptation of the craft to enable students to see whether the boards have been allowed to move after setting them, and in order to allow the teacher to check at a glance any such errors. This checking should be done before the press is finally screwed tight.

159

CHAPTER 11

Attaching Boards for 'Out-board Binding' and Hollow Back

Fixing Mull

All books 'cut out-of-boards' must now be strengthened down the spine with a piece of bookbinder's mull (muslin). Cut out a piece rectangular in shape, in width equal to the width of the spine plus about 2", and long enough to extend from one kettle-stitch to the other. Place the book in a lying press, having drawn

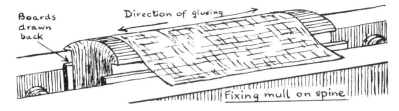

back each board a little, and glue the whole of the back from the centre outwards in both directions. Gluing in any other direction will result in runs of glue down the clean edges of the book, and thus ruin the work. Lay the mull down over the back, rubbing it down gently with a bone-folder, and pulling it slightly from each side in order to tighten it. When the glue has set, take all out of the press.

Attaching Boards

(a) Single boards glued on.

Lay the book on the bench, draw back the board about half-way across the endpaper, raise the mull, and trim off all the tapes (or frayed slips) about ¾″ from the back. Dab a little glue

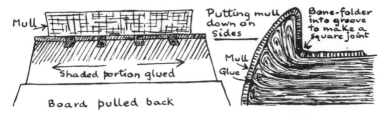

or paste under the tapes (or slips), put them down, and glue enough of the waste end-sheet to accommodate the mull, as shown by the shaded portion in the diagram. Put down the mull, and run a folder up and down the joint until it adheres. This retains a clean sharp groove. Repeat the process for the other side, and lay aside to dry by allowing the glued portions to project over the edge of the bench.

Take the boards and run the glue brush down the inside back edge so that the glued portion is approximately an inch wide, and working from the middle outwards in both directions. Place

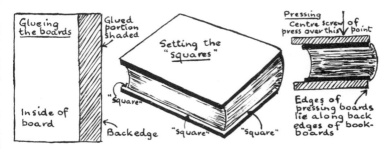

each board into the grooves of the book, and carefully 'set the squares' all round so that the boards project beyond the pages equally at the head, tail, and fore-edge. Then place all between pressing boards, and leave in the press for several hours. Note should be made of the position of these pressing boards in relation to the book. They should not extend beyond the back edges of the book boards, and when the whole is in the press the centre screw should be directly above the centre of the book when viewed from the front and side.

(b) *Attaching split boards.*

Cut down the tapes, glue them down, and fasten down the mull, as described in the section (*a*) above. Then lightly glue the upper side of the mull and the waste sheet, working outwards from the middle. Fold the waste sheet over until its edge fits neatly into the groove, and rub it down well, running a folder up and down the joint to retain a clean right-angled groove. When these 'flaps' have been completed they should be set aside to dry. If the waste sheets have been damaged when the front edge was cut, then trim off the torn portions before folding over. The flaps are now cut down until the width is a little less than the width of the 'split' in the boards.

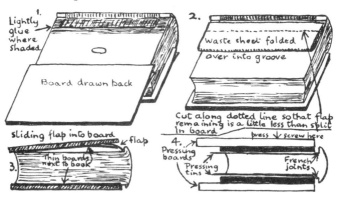

Take the boards and bend the thin board away from the thicker one in order to open the 'split' portion. Glue inside this split thoroughly on both sides, and lightly close it. It will be found that the thin boards spring away again slightly, i.e. just enough to allow the flaps to enter the splits.

Place the board on the book (thinner side inside) and slide the paper flap inside the split portion. Adjust the 'squares' of the boards carefully, and when both boards are in position insert a thin pressing tin between each board and the book. Place all between pressing boards, and leave in the press for several hours. If the squares have been properly set a small gap will be left between the back edges of the boards and the actual groove of the book, and this is known as a 'French joint'.

Making the Hollow Back

Books 'cut out-of-boards', with the exception of the library style, should have a hollow back. Books bound in calf style also need hollow backs, but this will be noted when that type is described. A hollow back separates the covering material from the backs of the sections, and serves two purposes. In the first place the cover is not creased on the spine when the book is

opened, and this preserves the tooling. The second, and more important reason, lies in the greater freedom given to the pages on opening. A book with a hollow back will lie much flatter than one which is flexibly sewn, and where it is necessary to write in a book the former style is much more convenient. The back is said to 'throw up' better, and music needs such a back if it is to lie flat when opened. Ledgers, cash books, and the like must open as flat as possible, and an even more effective hollow back is given. It is called a 'springback', and throws up very strongly indeed.

Good quality brown paper, or strong cartridge paper, is used in the making of the hollow. Take a piece of such paper, in length a little longer than the book, and in width no less than four times the width of the spine. Trim one of the long edges to make a straight edge, and lay this edge along one edge of the back, the book having been placed in a finishing press. Hold it firmly in this position and crease along the other edge of the spine with the thumb nails. Now lay the paper flat on the bench and fold it right over along the crease. Glue all along the back of the book, working from the middle outwards. It will be found that the hollow adheres more quickly if this glue is allowed to set for a minute or two before putting the paper on it.

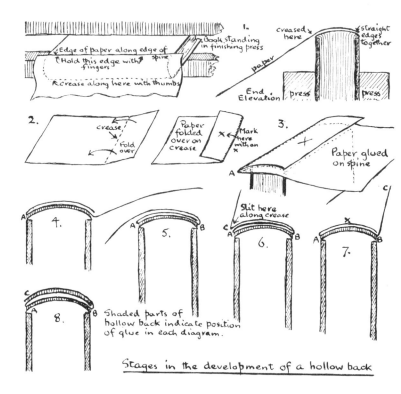

Stages in the development of a hollow back

The folded paper is placed on the back as shown in the diagrams, care being exercised to ensure that the fold A is exactly along the edge of the spine, and that it projects a little beyond the book at the head and tail. Rub well down with a folder until it is fast to the back. Crease the paper over again, as at B, along the book edge, making a clean sharp fold. Turn the remaining paper back again over fold A, as shown at C, and slit along this fold with a sharp knife. Turn back the top flap, and glue carefully the surface marked X. Hold this glued side down with the tips of the thumbs, and bring over flap C with the fingers. Rub all down thoroughly with a bone-folder until the glue has set. Further work on the hollow back will be dealt with under the heading 'Preparing to cover'. Fixing such a hollow back is often referred to as 'lining up', and this type is known as 'one on and two off'. In very heavy bindings the hollow back may start with two thicknesses glued first, and in this case it is known as 'two on and two off'.

The position adopted while carrying out the above operation is on the side of the book marked A. Some binders prefer to fold the hollow completely, on the bench, before attaching to the book, but I prefer the method already outlined.

CHAPTER 12

Lacing-in and Cutting 'In-board' Work

In order to keep the processes in the correct sequence for books which are cut 'in-boards' reference should be made to Chapter 9, in which the lining, squaring, and cutting of the boards were described. They must now be 'laced-in', i.e. attached to the cords on which the book was sewn.

Lacing-in

The boards are placed in position on the book, the 'lined' edges going into the grooves, and the double-lined side next to the endpapers. In the case of a 'made' board the thinner board is next to the book. Make quite sure that the front board is lying exactly in the position it will occupy when the book is finished. At this point the boards should be marked to indicate their positions, i.e. the front board is marked F near its head and the reverse board R, also near its head. This marking serves to indicate throughout the subsequent operations the head of the book, the outsides of the boards, and the sides to which they belong.

Mark along the back edge of the front board the exact positions of the cords. If double cords have been used, mark the points between each pair. Place both boards, as shown, back edges together, heads at the top, and mark the reverse board from the points already made on the front board. Using a try-square, lengthen all the marks to about 1″ long, and draw a line

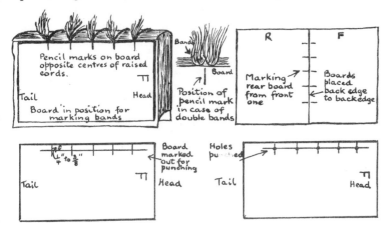

parallel to the back edge, from ¼″ to ⅜″ distant from it. This amount varies according to the size of the book, and large ones will require ⅜″. Take a fine awl and punch holes through the board at the intersections of the lines. This should be done upon a piece of hard wood, having a hole bored through it ½″ in diameter. The awl can then be pushed through, having the board over the hole in the wood as each point is bored. This support under the board prevents damage to, or bending of, the edge. Alternatively, the holes can be made over a cutting press by closing the jaws until a space of about ½″ is left between them. The line of the holes will lie over this 'slot' as the boring is done. Turn the board over, and punch another set of holes in the position shown in the diagram. There should not be more than

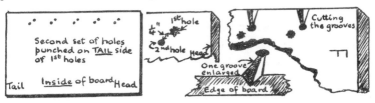

$\frac{1}{4}''$ between the first holes and the second ones, and the new holes must be on the tail side of the first ones. Do not make the holes any larger than is necessary to accommodate the slips.

Turn the board over, front side up, and from the back edge to the position of the first holes cut V-shaped grooves, using a very sharp knife. The groove is made by two slanting cuts; it should become shallower towards the hole, and must not be too deep at the edge of the board. This cut demands good judgement, for it should be only deep enough to accommodate the frayed slips comfortably. If too much is cut out the grooves will be seen as small hollows when the leather is placed in position; if too little is cut out, a series of lumps will be seen after covering. After cutting the grooves, run through the holes again with the awl to clear them. They will have become partially closed during the groove-cutting. I often cut the grooves before making the holes.

Now paste the frayed slips on one side of the book between the thumb and first finger, taking care not to twist them, and leaving $\frac{1}{8}''$ nearest the book free of paste. The pasting of this small portion at the base of the slip will lead to difficulty when the edges are cut. The movement required in the boards will tend to break the slips if they are stiffened with paste.

Take each slip in the left finger and thumb, and carefully twist the *final inch* to a point, using the right finger and thumb. Go on twisting until a stiff point is obtained. Cut off the fine hairs at the extreme end with a pair of scissors, to facilitate lacing-in.

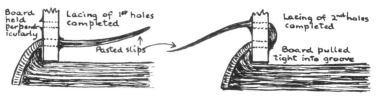

Place the board at right angles to the book, so that its edge rests in the groove, and lace each slip through the holes first made. When all the slips have been laced, pull them through until the upright board is standing close into the groove. Thread the slips back through the second holes, and pull all as tight as

168

possible, still keeping the board upright. Lower the board very gently until it is flat down on the book. This movement will pull the slips taut, so that the board is now tight in the joint. If the board is released from the pressure of the hand, it should 'spring up' a little at the fore-edge. If the 'springing' is more than a little, the board is too tight in the joint and must be eased off a little from the back until the 'springing' is correct. With a sharp knife, cut off the slips close to the board. While it is in this condition very great care must be exercised in handling the book. Take a backing hammer and gently tap the holes. This tapping will close the holes round the slips just enough for the book to be handled with greater safety.

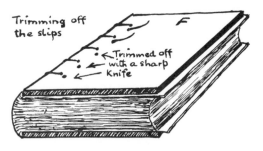

Trimming off the slips

Trimmed off with a sharp knife

Now place a knocking-down iron in the cutting press, and nip up the press so that the iron is firmly held. Place the laced-in board flat on the iron, supporting the weight of the book in the left hand, thus taking any weight from the newly laced slips. Give all the holes a smart tap as a beginning, and then go over each one carefully until the holes are completely closed. As the hammering proceeds, feel at the holes with the fingers, and when all sign of burr round them disappears, and the surface of the board is perfectly flat again, then turn the book over. The board is resting on the iron again, but this time it is the inner side of the board which is to be hammered. The tapping should be aimed at flattening that part of the slip which passes from one hole to the other. If the process has been correctly carried out the board should drop easily upon the book, and lie perfectly flat. In practice, it will be found that when the board is lowered from the perpendicular after lacing-in, it will be tight in the groove. The work would be spoiled if it remained like this, but the operation of riveting the slips causes them to 'give' a little, and the resulting condition is just right. The second board is laced-in, in the same way.

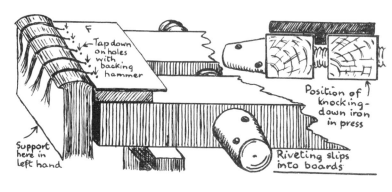

Cleaning off the Back

Stand the book in a lying or finishing press, and cover the whole of the spine with a thick layer of paste. Leave it like this for 10 to 15 minutes, by which time the glue on the backs of the sections will have softened. Have ready to hand a clean sponge, a band stick, and a pair of band nippers. A band stick is a piece of hardwood, preferably rosewood, rectangular in section. Its thickness is usually about $\frac{1}{4}''$, and its length $8''$ to $9''$. The width

varies from $\frac{1}{4}''$ to $1''$. The possession of three or four such sticks, of varying widths, is an asset. Using the edge of the stick, commence to scrape the back of the book, until the backs of the sections emerge clean and free of glue. Squeeze all possible water out of the sponge, and clean up the whole back with it. Do no more with the sponge than is absolutely necessary, as the sections must not be made too wet.

In the case of books having raised bands, the band nippers are now used to nip up and straighten the bands. Proceed with this until all the raised cords are equal in thickness, square across the back, and parallel to each other. Occasionally it may become necessary to use the end of the bandstick as a kind of chisel to make them parallel. The other end of the stick is gently tapped with a backing hammer.

Pressing

After the back has been cleaned off, and while it is yet damp, clean thin pressing tins are placed both inside and outside each board. The whole is then put between pressing boards, and placed in the press. Great care must be exercised in doing this because whatever shape the back of the book assumes while drying, it will retain as long as it remains a book. Check the

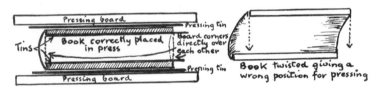

shape before putting in the press, and again after tightening, by inspecting the spine from both ends to ensure that no twisting has taken place. The pressure should be moderate, and at least 12 hours must elapse before the book is taken out.

Pasting Down Flyleaves

At this stage it is wise to paste down, if required, the flysheets in the endpapers. It will be remembered that an extra folded white sheet was sewn into the endpaper and one of the reasons for its presence now becomes apparent when this pasting down is done. Very often the coloured flyleaf of the endpaper has a reverse side which may not be entirely clean. This is often the case where thin marbled papers are used and pasting it down to

the white flyleaf, immediately next to it, surmounts this difficulty. In the case of a thin coloured leaf, it also provides some
necessary stiffening.

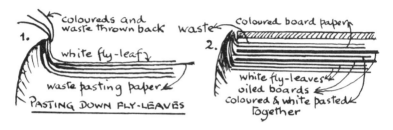

Place a piece of waste paper under the white flyleaf which is
now to be pasted all over. Withdraw the waste carefully and
insert in its place an oiled board. Bring down the coloured fly-
leaf upon the pasted sheet and place another oiled board over
this. Then close the book and quickly attend to the other endpaper. Place all between pressing boards and place in a press for
at least 24 hours, after which time the oiled boards may be
removed and the book replaced in the press until such time as
further work is done upon it. Reference should be made to
pages 223 ff., for the final pasting-down follows the same method
as outlined above.

Cutting the Edges 'In-boards'

It will be remembered that when cutting a book 'out-of-
boards' the fore-edge is cut before the boards are made, and
then the head and tail are cut with the assistance of the loose
boards. In the case of books sewn flexibly, whose boards are
laced-in, the cutting of the edges is done after the boards have
been attached, and the order of cutting is head, tail, and then the
fore-edge.

To insure against any possible breakage of the slips, damp
them slightly, with a sponge, where they are resting in the
grooves. Then very gently move the boards up and down until
the slips are free.

LACING-IN, AND CUTTING 'IN-BOARD' WORK

(a) Cutting the head

Place the book on the bench, and pull down the front board one 'square'. The slight amount of 'play' in the slips allows this to be done, and it is easier if the board is lifted to a vertical position, pulled down slightly, and then lowered into position. Place a 'cut-against' between the rear board and the book, in the same manner as employed in cutting 'out-of-boards'. Place all in the cutting press, and draw down until the edge of the front board is level with the press cheek. If the book is true

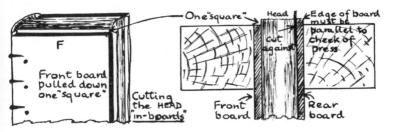

and square in the press then the top of the rear board will be parallel to the press cheek. No cutting must be attempted until this is so, and any correction must be made by twisting the book underneath the press, gripping it in both hands.

(b) Cutting the tail

Turn the book over, tail to the top, and draw down the rear board (now at the front) two 'squares' below the edge already cut. Slip in the 'cut-against' as usual, and lower into

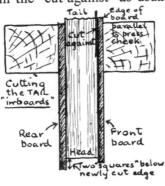

173

the press. Check the edge of the front board level with the press, and see that the rear board at the head is parallel to the press cheek. When all has been duly checked, the edge can be cut. It should be noted that when the head and tail are cut a certain amount of paper shavings adheres to the spine. These must be trimmed off with scissors after the book has been taken out of the press. They should never be pulled off, as such an action would leave the head or tail uneven at the back.

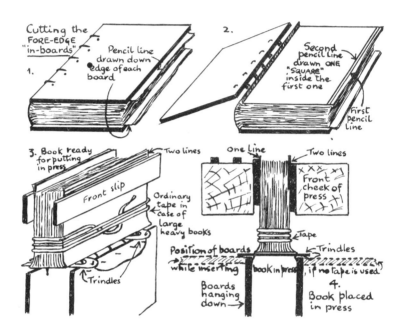

(c) Cutting the fore-edge

With a finely pointed pencil, mark a line on the endpapers along the fore-edge of each board. Open one board and draw a second line parallel to the line just drawn, and inside it a distance equal to one 'square' of the book. Take two slips of millboard (or other hard board) a little longer than the book and 2″ to 3″ wide. Each slip must have one edge perfectly straight. Place two small spots of glue or paste on these slips and lay them down exactly along the pencil lines. Shut down the boards, and place a weight upon the book until the slips have adhered to the waste sheets of the endpapers. It will now be seen that one piece is exactly level with the book board, whilst the other is one 'square' within the board edge. A pair of 'trindles' is now required. These are thin pieces of metal shaped as shown in the diagram. It is best to have them attached to each other by a thin cord about 9″ long. A hole is provided in each trindle to accommodate this cord.

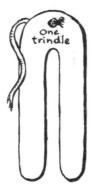

One trindle

The book is picked up by the fore-edge, the boards thrown back, and each trindle inserted across the back so that the two end cords of the book lie in the slots. This process will flatten the back, and if the book is a large heavy one, it will be advisable to pass a length of tape several times round in the position shown in the diagram, in order to hold the book firmly whilst handling it. If no tape is used to 'tie-up' the book, it should be gripped in both hands near the back, holding both boards at the same time, in a horizontal position, as shown at No. 4 in the diagram. Have the cutting press open, and slide the book upwards from underneath the press, and nip up lightly. When it is in the correct position for cutting, the lower slip at the front should be level with the press, and the rear slip one 'square' above the cheek and parallel to it. Inspect also the shape of the spine to ascertain whether it is still completely flat. Until these points are correct no cutting should be done. When the edge has been cut, take the book out of the press, remove the trindles, rip off the millboard slips and the back will resume its original curvature. It should be pointed out that the expert craftsman uses cutting boards instead of the millboard slips, but the process is sufficiently difficult for beginners without the complication of cutting boards, and with care the method outlined above will prove quite satisfactory until enough confidence has been gained. It is also usual for the craftsman to tie up the book ready for cutting, remove the trindles, and then lower it into the press from above, but my modification helps considerably where students are concerned.

CHAPTER 13

Treatment of Edges

Consideration must now be given to the methods used in the decoration of the edges. They may be left plain, gilded, marbled, or coloured. Any one of these treatments should be done immediately after the edges have been cut.

Edge Gilding

A gilt edge not only adds to the appearance of the book, but is a definite protection to the edges of the leaves. At the same time some discernment is necessary in the case of modern books, as the quality of the papers used makes gilding most difficult, if not nearly impossible. Books containing 'art' paper should be avoided at all costs. It is also very unwise to attempt edge gilding upon books which have had some amount of use. The edges of the leaves will have become slightly greasy, and the presence of grease in the paper is fatal to any success in the process.

Two alternatives present themselves, namely, gilding the head only, or gilding all three edges. For most books the gilding of the head is sufficient. Knock up the book at the head so that both boards are exactly level with the pages. Place a gilding board on each side, also level with the head, and lower all into a lying press until very little protrudes above the press cheeks. It cannot be emphasized too strongly that the book, boards, and gilding boards must be level, both across the width and along the length of the book. A small spirit level is invaluable here. Gilding boards are like backing boards, save that the tops are flat instead of bevelled. Some binders prefer to throw back the book boards for this work, owing to the risk of foreign matter being present in them, which, on being wetted, will affect the success of the work.

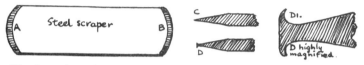

Having nipped up the press tightly, begin to scrape the edge carefully with a scraper. The tool I prefer is a piece, about 3″ long and 1″ wide, cut from a worn-out tenon saw blade. It is ground to the shape shown in the diagram. The ends A and B are ground like a knife edge, as at C, and this edge is then rubbed carefully in a perpendicular position on an oilstone until it assumes an edge like D. If examined under a magnifying glass it will be seen that two small burrs have formed as in D1, and on these depends the scraping power of the tool.

Other scrapers may be made suitable for use on a rounded fore-edge, but the principle remains the same whatever the

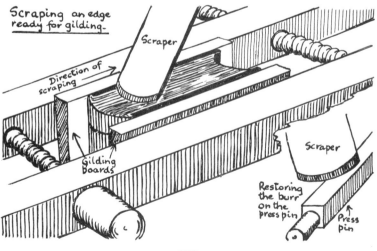

shape. The scraper is held in both hands, leaning at an angle of about 45° from the book. Scraping begins at the back of the book, goes along towards the fore-edge, and continues until a clean, smooth edge is achieved. Keep turning the scraper over, and when it ceases to scrape efficiently, restore the burrs by stroking the edge perpendicularly on the steel press pin. On no account must the edge of the book be touched by the hand, as the resulting grease will prevent the gold leaf adhering at that point.

The following items should be to hand for the next stage.

1. Two or three clean small pots—glass fish-paste jars are very useful for this purpose.

2. Armenian bole and powdered black lead.

3. Glaire (egg or blood albumen).

4. Two large flat water colour brushes, and a stiff hand-brush such as is used to apply polish when cleaning shoes.

5. Gold cushion, gold knife, a book of gold leaf, and a gilder's tip.

6. A sheet of clean bank paper, such as is used for guarding, and a little beeswax.

Take a little Armenian bole—a kind of red chalk—and a little powdered black lead, putting both into a pot, and add one or two drops of glaire together with a similar quantity of water. Mix them thoroughly with a paint brush. It should not be thinned down to a watery condition, but should have the consistency of thin poster colour. Working quickly from the back to the fore-edge, apply the mixture with the brush until the whole book edge is covered. The moisture will begin to sink into the edges of the leaves, and just before the wetness has completely gone, apply the stiff handbrush vigorously, and continue brushing until a black and shining edge is produced. Brush ACROSS the edge to begin with, until all wetness has gone and then do the rest of the brushing lengthwise. This prevents any splashing of the clean fore-edge.

Now put a few drops of glaire into a clean pot, and add to it three to four times as much water. Glaire is prepared by taking the white of an egg, adding a small teaspoonful of white vinegar, and beating it up thoroughly. This is allowed to stand for 24 hours, and then strained through a fine sieve or a piece of muslin, when it is ready for use in gold tooling. It is this glaire which is watered down for edge gilding. Blood albumen glaire is superior to egg glaire but see page 237.

Get out a sheet of gold on the cushion, estimate the width which will be required for the book edge, and cut it into strips a little wider than this estimate. The handling of gold leaf is described later when cover decoration is dealt with. Cut out strips of the bank paper wider and longer than the cut pieces of gold. Draw these strips across the hair, and lay them down on the gold strips. The grease from the hair will be sufficient to cause the gold to adhere to the paper, and these transfers should be placed gold side upwards near the book in sufficient number to cover the book edge. I only use this method when the edge is larger in area than can be covered with one leaf of gold. If sufficient strips of gold can be cut from one leaf to wholly cover the edge, I prefer picking up each strip as required with a gilder's tip. This is a camel-hair brush about 3″ to 4″ in width, and having a good length in the hairs. A stroke or two of such a brush across the hair will enable the gilder to pick up a strip of gold leaf flat on the tips of the hairs. All is now ready for the laying on of the gold leaf.

Pick up a strip of gold (either transfer or on the tip) in the left hand, and from the mixed glaire take a fully loaded brush in the right hand. Float the glaire very lightly and quickly along the edge from the back to the fore-edge. It is important that the edge be flooded with a full brush. Quickly bring the strip of gold right over the edge, and lower it evenly and gently until the glaire 'clicks' the gold. This should occur just as the brush (or transfer paper) is about to touch the wet edge if the downward movement were continued. The capillary attraction thus allows the gold to be put down without danger of wetting the tip. Pick up the next strip, and let it overlap the first one a little, and thus continue until the whole edge has been covered. On no account must the edge be touched in any way during this operation. If a break appears in the leaf, cut and pick up a small piece, and put down a patch large enough to cover the break. All this must be done before the glaire has had time to sink down into the pages. The edge should now be left to dry. The time required varies considerably according to the prevailing conditions. The weather has a considerable influence, and many rooms in which book-binding has to be taught are far from ideal from the gilder's point of view. The writer has in mind one room where an edge would be dry enough for burnishing in 20 minutes, whereas another required nearly two hours. A simple test can be applied to find out whether an edge is dry enough to burnish. Breathe on it lightly. When this is done a mistiness forms on the gold and dulls it. If this film of moisture dries off slowly the edge is still too damp, but if the film disappears almost instantly it is ready for burnishing. Another test which calls for rather more experience consists in tapping the edge delicately with the burnisher. If the sound given by such tapping sounds dead the edge is still too damp, but if it gives forth a ring it can be burnished.

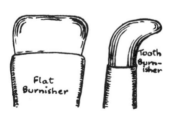

Take a piece of bank paper, somewhat larger than the surface of the edge, and rub upon it a little beeswax. Place it over the gold, waxed side up, and begin to go over the edge lightly with the burnisher. The direction of the strokes is from side to side, and not from the back to the fore-edge. The burnisher is made of agate or bloodstone. It is an expensive tool and it should never be dropped or scratched in any way. Always wrap it up in some soft material when not in use. The wax on the paper helps the burnisher to slip easily over the surface, and when the edge has been rubbed all over take the paper away, wipe the ball of the hand over the wax, and lightly stroke the gold edge with this portion of the hand. This will transfer a very small amount of wax to the edge, and will take off any surplus gold.

Commence burnishing direct upon the edge, working across the width, and gradually proceeding down the length. Let this initial rubbing be done very lightly, and test the edge for dryness by breathing upon it. As the gold on the edge becomes flattened, so the pressure upon the burnisher may increase until a bright surface is attained. Sometimes such an edge comes up bright, solid, and flawless, but in most cases it is better to give a second coat of gold after this first burnishing. The extra labour involved has its recompense in the resulting depth, solidity, and brilliance of the edge.

Take a wide flat sable brush which has been well washed, and place it in the mouth. Prepare the gold on the cushion as before, and by this time the brush should have been thoroughly wetted. Pick up a piece of gold with the left hand, and wet, with one stroke if possible, a piece of the edge a little larger than the piece of gold. Dab the gold down upon the wet edge without any hesitation. Wet the next patch and put down another piece overlapping the first a little, and so on until the edge has been completely covered. The whole of this operation must be done as rapidly as possible. It will be found that the burnishing can be done within a few minutes if this method is followed. If the second coat is put on by means of glaire it will mean waiting again for about an hour before burnishing can be attempted, and in addition there is a tendency for the glaire to produce a 'cloudiness' which shows through the gold. Small defects in a burnished edge can be repaired by the method outlined above, and no trace can be found of the patch. The piece of gold used to repair such a defect should be a little larger than the amount wetted with the brush. Two rules must be borne in mind in this edge-gilding. If the burnisher rubs the gold off, the edge is still too wet, whilst difficulty in obtaining a bright finish indicates that the edge has been allowed to become too dry.

Gilding the Fore-edge

The fore-edge may be 'gilt solid', i.e. gilt while round, or gilt flat. The latter follows the same procedure as is used for the head and tail, except that the book boards are hanging down below the press, and trindles are used to flatten the back. Reference to the section on cutting the fore-edge 'in-boards' will make this clear. In gilding in the round, the boards are hanging down, but no trindles are used. The scraping must be done with a more pointed tool and the gold laid on half the edge at a time, as shown below. The burnishing in this case is done up and down the length of the book, and a tooth burnisher is used.

Edges 'Rough Gilt'

The above term refers to edges which are to be left uncut. The section in Chapter 4 headed 'Trimming before sewing' indicates that the edges must be gilded before they are sewn. In such a case the fore-edge must be done first, and then the tail. In each case the sheets must be knocked up together so as to bring any shorter sheets level with the rest. Little or no scraping need be done. A gentle rubbing with fine sandpaper is usually sufficient, and then the method follows that already described for edges which have been cut. The term 'rough gilt' indicates that a shining bright edge is not to be looked for in this work, and the finished edge will be duller in appearance and more in keeping with the nature of uncut pages. If the head is to be also rough gilt the procedure is the same, but in most cases the head may be cut in the plough, and gilded in the usual way after the boards have been attached.

Gauffering and Edge-painting

Sometimes a gilt edge is tooled with warm tools, and this is called 'gauffering'. I do not propose to go further into this method, as I think that the decoration of a book is overdone by such means, and in any case such work is beyond the scope of this book. The same remarks apply to edge painting. It was a habit of binders in the seventeenth and eighteenth centuries to fan out the fore-edge, paint a picture upon it, close the pages, and often gild over the edge. Such a painting is only visible when the pages are again fanned out in the hand.

Coloured Edges

If an edge be sandpapered and scraped a little it can be done with plain colour. It is not vitally necessary to nip it up in the press for the colouring; if it be placed on the edge of the bench under a knocking-down iron it will be sufficient. Almost any water colour or dye will serve, but tube water colour mixed with a little Chinese white to bind it gives an evenly tinted edge. The colour must be thin and applied with a brush or a small sponge. Always work from the back to the fore-edge, and, on the fore-edge, from the middle to the head and tail. More than one coat may be applied to obtain depth of colour. When the edges are dry the book is placed in a cutting press and nipped up slightly. Rub over the edge with a rag which has been wiped on beeswax, and then burnish it with a bone-folder or an agate.

Fixing Markers

If book markers are required they should be fixed at this stage by gluing one end to the back of the book at the head, and bringing the marker over into the pages.

Capping up

When the edges have been gilded, coloured, or just left plain it is necessary to cover them up to prevent damage in subsequent operations. This is called 'capping up'.

Take a sheet of thin paper—bank paper is best—and cut it an inch or two longer than double the length of the book, and three

or four inches wider than the book width. Insert it between the
board and the waste sheet of the endpaper, as shown in the

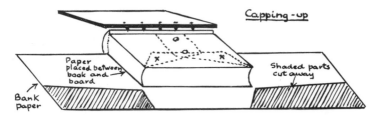

diagram. Cut out the shaded portions and wrap over at the head
and tail, placing dabs of paste at O, O to hold the flaps together.
Bring over the flap at the fore-edge and dab this fast at X, X.
Close the board and put the book under a weight until the paste
has dried. The final position of the 'cap' is shown by the dotted
lines. Thin adhesive paper, or self-adhesive tape, may be used
instead of paste, and there is less risk with it in the way of damp
staining the endpapers.

In the case of books having leather joints in the endpapers
there is always a grave risk of staining by the leather. The natural
oil in the leather tends to make a dark mark down the length of
the endpaper which it faces, and as the book remains closed
during most of the operations, often under pressure, such a risk
is increased. To avert this damage pieces of clean paper are
attached to the face of the leather joints with small spots of paste
so that they come between the leather and the endpapers. They
should be cut to the same size as the book, and placed in position
before the capping up is done. The spots of paste should be
placed near the outer edge of the joints. It is infinitely better to
do this at an earlier stage, as described on p. 67.

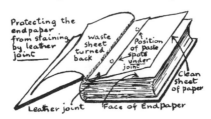

CHAPTER 14

Headbanding and Lining-up

Headbanding

Two kinds of headbands are used in bookbinding; one which is sewn on, and another which is ready-made and merely glued on. As the chief purpose of a headband is to give strength to the head and tail in order to combat the strain imposed when a book is pulled from a shelf, the glued-on variety is just useless. Its only function is to provide added decoration without constructive value. It is better to use a French headcap, if a sewn headband is not contemplated. A properly sewn headband not only gives strength to the book, but also adds to its beauty, and it is this type that is worthy of the craftsman's attention.

The foundation of headbands may be gut, vellum, or cord. The gut and the cord will give a round band, but the vellum produces a flat one.

(*a*) *Gut.* A selection of 'cello strings which have been discarded (or even double bass) should be collected together when opportunity offers.

(*b*) *Cord.* A selection of good Italian line in several thicknesses should be kept in stock. In choosing such cord bear in mind the dimensions of the 'squares' of the books likely to be bound. Such 'squares' vary with the size of the book, and allowance should be made for this variation in selecting the different cords.

(*c*) *Vellum.* Pieces of vellum are often left over when books are bound in this material, and for headband work they should be glued between sheets of good cartridge paper and pressed thoroughly until completely dry. Illuminators often have clippings to dispose of, and worn-out drum-skins can also be used.

Set one of the 'squares' of the book, and test by this projecting piece which cord or gut is just a slight fraction less in thickness. In the case of vellum a strip is cut to fit such a measurement. Draw back the 'capping up' a little way from the groove and pull down the right-hand board until it is level with the book edge. This is necessary to prevent fraying of the sewing silk as it passes round the headband. It is better to begin with the tailband. Place the book in a finishing press at an angle as shown in

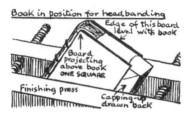

the diagram. Cut off two pieces of the foundation material a little longer than the thickness of the book. Choose two contrasting colours of silk, each about half a yard long: both colours should harmonize with the colour of the leather selected for the cover. Tie the two lengths together to form one continuous thread and thread a fine needle on one end. The needle must be tied securely to the silk. A coin—a penny is best—is a necessity for headbanding; especially is this the case for beginners.

Push the needle down just inside the first section, avoiding the endpaper, and come out a little below the kettle-stitch as in diagram 1. Pull through until the knot, joining the two colours, reaches the back of the section. If at all possible, pull the knot through to the outside. Put the needle in again at the same place and pull until a loop is left at the head as in Fig. 2. Through this loop place the foundation piece; it is more easily dealt with if a pin be put through it into the edge of the book board. Pull the loop tight and bring up the needle cord alongside it as in Fig. 3. Pass the light over the dark, under the right-hand end of the foundation, and bring it over next to the dark. Repeat this to make two darks and two lights on the cord. As the last light comes over, cross it with the dark, and pass under the cord again. Repeat this to give two darks; cross over with the light, and make two of these. Cross over again with the dark, pass round the cord, and then put the needle into the leaves of the book opposite the last stitch; come out just below the kettle-stitch and over the cord again, thus making the second dark. The

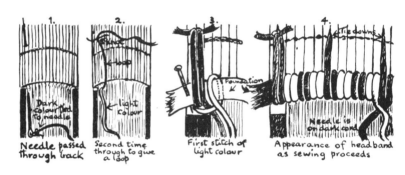

1. Needle passed through back
2. Second time through to give a loop
3. First stitch of light colour
4. Appearance of headband as sewing proceeds

last stitch mentioned is called the 'tie down', and this should be done at frequent intervals across the back in order to fasten down the headband in an even manner. When the right-hand side of the book back has been reached the headband is finished off by a 'tie down', and the two colours tied in a knot at the point where the tie down emerges below the kettle-stitch. Cut both threads $\frac{1}{4}''$ away from the knot, tie them together again, and retie the needle on the opposite colour ready to do the head of the book.

The above method gives two dark threads and two light ones alternately across the headband, but this may be varied if desired to produce a different pattern. If the foundation be vellum it must be kept upright during the sewing, and in all cases the headband must be made to follow the line of the curve of the book back. It is very essential that, during the whole operation, a light tension be kept on both colours; it is also most essential that the crossovers, which form a small 'beading', be kept down at the base of the band.

Lining up

It is now necessary to back up the head and tailbands with strong brown paper. The variety known as Kraft (unglazed) is admirable, but strong cartridge paper may be used as a substitute. Cut two pieces about twice as wide as the back of the book and approximately 2″ long. The latter measurement will vary somewhat according to the size of the book. Place the book in a finishing press, and apply glue to the back at each end. In the case of raised cords the glue should extend to the first band, as at A, but where a book has been sewn on cords sawn-in, glue enough to cover all the silk stitches plus an amount approximately $\frac{1}{4}″$, as at B. Hold the strips of brown

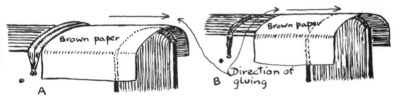

paper down in the position shown, and rub down thoroughly with a bone-folder until the glue has set. Inspect the headband frequently as it is most essential that it should be kept close to the brown paper all the time. The book should now be put on one side until the lining-up is thoroughly dry.

Take a piece of fine sandpaper and wrap it round a bandstick, or some other firm base, which will give a flat side to the sand-paper. Rub down the brown-paper backings gently until a smooth surface is attained. During this process the overhanging pieces at the ends and sides should drop off, but the rubbing down must not proceed so far as to lay bare the silk threads.

In the case of large heavy books, the lining-up is carried a stage further. To give added strength, they are lined up between all the bands, and thin leather, linen, or strong brown paper may be used for the purpose. The method is the same as that used in backing up the head and tailbands. Smaller books bound in this style do not need this extra work, and the covering leather is pasted directly upon the backs of the sections.

Books sewn 'sawn-in' (usually called calf style) may be 'fast backs' or have hollow backs. If calf leather or vellum be used for covering, a hollow back is essential, and reference must be made to Chapter 11 for the making of such a hollow back.

CHAPTER 15

Covering

★

Preparing to Cover

Books with hollow backs bound in cloth

This group comprises books having single boards attached with glue, and those done in a semi-library style having split boards. Reference must be made to Chapter 11 in which such books had been forwarded as far as the fixing of the hollow back, and from this point they are now prepared for covering.

Using a pair of scissors, cut off the projecting ends of the hollow back level with the edges of the boards, and slit down the

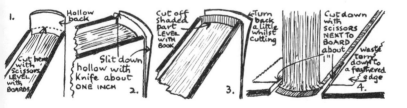

sides with a knife a distance of about 1″. Turn back the outer side of the hollow a little and cut off the inner piece flush with the head and tail of the book. Open the boards, and cut down the joints (with scissors) *close to the boards*, a distance of about 1″. At the

191

same time tear down the waste end sheets from head to tail in order to feather off the edge of the paper already glued to the boards.

Covering in Cloth

1. *Quarter-cloth and paper*

Cut out a piece of cloth 1½″ longer than the book and wide enough to cover the spine and about one-third of each side. This will allow sufficient for trimming as the orthodox proportion of cloth to paper on the side of a book lies between one to four and one to three, i.e. the cloth is usually between a quarter and a third of the total width of the book. This proportion is by no means arbitrary, as much depends on the personal taste of the binder, and the nature and purpose of the book, but the width of the cloth upon the side should never be greater than one-third.

Glue the cloth all over, having first placed it on a waste sheet. Place the back of the book in the middle of the cloth and lower it carefully upon one side until it rests on that side of the cloth. Bring the cloth over on to the upper side of the book and rub it down. Turn the book over, lift up the cloth, and lay it down again to tighten it a little, and rub down. Open the boards and insert a small piece of waste paper on the portion of glued cloth projecting at one end. This will prevent the glue from soiling the clean edge of the book. Stand the book up on this end with the boards thrown wide open, and grip firmly in the left hand. The right hand should be outside the cloth at the head of the book with the thumb in the centre. Turn the projecting piece over the hollow back, and push it down between the back and the hollow, forcing back the boards slightly to facilitate a clean turning-in. Insert a thin bone-folder down the hollow to straighten out any creases, and make sure that the cloth is turned over the edges of

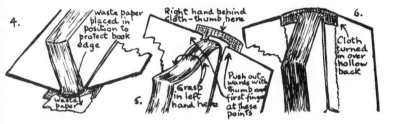

the boards tidily and tightly. Turn the book over, strip off the small piece of waste paper, and repeat the process. Close the book and generally neaten the cloth all over with a bone-folder, creasing a little down the joints. Finally, stand the book upright upon its spine and flatten the turn-in with the point of a folder, rotating it slightly during the operation. Square the cloth on the edges of the boards at both head and tail.

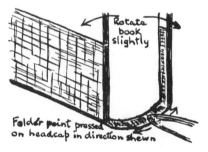

The cloth on the sides must now be trimmed. Take a pair of dividers and select a point where the cloth sides appear to be narrowest in width. Set the dividers a little less than this width, and mark points at the head and tail on both sides, measuring from the joint of the book. Place a straight-edge on the cloth up to the marked points and cut with a sharp knife from head to tail. Little experience is needed to perceive when the knife has passed through the cloth, for cutting into the board must be avoided at all costs. Cut the cloth at the tail, as shown in the diagram, and strip up the waste piece smartly as far as the head,

N
193

where it is cut off neatly with the knife. Run the finger down the roughened part of the board, this action being sufficient to smooth down the effects of the glue on the piece just stripped off.

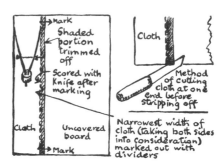

Repeat the process on the other side. It is not necessary to trim off the cloth on the edges of the boards at the head and tail, nor the turn-in of the cloth inside the book.

Choose a suitable paper for the sides, and cut out a piece equal in length to the book plus 2″, and twice the width of the uncovered part of the board plus 2″. Fold this piece, right side inside, and lay the folded edge $\frac{1}{32}$″ over the edge of the cloth. Hold it down firmly and crease all round the edges of the board. Remove the creased paper from the book and outside the creases mark parallel lines at a distance of $\frac{3}{4}$″. Trim these three sides

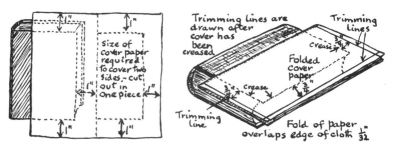

along the lines just marked, with a knife and straight-edge, and finally cut off the folded edge thus giving two separate pieces of cover paper, each with a turn-in of $\frac{3}{4}$″. In trimming off this fold no more must be cut off than the actual fold itself. Each sheet is now pasted all over on a clean sheet of waste, and laid down on the sides of the book in such a way that the straight edge of the paper extends $\frac{1}{32}''$ over the edge of the cloth. Smooth down the

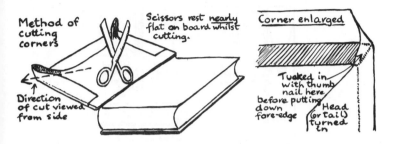

surface, lift up the board and turn in at the head, tail, and middle of the fore-edge. Nip up the corners with the finger and thumb so that they roughly bisect the right angle formed by the corners of the boards. Place the scissors nearly flat on the book board, and cut off each corner OUTWARDS. Lift up the fore-edge turn-in, put down those at the head and tail neatly, tuck in at the corners as shown in the diagram, and turn in the fore-edge. The tucking in should be done with the thumb nail. Neaten all with a folder, and square the paper round the edges of the boards. When both boards have been covered stand the book on its end until the sides are nearly dry, and then place between clean boards under a light weight. The craft term for this process of putting on the paper sides is 'siding'.

2. *Half-cloth and paper*

Cover the spine in cloth in the same manner as was done in the case of quarter-binding. Proceed as far as trimming both sides equally. On one corner mark two lines, A and B, with the dividers so that both lines are parallel and equidistant from the edges of the boards. Draw a line C from the corner to the intersection of A and B, thus bisecting the corner angle of the book. Measure with the dividers the distance D from the back of the book to the trimmed edge of the cloth, and transfer this to the line C so that distance from the corner to X equals D. Swing the dividers from the centre X to the edges of the boards, thus marking Y and Z. Join X, Y, and Z.

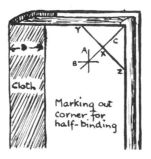

Marking out corner for half-binding

Take a piece of cartridge paper, having a straight edge, and place it over the corner; the straight edge should coincide with XYZ. Crease along the edges of the board, and outside these creases allow $\frac{3}{4}''$ for turning in, and cut off the corner $\frac{1}{4}''$ away from the corner formed by the creases. Using this paper pattern mark out the positions of the three remaining corners on the book, and, again using the pattern, cut out four corners from the same cloth as was employed to cover the spine. Glue the corners on a waste sheet, and place them in position on the book. They are turned in and trimmed with the scissors in exactly the same manner as that described for the siding in quarter-binding.

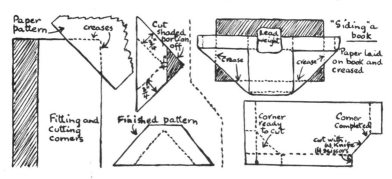

When covering the sides proceed in the same way as for quarter-binding as far as the separation of the folded sheet into two separate pieces. Then place one of the sheets with its straight edge just over the edge of the cloth, and place on it a small weight to hold it in position. Turn back both corners, and crease them carefully in such a way that the paper just overlaps the edges of the cloth corners. Both the turned-back corners should be level with each other, and square with the edges of the boards. Crease the paper well along these edges, take the piece off the book, and cut off the corners as shown in the diagram, using scissors for the right-angled creases, and a knife and straight-edge for the diagonal creases. Paste all over, lay on the book in position and turn in the edges neatly, squaring them round the edges of the boards. Repeat for the remaining side of the book.

3. *Full binding in cloth*

Lay the book on the wrong side of the cloth, and mark along the edges of the board at the head, tail, and fore-edge with a pencil. Roll the book over on the cloth without moving the position of the spine, and again mark round the board. Allow a distance of $\frac{3}{4}''$ to $1''$ outside these lines for turning in, and then cut out the whole piece. Glue the cloth all over, place the book

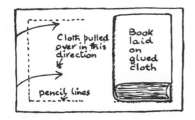
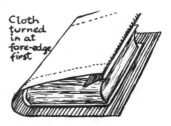

on one side up to the lines already marked, and pull the remaining cloth over the upper board. Lift this board slightly and turn in the cloth along the fore-edge. Turn the book over, lift the cloth, pulling it gently and putting it down, again turning in the fore-edge. Stand the book on its tail, boards thrown back, a piece of waste paper placed in the tail to prevent any soiling of the pages, and turn in the cloth in the manner described for quarter-binding. Repeat at the tail, nip up all corners, and cut from the inside with the scissors. Lift up and tuck in, and neaten all the surfaces, the back, the board edges, and the head and tail turnings-in, using a bone-folder. The book may then be given a light nip in the press, after which it should stand up on one end until dry.

The Paring of Leather

Before going on to describe the covering of books in leather it will be necessary to devote some space to the question of leather paring. My own favourite leather is Oasis Niger Goat, manufactured by Messrs G. W. Russell & Son Ltd., of Hitchin, and supplied by Russell Bookcrafts, Hitchin. It is this type to which the following methods are directed in particular, though generally applicable to other leathers.

Two knives are necessary, one an ordinary paring knife, and the other a French knife. The underside of both types is ground flat, whilst the upper side is bevelled so that in fact they assume

the appearance of a wood chisel though on a smaller scale. Both depend for their cutting power upon the retention of a very fine burr on the underside of the edge. If this burr is too coarse it will not cut efficiently; on the other hand, if it is too fine, or not present at all, the result will be the same. So that skill in paring is wholly dependent on the student's ability to retain this burr in the right condition. A fine oilstone should be at hand to restore the edge as the paring proceeds. On no account must this oilstone be near the leather as an accidental spot of oil will ruin the skin. The blades should be turned over, flat side uppermost, and given a gentle wipe over the stone. If the burr becomes too coarse the knife must be ground with the flat side down on the stone, until the burr has disappeared, and then turned over again and given another slight wipe on the bevel until the burr begins to appear again. It is possible for the student to obtain an ordinary cobbler's knife and have one side ground flat; a French knife can be bought for a few shillings.

After a piece of leather has been cut out it must be trimmed round the edge with the ordinary knife. No paring with a French knife must be attempted until this is taken off. The knife must be held at a very slight angle from the horizontal, and the edge of the leather pared off, giving it a bevel all round. This applies to all pieces cut out for covering purposes.

Paring for Quarter- and Half-binding in Leather

The piece required should be cut out as long as the book plus an amount at each end sufficient for turning in. This amount varies slightly with the size of the book, but for the most common sizes, $\frac{3}{4}''$ at each end is sufficient. After running round it

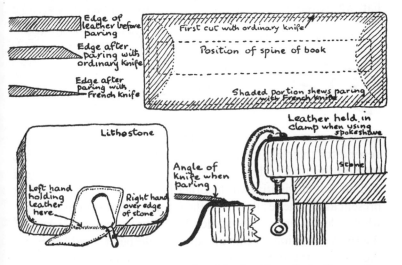

with the ordinary knife, pare it with the French knife on the areas shown in the diagram above. The position of the book back should be marked on the leather with a pencil, preferably of the solid ink type.

The best base for paring is a litho-stone, but if this is not obtainable, a piece of marble or sheet of plate glass, the edges of which have been ground off smooth to prevent damage to the leather. The piece to be pared is placed flat on the stone, and the knife held nearly flat, with the hand not quite over the stone.

A much more efficient and speedier alternative to the French knife is the spokeshave; the former is of course useful for small pieces, such as the corners in half-binding. 'Record' or 'Stanley' metal spokeshaves of the type fitted with two adjusting screws are very suitable. The blade must be removed and REVERSED, before paring leather, so that its bevel is uppermost—as in the French knife. The edge in this case is NOT to be provided with a 'burr', but kept 'razor sharp'.

The leather is held in a 'G' cramp, as shown in the diagram. A piece of hardwood, roughly 4″ to 5″ long, 1″ wide and about $\frac{3}{4}$″ thick, should be used between the cramp top and the leather; the paring should never proceed too far away from the cramp head and laziness in trying to avoid moving the leather along often enough, usually results in disaster. Never allow the leather to come between the stone and the cramp screw UNDERNEATH. The paring should be done very evenly, and if the portion being pared is frequently run between the thumb and forefinger, any unevenness will be easily detected. Parings tend to get under the leather, but they must never be allowed to remain there. Frequently clearing out of such parings is necessary. It should be carefully noted—see diagram—that the strokes of the spoke-shave blade should always be taken as radii from the cramp; the position of the blade, while cutting, is not at right angles to the stroke, but at an angle of about 30 degrees; this gives a slight slicing action, but it must not be overdone. A piece of hardwood, provided with a saw-cut to accommodate the blade, is necessary for sharpening purposes; this is shown in the diagram.

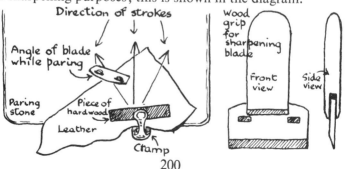

The final thickness at the points where the leather is turned in on the book, should be half the original thickness, tapering down to a very thin edge all round the piece. This work requires patience and care and facility in the use of all the tools only comes when the student has acquired, through experience, the 'feel' of these things. If an edge is allowed to become blunt, there is a much greater danger of cutting through the leather. Left-handed students really need an ordinary paring knife, the grinding of which is reversed.

Finally, it makes for much tidier work in paring, if a wooden tray can be provided. A three-ply base, of sufficient size to take the paring stone and a reasonable space for the parings, is surrounded on three sides only by sides about 3″ high. The diagram will make clear the whole arrangement. Students often feel that the disposal of parings into the refuse bin seems wasteful; and so it is. Dug into the garden, they make good organic manure.

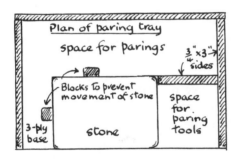

Paring for Half-binding in Leather

For half-binding the leather corners should be cut out, using a paper pattern for the purpose, in the same manner as that used for half-binding in cloth. They are run round with the

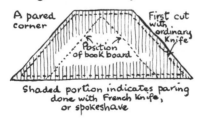

201

ordinary knife, and finished off with the French knife, thinning them down on the shaded portions shown on the diagram on this page. Particular attention must be paid to the small portion which will be turned over the board corner. If the leather is too thick at this point it will be impossible to avoid a clumsy corner. An alternative method of half-binding, illustrated in Chapter 1, requires a strip of leather down each fore-edge. Such strips should be pared in a similar fashion to the piece for the spine, making it thinnest at the points where the book corners will come, so assuring a neat turn-in.

Paring for Whole Binding in Leather

When cut out, the leather should appear as shown in the diagram, marked with a pencil to leave a margin outside the book size of approximately 1″ for turning in. When it has been pared all round with the ordinary knife, the work should be continued with the spokeshave in such a manner that the beginning of the paring comes a little within the line of the book position. Proceed a little further inwards from each

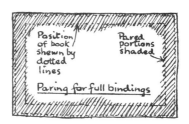

corner and at the head and tail, as shown by the shaded portions in the diagram. Where a book has leather joints in the endpapers, it will be necessary to pare the turning-in to the same thickness as the joints. This will be appreciated when the mitring is done, as two differing thicknesses of leather inside the boards cannot be successfully mitred. When the whole of the cover has been pared, replace the book upon it, re-mark its position again by a pencil line to assist in correct placing when covering.

202

The Fixing of 'False Bands' on a Hollow Back

In the case of leather bindings having a hollow back, it may be desirable to have raised bands under the leather. The material for this purpose is made by placing odd scraps of leather upon a piece of strong brown paper which has been glued all over. The pieces are arranged on one half of the paper, and the remaining half is folded over them, so that the leather is enclosed between the two thicknesses of paper. This is left in a press between pressing boards for some hours until it is dry. Strips can then be cut from it with a sharp knife. Such strips should not exceed $\frac{1}{10}''$ in width, and must be a little longer than the width of the book spine. The latter is marked out with pencil lines to indicate the desired positions of the bands, and the whole of the back run over with a very thin coat of glue. If calf is being used for the cover, the glue must be applied only on the portions of the hollow back which will be covered by the bands, and not over the whole of the back. Glue the strips themselves, and leave both the book and the bands until the glue has become tacky. If the bands are now taken one at a time and damped slightly on the glued surfaces by wiping over a wet sponge, they can be placed in position, and held down until they adhere. When they are completely dry, cut off the ends, flush with the book, in a vertical direction, using a very sharp knife.

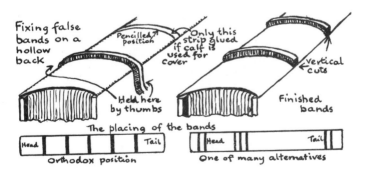

Fixing false bands on a hollow back. Pencilled position. Only this strip glued if calf is used for cover. Held here by thumbs. Vertical cuts. Finished bands.

The placing of the bands

Head — Tail — Orthodox position

Head — Tail — One of many alternatives

There are two ways in which such bands may be placed on a hollow back. The first one is the orthodox division into six panels having five bands, such as is used in flexible sewing on raised cords. The second method departs from orthodoxy, and allows the bands to be placed in any position the binder desires. The above example is only one of the many variations which may be used, and the governing factor will be the design intended for the book when the tooling comes to be done. In the case of full leather covers this variation gives much greater scope for freedom in the design, and is much favoured by French and German binders of today. I see no reason why such greater freedom should not be attained by this means, as the bands have no constructional value and are merely decorative. It is, however, not quite honest to use false bands in the orthodox position. It would be better to leave a plain hollow back, using no bands at all.

Back Cornering

All books bound in leather should have the boards 'back-cornered'. Lift the board and place a cutting tin under the back corner; shut down the board again. Take a very sharp knife, and cut off the corner of the board in a slanting direction. The inner corner nearest the book should only have

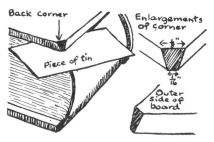

$\frac{1}{16}''$ cut off, whilst the upper or outer corner should be approximately $\frac{1}{8}''$. All four back-corners should be similarly treated, and the purpose of the operation is to give more room for the boards to open when the leather is turned in, and to help in the forming of the head caps.

Setting the Squares

In all cases where the boards have been 'laced-in', the book is placed with its back along the edge of the bench, and the upper board turned back until it hangs down. The small wedge-shaped grooves cut into the boards to receive the slips can now be seen, and they are now carefully filled with a little paste placed on the end of the finger. Turn the board back

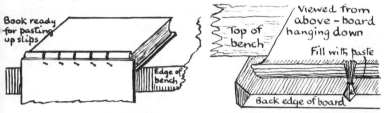

over the book and the slips will now be resting in the paste. Rub the surplus paste off with the finger, rubbing it also into the slips at the same time, and set the 'squares' of the book. When both boards have been thus treated, enclose the book between two clean pressing tins, place a pressing board on each side, and leave all in a press overnight. By this means the slips are pressed firmly into the grooves, leaving the surface of the boards smooth.

Covering with Leather

Quarter- and half-binding

Two groups must be considered, namely: (*a*) Books which have no sewn head- and tailbands. (*b*) Books with sewn head- and tailbands.

Books included under (*a*) may have hollow backs or fast backs, including library-style bindings, and it is usual to give them French headcaps. Instead of a visible headband, the head and tail are provided with a band placed underneath the leather when covering. For this purpose a small stock of good Italian line is necessary. It should be kept in a few different thicknesses. It is a strong hempen line, well sized, and sufficiently hard to provide the necessary support for the head and tail caps. First ascertain the dimensions of the 'squares' of the book, and select a piece of line the slightest fraction less than this measurement in thickness. Cut off two pieces exactly the same length as the curve of the spine, and roll them in a little paste.

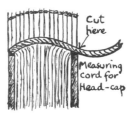

Take the pared piece of leather and damp it on the face side with a clean sponge. Allow this moisture to sink in, and then turn it over upon a clean sheet of waste paper, and paste it thoroughly all over. Give it a coating of paste rather thicker than that which is required in paper work, and leave it aside to soak. Coat the whole of the spine of the book with thin glue, but on no account do this if calf is being used. Allow the leather to continue soaking for about 15 to 20 minutes. The moisture in the paste will have been absorbed by this time into the skin, and it may be necessary to paste it again very lightly with thin paste.

Place the spine of the book in position in the middle of the pasted leather, lower the book upon one side, and pull the leather over in the manner employed in covering with cloth. Whether the book has raised bands or not, stand it on its fore-edge and tighten the leather over the spine, but not down the sides. This is done by using the ball of each hand at both sides of the spine simultaneously. It is most important to have the leather tightly stretched over the back in this way. If the back has raised bands, a pair of band nippers must then be used to nip up the leather on each side of the bands. The best nippers are chromium-plated to prevent injury to the skin, as plain steel is very apt to cause staining. The nipping should be carried out evenly and gently, working the nippers from one side of the back to the other. Smooth down the leather on the sides now, working over it with the hands, but avoiding any tendency to stretch or indent it.

When turning in at the head and tail follow the same method as is used in cloth binding, remembering to place a piece of waste paper between the leather and the pages of the book to

206

prevent soiling them. Before the leather is actually turned in, place a piece of the pasted Italian line just above the head of the book. The turn-in will then enclose the cord, which can be felt as the turning-in is done, and a sliding motion by the finger and thumb will retain the cord in position under the leather. There is no difference in the method if a hollow back is present. When completed, this cord should be sitting neatly on the head (or tail) of the book. Before finally closing the book, open each side and push the boards against a pressing board which has been placed up to the joint, as shown in the diagram. Close each board carefully after it has been set in this fashion.

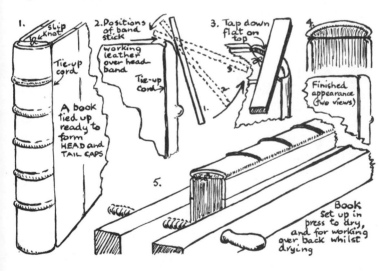

The bands must be gone over again with the nippers, and the panels between the bands worked over with a rosewood bandstick, particular attention being paid to the leather immediately over the joints of the boards. This process must be repeated at

207

intervals during the next hour, until it is seen that the leather is securely set on the back. Before setting it aside to be attended to in the above way, take a length of fine cord, such as 3-cord sewing thread, or printer's page cord, and tie up the head and tail caps, the cord running through the grooves formed by the back-cornering. In doing this, use a slip knot, and this knot should be placed at one end of the book so that it will not rest on the damp leather. After tightening the cord, make it fast and cut off the loose ends. Take a broad bandstick, stand the book on one end, and work over the leather towards the book as shown in the diagram. When it has been well moulded in this way, give the cap a final tapping to flatten the top of the cap, and repeat at the other end. If these have been well done, the book should stand square on the bench so that the edges of the boards and the head caps are flush with the surface of the bench. The tying-up cord should be left in position until the leather has dried, and then it can be cut off. In quarter-binding of this type the book is now placed standing on its fore-edge and nipped up in a finishing press, and it is whilst drying in this position that the bands are attended to at intervals, as previously mentioned.

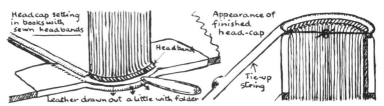

There is little difference made in the covering of books under the heading (*b*), i.e. those with sewn headbands. The variation lies in the turning in of the leather at the head and tail. It is carried out in the same way as turning in cloth, but after the turning-in has been done the book is placed with its spine on the bench, the boards lying open. Then a little of the turned-in leather is drawn out again gently with the point of a fine folder. This requires considerable judgement, for the amount drawn out should be just sufficient to be worked over the upper edge of the headband, and yet leave most of the headband stitching visible.

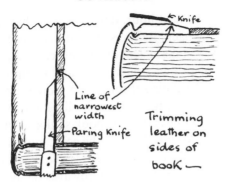

Trimming Leather on Sides

When the leather on the spine is dry, it must be trimmed, but, unlike the method used with cloth, it must be done with the paring knife; marks, showing the narrowest width from the back, are made (as on p. 194) and joined by lines made with a fine folder. The surplus leather is then pared off in a gently sloping fashion, as shown in the diagram.

Half-binding in Leather

In half-binding the corners are marked out on the book. The usual paper pattern is made and the leather cut out and pared. All four are pasted, allowed to soak a little, and placed in position, turned in, cut and smoothed off in the way already described for half-binding in cloth. 'Siding' for both quarter and half-leather work follows the same procedure as that already outlined for cloth work.

Covering for Library-style Books

Nothing has been said yet concerning the covering of books done in a library style. The variation in this style occurs in the putting down of the leather on the sides. After tightening it over the back, a bone-folder is run down the groove left between the back and the back edge of the boards. This groove is known as a French joint and the leather is pressed well down into it with the folder. Turning-in, tying up the caps,

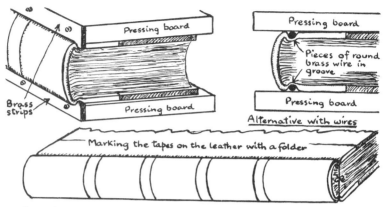

and setting them is carried out in the usual way. Some binders have special pressing boards for this style, which ensure that the leather is held down in the joint while drying proceeds. They are furnished on one edge with a strip of brass which projects into the joint. If such boards are used the head and tail caps should be allowed to set first, and the tying-up cord removed. An alternative is to be found in the use of pieces of round brass wire of sufficient thickness to fit exactly into the French joint. These are covered by the pressing boards, and so pressed down upon the leather in the groove.

Before leaving the subject of library-style binding, mention must be made of the marking of the tapes on the spine. It is usual to mark the positions of the tapes whilst the leather is still damp. This is done with the edge of a fine folder, or the corner of a bandstick, and is a form of blind tooling. Use is made of the fact that a book sewn on tapes, having a fast back, will naturally have slightly raised bands on the surface of the leather where the tapes occur. The rubbing of the folder upon the damp skin will cause a darkening of the leather and so produce blind lines.

Covering in Full (or Whole) Leather

The leather is pasted and soaked in the usual way. Then the book is placed in position on the lines already marked on the skin, the face side having first been inspected to ascertain which portion of the leather has the best appearance. The

210

front side of the book should be placed on this half. Draw the leather over the book, turn the fore-edges *outwards*, and stand the book upright upon a sheet of waste paper. Pull the leather tight over the spine, as in quarter-binding, and nip up the bands. Lay the book down, lift the leather on the side, and put it down again without stretching it. Smooth it down with the hands, and turn in at the fore-edge. Repeat for the other side.

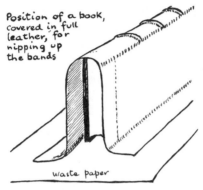

Position of a book, covered in full leather, for nipping up the bands

Waste paper

Turn the leather in at the head and tail; stand the corners up and cut with the scissors, leaving rather more to put down than in the case of cloth, i.e. raise the scissors a little away from the book so that when the leather is put down there is a good 'wrap over' on each side. This facilitates mitring at a later stage.

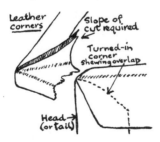

Leather corners

Slope of cut required

Turned-in corner shewing overlap

Head→ (or tail)

Close the boards after drawing out the head and tail for the caps, and forcing each board against a pressing board placed in the joint. Go over the bands again with the band nippers, tie up and mould the head and tail caps, and at the same time square the leather round all the edges of the boards with the bandstick. Carefully insert a piece of waterproof paper in each end of the book between the boards and endpapers in order to prevent any staining or cockling of the pages while the leather is damp. The material sold for lampshade making is quite good for this purpose. Go over the bands at intervals until they are set, and leave the book standing upright for some time until the leather begins to dry. It usually takes twelve hours or more to dry out, but it must not be left standing all this time, as the boards would be warped too much by the pull of the drying leather. When the bands and caps are set, take off the tie-up string, and place the book between clean oiled boards. Over all place clean, smooth pressing boards, but on no account put the book into a press. It will be sufficient to place it under a light weight. During this drying-out process nothing in the nature of pressing tins or metal plates should be allowed to come into contact with the leather. The results of such a contact are disastrous.

Varieties of Bookbinding Leather and its Preservation

It will be convenient at this point to say something concerning the leathers used for the covering of books. During the past hundred years one of the great problems besetting all librarians has been the rapid decay of leather used for books. This difficulty arose from the use of acids in tanning and dyeing. Once a skin has been treated with sulphuric acid it is wellnigh impossible to free it of such acid, and the rot literally sets in. Experiments during this century have produced leathers which were guaranteed acid-free, but even then it was discovered that after a book had been exposed to the atmosphere for some little time, it was found to contain free sulphuric acid, and the obvious conclusion presents itself that such acid had been absorbed by the leather from the air. Further research by the British Museum has brought to light many of the causes of such decay, and the means which can be adopted to protect leather by restoring the natural protective oils which it possessed before tanning and dyeing removed them. For details concerning the measures adopted, the student is advised to obtain a copy of the publication issued by the British Museum on the subject. It is entitled *The Preservation of Leather Bookbindings*, and is written by Mr. H. J. Plenderleith, of the British Museum Laboratory, who has set forth the whole problem in a clear and unmistakable fashion. It is no satisfaction to any binder of beautiful books to have to wonder how long the leather he has used will withstand the action of acids, and once he has parted with such books he may never see them again. He is not in a position to assess the lasting power of the leather, and therefore his thanks are due to the Museum Laboratory for the patient research which gives him a greater certainty that his work will be more enduring.

Among the many kinds of leather used in bookbinding the most familiar are Calf, Sheep, Pig, Seal, and Goat. As this book is mainly concerned with bookbinding carried out in schools and colleges, it is wise to confine the choice of leather to those skins which prove to be the most useful from the students' point of view.

Calf skin is difficult to handle, especially when wet, is very easily marked, and should be avoided. Pigskin is an excellent leather but difficult to work, and dyeing often spoils it from the bookbinding angle. Sealskin is a beautiful leather, but precautions have to be taken against the very oily nature of this skin. The writer's preference, from all points of view, is for Goatskin, commonly called Morocco. There are a number of varieties, but Oasis Niger Goatskin is a most beautiful leather, giving the best results in every way. The natural undyed skins, and those of a natural red, given to it by the natives during tanning, are most satisfying in every way. The sole manufacturers of Oasis Goatskins are Messrs. G. W. Russell & Son, of Hitchin.

One of the great difficulties young pupils have to meet lies in the paring of the leather, but a large percentage can cope with those skins known as Niger Kid. Such skins are naturally small, but they are thin, and need very little paring. If the teacher feels that these skins are too expensive, rather than relinquish the opportunity of binding books in leather, he can fall back upon skivers, either of sheep or Persian goat. These should be plain, i.e. having no artificial grain. It should be clearly understood that such skins are very thin, with little strength, and of poor wearing quality. In spite of such drawbacks, I do not hesitate to use them for younger pupils for one very important reason, namely, that even the use of skivers opens out for the pupil the whole field of finer binding, which can only be attempted when leather is used.

One reason for the fading of interest in schools, on the part of teacher, pupil, and those in authority, is the constant round of books sewn on tapes and bound in cloth, often only case-bound in a kind of pseudo-commercial fashion without the tools of trade binding. No flexible binding can be done under such limitations, and little opportunity is possible to explore the interesting vistas opened out by the use of leather, with all the delight of tooling and design that accompanies it. A little experience with skivers will open the way to Niger Kid in the majority of cases, and pupils are always very willing to purchase this leather once their interest has been aroused. If the teacher buys a few skins himself for this purpose, he must exercise care in cutting them up if he wishes to refund the money he has laid out. The method of measurement used in calculating the square feet in any particular skin is complicated, and in practice it will be found that a skin marked 4 feet will by no means give that area in cut pieces for books. The footage charged by the supplier is usually marked on the back of the skin, and is reckoned in whole feet, and quarters of a foot. For instance, a skin of $4\frac{1}{4}$ square feet is marked 4/1, $4\frac{1}{2}$ is given as 4/2, and $4\frac{3}{4}$ as 4/3. Before any pieces are cut from such a skin it should be roughly measured up to find the actual area available for cutting, and the price per foot calculated on this basis. An example may be taken from the 4-foot skin just mentioned. This may only give 3 effective square feet; so that if it were purchased at 8s. per foot the price would be 32s. The actual price charged for cut pieces, excluding all ideas of profit-making, should therefore be 32s. divided by three, i.e. 10s. 8d. per foot. Only when half or quarter skins are sold could the price be the same as the invoiced figure. The irregular pieces round the edges, such as the legs, can be used for the corners in half-binding. The skins under consideration are usually classed as first and seconds, and the seconds are further subdivided into seconds and good seconds. Firsts should be perfect skins, free of marks and holes, but they are more expensive for this reason. Good seconds are a little cheaper, and admirable for students. The flaws are not numerous, and can often be avoided by careful cutting. When skivers are used it is not necessary to use the French knife. If the edge is shaved with the ordinary knife, it will be sufficient.

CHAPTER 16

Mitring, Trimming-out, and Polishing

Care must be exercised when opening the boards of a newly covered book for the first time. If the boards appear to open very stiffly, and threaten to pull the cover away at the joint, the leather along the hinge outside must be damped with a clean sponge. When the moisture has penetrated the leather a little, begin to open the boards a little at a time until they are fully extended and move freely at the joint.

Putting Down the Leather Joints

Where a book is provided with leather joints in the endpapers, these pieces of leather must now be pasted down. Place the book on a clean duster, and arrange a sufficient number of pressing boards underneath the opened board to support it horizontally. A more convenient form of equipment to take the place of pressing boards is a book block. This is a piece of wood having one edge rounded like the fore-edge of a book, but a number of such blocks will have to be kept in stock, varying in thickness to accommodate the differing thicknesses of books.

Open the board until it rests on the pressing boards (or the block). Take a very sharp knife and cut the covering leather at the head and tail on the back edge of the board, as shown in the diagram. Do not allow the cut to extend beyond the end of the

216

leather joint. This operation will facilitate the removal of the under piece of leather when the mitring is done.

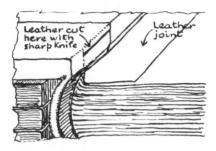

Tear out the waste sheet, and clean out any bits of paper or glue remaining in the joint. Place a piece of waste paper under the joint, and paste it well. Allow it to soak for a minute or two, remove the soiled waste and insert a piece of oiled board in its place. Bring over the book board and close it down upon the leather joint. Apply pressure, on the outside down the joint, with the hand and then place a pressing board and a knocking down iron on the book. Leave it thus for about 5 minutes. Now open the board gently until it is in a perpendicular position and very slowly close it, watching the back edge of the leather joint all the time. If there is any tendency for the joint to crease on the back edge, raise the board again and pull the joint, very gently, a little further over the board. Test again until no crease appears. Close the board and perform the same operation with the other joint. It will then be necessary to turn back to the first joint which will, by this time, be sufficiently set. Open the board carefully until it rests on the pressing boards and place a strip of bank paper over the joint. Over this paper go up and down the

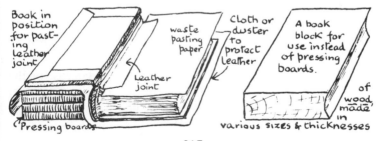

back edge of the board with the finger and thumb to give a good square finish to the joint. Continue until the leather appears to have adhered to the edge of the board. Then the book board should be gently closed and the other end of the book treated in the same way. See that the oiled boards are in position; then place the book between pressing boards and leave all under a weight, a knocking-down iron is adequate for this purpose. Three or four hours should elapse before the book is ready for the next stage.

Mitring the Corners

After the joints have dried out completely, the corners are mitred. Take a pair of dividers, and at each corner make two marks on the leather, as at A, by running one leg along the edge of the board, while marking with the other leg. A line running from A to B would of course bisect the angle formed by the corner of the board and it is along this line that the mitre is made. Where a leather joint is present, the line of the mitre CD should not go to the corner of the board, but to the edge of the leather joint.

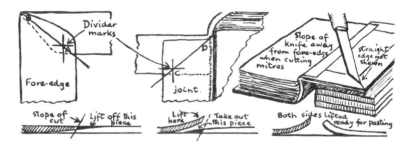

Take a sharp knife and a straight-edge, and cut through the leather at a slight angle along AB, CD, etc. It will be seen that the slope of this cut will give an almost invisible joint when the mitre is finished. It is best to work systematically in the cutting, and always have the knife sloping away from the fore-edge or the leather joint.

When all the corners have been cut, dab them with a damp sponge until the leather has absorbed enough moisture to soften the paste underneath. Lift off the small overlaps and open out the two sides of each mitre. Moisten the small piece still left underneath, and take that out too. Repaste all the opened corners with the finger and allow them to soak for a few minutes. Put down the head and tail sides of the mitres first, and then the fore-edge and joint sides, working carefully with a folder until a neat and level joint is formed. Sponge off the paste which is squeezed out in the process, and also any paste marks left on the leather where the overlaps were taken off. Leave the boards open to dry out the mitres. It is wise to place a sheet of waterproof paper inside the first board while the second one is being done. I often only lift the fore-edge and joint pieces for pasting, leaving the others *in situ*, but difficult corners should have both sides lifted.

Trimming out and Filling in the Boards

In the best work it is necessary to 'fill in' the insides of the boards so that the edges of the turned-in cover will not be visible under the endpapers. Very thin manilla, sold as 100 lb. weight, or stout cartridge paper may be used for this work, and two pieces should be cut out a fraction less than the size of the book boards. Ascertain by inspection the point inside the boards where

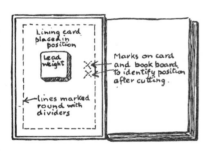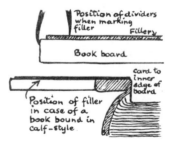

the turned-in leather is narrowest, and set a pair of dividers to a fraction less than this width. Open one board out flat upon pressing boards or a book block, in the manner adopted for mitring the corners, and place the manilla or cartridge card in the centre of this board. Upon it place a lead weight to hold it in position. An alternative to the weight is the placing of two tiny spots of glue on the back of the filling-in card to fasten it temporarily to the board. It must remain under a weight until the glue has set.

Take the dividers, already set to the required width, and run them round the board, with one leg over the edge and the other on the card, thus making a mark equidistant from the edges of the board. On no account must any movement of the card take place during this and the following operation. With a knife and straight-edge cut through the card and the leather on all four sides. The resulting cut-out rectangle is lifted and its position marked before finally removing it from the book, i.e. a pencilled mark of some kind is made on the back of it near the inner edge, and also on the book board itself, to indicate its position when finally putting it down. Strip off the pieces of leather left inside the line of the cuts. GLUE the filling-in piece, place it in position and rub it down thoroughly all over with a folder until it sets, paying special attention to the edges where leather and filling-in piece meet. This joint should be level, and considerable judgement is necessary in assessing the thickness of card or paper required to make it a good one. This judgement only arises from experience and familiarity with the thickness of the leather after paring.

In the case of calf-style bindings where no leather joint is present, the filling-in piece should have one edge cut perfectly straight. This straight edge should lie along the back edge of the board, and the three remaining sides should be marked and trimmed out.

It is not necessary to fill in cloth bindings, but they are often trimmed out only, to give a somewhat neater appearance after the endpapers have been put down.

Polishing the Leather

The varnishing of leather in order to produce a polished surface should be avoided. It may produce such a surface quickly and with little effort, but eventually the varnish deteriorates and goes white in the joint. The polishing of leather with a polishing iron entails much more labour, but is far more satisfying when done. The iron is shaped as shown in the diagram. The under-side should be very slightly convex, and if, when purchased, this is not so, it should be ground slightly to put it right. Round off the edges too. It is a very great advantage indeed if this tool is chromium-plated, and the cost of plating is not great. If left as plain steel it quickly becomes rusty, and has to be cleaned with fine emery cloth every time it comes to be used.

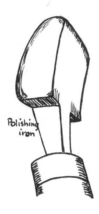

Polishing
iron

The iron is placed on a finishing stove, and made no hotter than can be borne by touching it quickly with the palm of the hand. Meanwhile the book is placed upon a clean duster and sponged over with clean water and a little white vinegar. The damping should be even and not overdone. Place a clean piece of thin bank paper over the leather and work the polishing iron over it, both down the length of the book and across the width. The iron must be kept moving all the time, and when the leather has dried a little, it can be applied directly upon the leather itself. Put little pressure on at first, but increase it as the polishing proceeds, and the iron can be a little hotter as the leather gradually dries. When both sides are polished, go over the back in a similar fashion. If raised bands are present, it will be necessary to turn the iron over in order to go right up to the bands. Complete the back by running over the bands themselves, the edges of the boards, the head and tail caps, and the margins of leather inside the boards. From this point, until the book is completely finished, it should be kept in a duster to prevent scratching of the polished leather, and, when work is not being actually done upon it, kept under a moderate weight.

Two faults are very common amongst students doing polishing. One of them is evident when the iron is not held firmly, but allowed to wobble slightly on the leather. Instead of getting a fine polished surface, too often the book is covered with lines made by the edges of the iron, and these are very difficult to remove. The handle of the tool should rest on the shoulder, and the whole body down to the waist should move with the iron as the strokes are made. The other fault is concerned with the heat of the iron and the dampness of the leather. It should be firmly fixed in the mind of the would-be craftsman that damp leather should never be treated with a hot tool, and that the wetter the leather the cooler the tool. Only as the skin dries should the heat be increased, and that very gently indeed. A hot iron on damp leather will leave dark marks wherever it is touched, so that the beginner would be well advised to err on the side of too much dryness and too little heat until he has gained more experience, even at the expense of less polish on his book. Patience is also a necessary item in this work, as it is a process which cannot be hurried if the desired result is to be obtained.

CHAPTER 17

Pasting Down and Pressing

It is wise to leave the pasting down of the endpapers until all the decorative work on the book is completed, particularly so in the case of leather bindings. For convenience, this chapter is inserted here, in order to keep all the matter concerning finishing, i.e. the decoration of the book, in one complete section to itself. Pasting down the endpapers falls into two distinct divisions, viz.,

(a) pasting down 'shut';
(b) pasting down 'open'.

Pasting down 'Shut' for books Bound 'out-of-boards'

The majority of cloth bindings fall under this category. An exception is found in the case of a binding which has a separate 'board paper'. Library bindings done in quarter leather are also pasted down shut. When using this method it is not usual to trim the board endpapers before pasting down, but if this is desired reference must be made to the way in which calf-style bindings are prepared for pasting down. This will be found later in this chapter.

Open the board, and place a piece of clean waste between the endpaper and the book itself. This waste paper must be somewhat larger than the book. Hold the endpaper and the waste

223

down at the point indicated in the diagram, and paste outwards until the endpaper is given an even coat. Finish off the place where the finger has rested, and close the board down on the pasted paper. As the board is closing, it should be bent slightly

outwards to lessen the risk of leaving air bubbles between the two surfaces. If the board is now lifted very slightly, the pasted endpaper will adhere to it sufficiently to make it possible to withdraw the waste sheet. This should be done rather smartly, taking care to avoid touching the endpaper with the surplus paste. Close the board again, and quickly put down the other side in the same manner. Place the book between pressing boards, the edges of which must only come up to the joints, leaving the spine clear. Leave all in the press until drying is complete. This period should be no less than 24 hours, and if a book can be left longer than this time, it is better to do so, as drying out under pressure is a slow process. Taking the book out prematurely only results in warped boards. Students often fall into the habit of placing clean waste paper in the endpapers before putting the book into the press, but this is entirely unnecessary, and often causes trouble. On the other hand the placing of oiled boards in the ends is a good thing and must be done if the pages of the book are at all likely to 'cockle' from the dampness of the endpaper.

Sometimes, owing to defective backing or gluing-up, the fore-edge of the endpapers protrudes a little beyond the leaves. This should be cut off, using a knife and a very thin steel rule, before any pasting down is done. The strip of cutting board between the side of the book and the book itself must not be forgotten. Its function is the protection of the book board from the

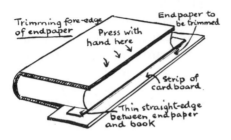

knife. It will be seen that the steel rule is placed between the last page and the endpaper to be trimmed and the pressure on the book, while cutting, must be firm.

Pasting down 'Shut' for books Bound 'in-boards'

Consideration is now given to all books bound flexibly, having laced-in boards and with endpapers having no leather joint.

These books may be sewn on raised bands or on bands sawn-in, and the endpapers will be of the ziz-zag type. It will be remembered that such endpapers have a concertina-like fold forming the zig-zag. It is this fold which must be first cleaned out

before any pasting down is done. Take the book, and tear out both the waste sheets carefully and in a clean manner. It should now be possible to insert a fine folder into the joint in order to open it and clean it free of any particles of glue. Theoretically it should be completely free of glue, but occasionally some may have squeezed through the stitching. An eighth-of-an-inch of the waste sheets will be left adhering to the coloured sheet, and this must be left undisturbed.

Bring the board paper over the opened board, now resting on pressing boards or a book block, and, keeping it tight, rub down

P   225

the back edge gently, fitting it into the joint. After deciding how much of the cover turn-in is to show round the inside of the board, set the dividers to this width, and still holding the endpaper in position, run round the edges of the board, thus marking the endpaper parallel to the head, tail, and fore-edge. Place a cutting tin on the book; bring over the board paper, and cut with a sharp knife along the marks made by the dividers. A small piece must be left at the head and tail to cover the edge of the board, and it requires some experience here to allow for the expansion of the paper on being pasted, for the small piece should only come level with the upper edge of the board. The diagram will make this clear.

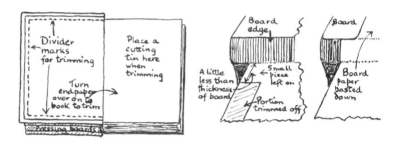

The endpaper is now thoroughly pasted and the board brought over upon it, in the usual manner, lifting slightly to extract the waste paper. Give to it the same test as that used in putting down leather joints, i.e. open the board enough to inspect the joint. If the paper shows any creasing here at all it must be pulled a little further over the board, and closed down again. Sometimes this extra pulling, or the fact of the paper's stretching while wet, causes the fore-edge to come over too far, thus making the margins unequal. If a knife is made extremely sharp the paper may be successfully trimmed back whilst wet, but great care must be used in doing this. The secret lies in a good pressure upon the straight-edge, and very light strokes of the knife. Place oiled boards inside the endpapers and pressing boards outside the book and give a nip in the press for two or three minutes. Take out and inspect the joints again and rub

226

down under paper, if necessary. Then return all to the press and leave there as long as possible.

Pasting-down 'Open' for Books having Separate Board Papers

Leather jointed endpapers come into this category and in such cases the board papers are two single sheets. Both must be trimmed approximately $\frac{1}{16}''$ less than the size of the boards. Open a board and support it in the usual way by pressing boards. Place one of the single sheets upon the opened board, putting a small weight in the centre. Run around all four sides with the dividers set to the chosen margin. Take off the paper and trim it along the marked lines, paste it and lay it in position, rubbing it down carefully under a clean sheet of paper. When both sides are completed, stand the book upright with the boards open, and held by a slotted card, as in the diagram, until the endpapers begin to contract and pull the boards straight. Then place be-

Drying endpapers in a book pasted down OPEN

tween boards in a press and leave as long as possible. If the book be covered in full leather, and chromium pressing plates are available, it is an advantage to use these next to the book when pressing. Only a light pressure is needed; heavy pressure would tend to crush the spine and detach the leather by wrinkling it.

It should be noted that where leather bindings of the in-board types are concerned, the pressing boards are placed over the joints and not just up to them.

Opening up

All good books should be carefully opened up after the whole of the work has been completed. This section should therefore come at the end of Chapter 19, but is inserted here for greater convenience. The book should be placed flat on the bench and opened gradually from the front, a few pages at a time, until the middle is reached. Then it is turned over and the same process repeated from the end of the book to the middle. At each turning of a few pages the hand should be run down the middle of the opening with a moderate pressure. The purpose of this process is to ensure that subsequent opening of the book will not do any damage to the back, and to make it open easily and evenly. Pressing follows when the opening up is complete.

CHAPTER 18

Tools and Materials for Decoration

☆

The decoration of books is known as 'finishing', and the tools used are called 'finishing tools'. Such tools fall into different classes, viz.,

(a) Handle lettering tools and brass type.
(b) Fancy hand tools.
(c) Pallets and gouges.
(d) Rolls and fillets.

Handle Lettering Tools, and Type

Such handle tools are sold in sets of about 38, giving the letters of the alphabet, numerals, full stop, and comma. They are manufactured in different sizes and type faces, and it is useful to have a small, medium, and large size in a good Roman character; 12 point, 18 point, and 24 point are the sizes which cover

Name of tool printed on paper band and covered with band of sellotape.

A brass handle letter

Nick to indicate top of letter.

most of the work attempted by students. Modern type faces, such as Gill Sans Serif, may be added as funds permit. One disadvantage of the Sans Serif letters was felt by designers to lie in the fact that as the height of the letter increased so did the actual

229

thickness of the letter. On using such letters in conjunction with a modern design built up from line tools, the lettering appeared to be clumsy and not in harmony with the general feeling of the design. It is fortunate now that the makers have appreciated this difficulty, and such tools can be obtained which correspond in thickness with the usual thickness of line tools, whatever the height of the letter.

As all finishing tools are made of brass the students should use the utmost care in their employment and storage. Dropping them on the floor or knocking them in any way on a hard surface will ruin the face of the tools. They should be kept in round boxes, or standing in a block of wood which has been bored to provide a hole for each tool. Each alphabet or other set of tools should have its own box or block duly labelled.

Cases of brass type cast in various sizes and faces can also be used. A typeholder is needed, and the type is set up in such a holder in the manner that a compositor sets up type for printing. In this way one or two words can be tooled as a whole, instead of letter by letter. I have always avoided this method of tooling where students in schools are concerned. It is not only unsatisfactory in the hands of the beginner, but eliminates that individuality to be found in the use of handle letters. For the same reason lettering built up from individual pallets and gouges is to be preferred to handle letters. The use of the typeholder really belongs to commercial bookbinding and there it should remain.

Fancy Hand Tools

This title covers a very large range of tools having some device or design cut on the end of the brass shank. They may be used separately or in conjunction with each other and with line tools to form patterns. They may also be 'solid' or 'line' in form, but should not exceed $\frac{3}{4}''$ by $\frac{3}{4}''$ in size, as they become difficult to use above this dimension.

The use of such tools has declined in recent years in favour of the simpler gouges and pallets, chiefly owing to the different conception of design prevailing today, but the same principle of building pattern from separate tools remains as evolved by Roger Payne in the eighteenth century. Many such simple devices can be made for use in school by screwing large brass screws into wooden handles, and filing down the head to the desired shape.

Pallets and Gouges

Pallets are straight-line tools of various lengths, and a complete set for the building of design ranges from $\frac{1}{16}$" long, increasing by $\frac{1}{16}$" at a time to a maximum of 2". The edges should be very slightly convex in order to avoid the cutting of the leather by the extreme ends when tooling. It is possible to make a set of small straight tools from brass screws, as already described, and these can be quite effective for beginners, giving them experience in the handling of finishing tools. There are also longer pallets for use in working over the backs of books; some of these have double lines on the edge, and others

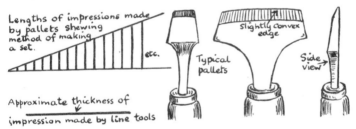

Lengths of impressions made by pallets shewing method of making a set.

etc.

Approximate thickness of impression made by line tools

Typical pallets

Slightly convex edge

Side view

may have a repeating design engraved thereon. The latter have little appeal today in view of the emphasis in modern design upon the simple line.

Gouges are single-line tools, like pallets in appearance, giving curved lines. The ideal collection for design comprises three sets, each set having a different curvature. If a series of concentric circles be drawn about $\frac{1}{10}$" apart, the lines given by the tools are obtained by taking different sectors, e.g. No. 1 set would give quarter-circle tools, No. 2 set in a sector of about 60° would give

231

less curvature, and No. 3 set in a sector of 30° would give fairly flat curves. Each set should range from about ⅛″ wide to approximately 2″. It should be clearly understood that the above sets of pallets and gouges represent the ideal, and few classes in bookbinding are so equipped. They have to be content with a small selection, with the consequent limitation in the scope of the designs attempted. If, however, the craftsman is determined to have a complete set, as outlined above, the cost of making such a set to his own specifications would be prohibitive. Given

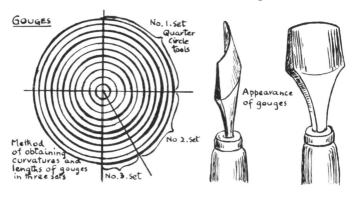

time and patience, there is the alternative of making them himself. With the aid of the concentric circles, it will be seen that there are in each set about twenty tools, and if the sizes of the largest tool, the 7th tool, and the 13th one be noted, together with the largest pallet, the 8th, 16th, and the 24th, patterns of these particular tools can be made in hardwood. Such patterns are not very difficult to shape out with the aid of a fretsaw, files, and sandpaper, and an additional pattern should be cut out which is ¼″ square. A tang 1″ long and a shoulder piece should be incorporated in each pattern. After the finished patterns have been dipped in shellac they can be sent to a brass founder, with instructions to cast a number of each pattern, e.g. the largest pattern of each set should be repeated to give the number of tools down to the size of the next smaller pattern, and so on throughout the set. When they are returned cleaning up and filing down to the required sizes is carried out, a very accurate drawing being used to act as a template for curvatures, lengths, and thicknesses. The use of more than one pattern for each set reduces the waste of metal and a considerable amount of filing. The $\frac{1}{4}''$ square blanks are used to make small tools such as solid

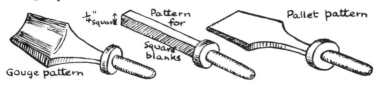

and hollow circles and squares, and two or three dozen castings will prove very useful for such tools. The handles are made from $\frac{5}{8}''$ dowelling, bored a little smaller than the tangs and driven down to the shoulders. A spokeshave and a file will shape these handles to the shoulder size. While the handles are being driven on to the tools the face of the latter must be protected. This is most easily done by resting the shoulder upon both jaws of a vice, having the tool itself between the jaws but not gripped by them. The handle is then tapped down to the shoulder. Such tools are worth all the care and time required to make them, and add greatly to the scope and quality of design.

One great advantage of the above sets of tools is to be found in the possibilities of built-up lettering. Though more time is occupied in its execution, such lettering forms an integral part of the design, and gives more scope for that individuality which is one of the marks of the true craftsman.

Rolls and Fillets

Rolls and fillets are circular pieces of brass, usually 3″ to 4″ in diameter, mounted in long handles which rest on the shoulder while tooling is being done. They are used for long continuous lines in design, and must be very true round the circumference. Rolls often have a repeating pattern engraved on

233

the edge, but designs made by this method are very mechanical. The fillet has a notch cut out of the edge to enable the craftsman to form his corners neatly. Variations of both rolls and fillets are to be found in the two-line tools. These have two lines on the

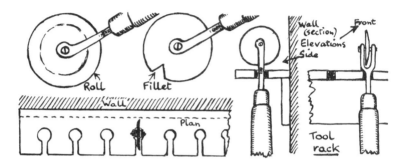

circumference instead of one. These items in the equipment of a bookbinder are expensive and damage very easily; therefore they should not be left lying about, but kept in a wooden wall rack, slotted to receive them. When they are in use they must never be carelessly handled or knocked upon a hard surface.

A small roll about 1″ in diameter is often used to tool lines which cannot be successfully done with a gouge.

Finishing stove

A bookbinder's finishing stove has a circular plate in the centre which can be heated, and an outer notched ring to support the tool handles. One heated by gas is convenient, and very easily controlled. The handles must be kept clear of the hot centre plate; beginners invariably forget this important point, and allow the handles to become charred. Asbestos handles are

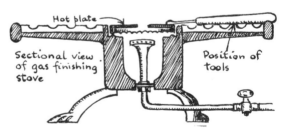

expensive and seem to me to be an admission of lack of care or even defeat. Each tool must point towards the hole in the centre of the plate. The diagram indicates one of the bench variety.

If an electric stove is preferred to gas, the best one available is that designed by Sydney Cockerell of Letchworth. It is fitted with a simmerstat and can be regulated to the heat required. Some stoves in the past have been sold as finishing stoves, but they could never have been designed by a bookbinder. This stove, however, has been thought out and made to the specifications of one who knows the craft intimately and it is well worth the extra cost involved.

If it is felt that funds will not allow for the purchase of a finishing stove, a quite effective substitute can be made with the assistance of the metal-work class for use in school. A piece of sheet metal about $\frac{1}{10}''$ thick must be cut out and bent round to form a cylinder about 4″ high and 4″ in diameter. It is wise to have this properly welded at the joint, and at the same time to weld on at one end a circular piece of the same metal. In the middle of the latter cut out a circle 1″ in diameter, and bore six $\frac{1}{4}''$ holes, three near the top and three near the bottom, arranging them alternately to form a hexagon in plan.

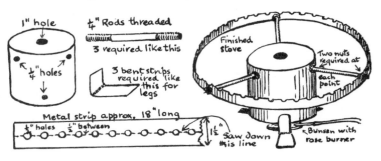

A metal strip $1\frac{1}{2}''$ wide and about 18″ long, is bored with $\frac{1}{2}''$ holes, $\frac{1}{2}''$ apart, down the centre. This strip is then sawn down the middle along the whole of its length; the pieces are bent round to form semi-circles and then welded to form a complete circle. Three $\frac{1}{4}''$ round rods and three bent strips to act as legs are needed, and then the whole can be assembled as shown in the diagram. A small rose burner adapted to screw into an ordinary bunsen burner will provide the heat under the plate.

Gold cushion and gold knife

The gold cushion is a piece of wood covered with calf skin. The flesh side of the leather is uppermost, and a thin layer of cotton wool lies between the wood and the leather. A convenient size is 8″ by 6″. It must be kept scrupulously free of grease of any description, and a regular rubbing over with a little powdered bathbrick will overcome any difficulty of this nature. The gold knife should be rubbed at the same time for the same reason. Such a knife has a semi-blunt cutting edge, so that the leather pad is not damaged when the gold leaf is being cut up.

Cotton wool

A supply of cotton wool should be kept in stock. It is used for greasing the leather when tooling, and also for picking up the leaf from the cushion.

Brushes

One or two fine sable-hair brushes are necessary for the application of the glaire, and for use when blind tooling.

Grease

Grease is necessary when applying the gold leaf, and Vaseline, sweet oil of almonds, or coconut oil may be used. The last is superior to the first two.

Glaires

Glaire is the name given to the preparation employed to fasten the gold leaf to the leather. It is made by beating up the white of an egg to which has been added a teaspoonful of white vinegar. This is allowed to stand for 24 hours, and the liquid poured off and strained into a bottle. It is then ready for use. As time goes on it becomes cloudy and small lumps form; it should then be re-strained. The fact that it eventually goes bad does not seem to affect its working quality, but it is unpleasant for the binder. It can be purchased in dry form, known as Dry Albumen, and mixed up with water and a little vinegar, but it does not seem to be quite as reliable as the natural white of egg.

Superior to the above Egg Glaire is one recommended by Mr. W. H. Langwell, F.R.I.C., author of *The Conservation of Books and Documents*. It gives a very bright finish in gold tooling and does not require as much heat in the tools as in the case of Egg Glaire. The formula is:

Blood albumen, 10 per cent

Phenol B.P., 0·5 per cent w/v

Purified water B.P. to 100 per cent

Messrs. Boots Chemists make up the above under recipe No. CP12903 and half a pint will go a very long way. For general work in tooling, it should be diluted, as required, with equal quantities of water. For B. S. Glaire, see appendix.

Gold leaf and tooling leaf

The best gold leaf for bookbinding is that known as 'double gold', i.e. it is double the usual thickness. It is, of course, more expensive, but is much more satisfactory in every way. The introduction of gold and coloured tooling leaf has extended the scope of tooling, especially on cloth. Whereas in the past the hand tool could not be used with the ordinary metal foils, the floating of metallic compositions and glaire upon very thin cellophane has opened out a new field in the use of handle tools. It should not be regarded as a substitute for gold leaf in the best work, but it does offer opportunities to young students who would find much difficulty in handling gold leaf under conditions which may be far from ideal. It is useful also to have a roll or two of ribbon gold in stock; this proves convenient at times for long lines tooled in gold.

Whiley's of Ruislip have brought out a very useful series of tooling foils under the name 'Coloured pigment foils'. The medium is actual pigment, not metal, deposited on cellophane and is available in a very large range of colours. Quite unusual and striking effects can be produced on leather. Their 'gold film' is very good too.

Gold rubber

This is a form of virgin rubber treated with paraffin, and it is used to pick up the surplus gold from the book on the completion of the tooling. When such a rubber becomes loaded with gold it can be recovered by the refiners.

Vinegar

A bottle of white vinegar should be kept in stock. This is a 5-per-cent solution of pure acetic acid in water.

Benzine

This is used for cleaning the grease from the leather after tooling.

Testing pot

If a pottery is accessible a very useful and simple pot can be made to hold the tool testing pad. The pad is kept constantly wet by this device and it is further improved by the addition of a lid, when not in use.

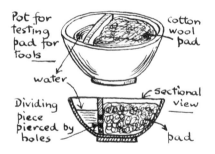

CHAPTER 19

Decoration

Lettering and Tooling on Cloth

It has already been noted that since the introduction of cellophane tooling leaf, the problem of decoration on cloth bindings has been greatly simplified, bringing such work within the scope of the modern school.

The first example to be considered is one where lettering is placed on the spine. According to the sizes of the tools available, a decision has to be made whether the lettering shall go across the back or down its length. A piece of thin guarding paper should be cut about the same size as the spine.

If the tooling is to be placed along the length of the back, rule a pencil line down the length, approximately in the centre of the width. Having selected the tools required, place a piece of strawboard under the pattern paper, and mark out the title with the tools. The strawboard protects the soft brass of the tools from damage. Several methods of making visible impressions with the tools are used. An ordinary endorsing pad such as is used in connection with rubber stamps; a piece of soft paper over which an inked roller has been passed; a piece of strawboard which has been held over a candle flame until sooty; a printing roller itself having on it a thin film of ink; these are among a number of suggestions for this work. If the beginner is not satisfied with his

239

first attempt, another line should be ruled and a fresh title marked out. It should be noted that the letters 'hang' on the line, and that the space A at the tail is a little larger than B at the head.

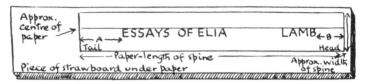

Two ways now present themselves of carrying out the tooling on the book, viz.,

(a) blinding an impression first; or

(b) using tooling leaf.

For 'blinding in' take the pattern, position the lettering on the back and fasten it to the book with small pieces of self-adhesive tape. The invention of these pressure sensitive tapes has revolutionized the fixing of patterns for tooling. Place the book in a finishing press, and arrange the tools in the proper order upon the stove. When only a few tools are required, follow the order of the letters in the words of the title. In the case under con-

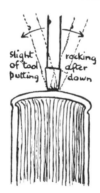

sideration they would be in this order: E, S, A, Y, O, F, L, I, M, B. When they are warm, but not yet hot, proceed with the tooling in the following way: All lettering tools are provided with a small nick across the shaft to indicate the head of the letter. Take the first tool, checking off the nick, and lower it over the letter on the paper pattern. Do not actually touch the paper until the correct position is attained, and then put it down smartly, rocking it slightly backward and forward to obtain an even impression on the curved spine. On no account linger on the work once the tool has touched the paper. When all the letters have been impressed, take away the pattern, and a 'blind' impression of the tools will be seen. A quick method of finishing this work on cloth is found in the use of a candle. Allow the tools to become hot enough to hiss a little when tested on a pad of wet cotton wool. When testing, do not, as many beginners do, put the 'face' of the letter on the pad. The 'shaft' is laid flat on the pad for a second. Hold the letter in the end of a candle flame until it is evenly blacked, and tool it straight down into the blind impression on the book. The heat of the tool will fasten the lampblack to the cloth. It is essential that tools used in this way are cleaned after the work is done.

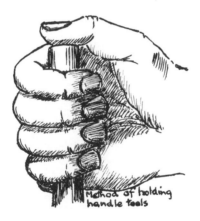

Method of holding handle tools

A much cleaner method is found in the use of typing carbons. They can be had in a variety of colours and the piece selected should be fastened down on a piece of strawboard. Press the hot tool upon it, when sufficient colour will be picked up to give a clear print in the blind impression. The tool must be hot enough to 'fasten' the colour.

A golden rule for all tooling is to hold the tool perpendicularly when put down and held in the manner shown in the diagram.

The thumbnail of the left hand is used to guide and steady the tool as it descends into position. The line of sight is down the head of the tool past the nick.

The second method involves the use of tooling leaf. Cut enough leaf to cover the lettering. Turn the pattern over, and fix the strips with tiny spots of paste or tiny pieces of sellotape. Make quite sure (*a*) that it covers all the lettering, and (*b*) that the leaf is the correct side out. The cellophane side goes next to the paper, leaving the dull, glaired side face up. Fasten down the pattern on the book in the manner already described for blind tooling, and tool the letters. For this kind of work the tools should be a little hotter, i.e. when tested they should hiss a little more. The heat of the tools is a vital factor, and its correct assessment is only gained through practical experience.

Detach the pattern, and it will be seen that small portions of the foil may have adhered round the letters. If the whole of the tooling is rubbed over with a piece of worsted cloth, most of this superfluous metal will be removed. If some still remains it is an indication that the tool has been too hot, or that the student has lingered too long on the impression. If, after rubbing, portions of the lettering have been removed, it is a sign that the tools have not been hot enough. It is rather difficult to patch places which have been missed in the tooling. Suppose, for example, the left side of an A is missing; place a little of the foil over the defect, and bring down the tool upon the letter, using the uncovered portion as a guide for correct placing.

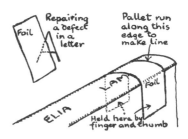

If tooled lines across the back are desired it is a simple matter to hold a piece of the leaf across the spine, and bring a pallet down along its edge. After each line is tooled, cut off the used piece, thus leaving a straight edge ready for the next line.

When the title is to be placed across the spine a similar procedure to that already outlined is followed, with a slight difference in the paper pattern. This paper need only be of sufficient size to accommodate the number of lines required plus a small overlap, about ¼″, on each side of the book.

Place the middle of the strip over the back of the book and mark it with a pencil down each side to mark the exact width of the spine, as at X, X. Within this space the lettering must be planned. If the space between X, X be folded so that X is over X the resulting crease will be in the centre of the space and is used as a guide to centre the words. The words are mapped out roughly in pencil on a piece of spare paper to obtain some idea of arrangement together with a rough approximation of the middle letter in each line. A knowledge of the relative widths of the letters of the alphabet is invaluable at this stage. Where two or more words occur in one line the space between them should be equal to an 'O'.

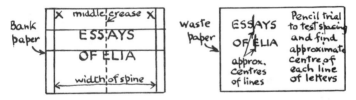

Begin marking out the letters with the tools from the centre crease, e.g. ESSAYS should begin with S on the left of the centre crease, followed by S again and then E. A, Y, and S follow in their proper order. If the word does not appear to be quite central adjustments should be made, working over the first impressions. Slight discrepancies such as letters not being quite upright should not be altered on the pattern, but adjusted as the actual tooling is done. The presence of such a slight error is often helpful in getting that particular fault corrected.

The tooling is then done in the manner already outlined. If a binding be done in full cloth, some decoration may be required on the sides. The procedure is the same, save that the book is laid flat on the bench while the work is carried out.

Tooling on Quarter- and Half-leather Bindings

On cheap leathers such as sheep skivers it is wiser to carry out the decoration with tooling leaf attached under the pattern, finishing in one operation, in exactly the same way as that used for cloth. Where the better leathers are concerned, a pattern of the lettering and design is carried out, and then tooled in blind.

The pattern is taken off and, if gold tooling is intended, the leather is washed over with a little white vinegar or paste-water on a sponge in the case of Morocco, and with paste-water if calf is used. Paste-water is made by adding a little paste to water until it has the appearance of thin milk. The purpose of this washing is two-fold; it cleans the leather and seals up the grain so that the glaire will not be absorbed. Indeed, any leather of a porous nature should be paste-washed.

Finishing in 'Blind'

If part of the work is to be finished in blind tooling, i.e. without gold, this must now be done whilst the leather is damp, after sponging. The whole idea behind such work is to go over the impressions with warm tools until they assume an even depth of dark brown colour and become polished. If the leather is of a dark colour little difference will be made by such tooling as far

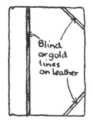

as colour is concerned, but in the lighter leathers much skill is needed to retain the same tone throughout the work. Two very important factors govern the process, namely, the heat of the tool and the dampness of the leather. A very good maxim to bear in mind all the time is 'the wetter the leather, the cooler the tool'. The tools used must not by any means hiss when tested, and the beginner would be well advised to damp any odd scrap of waste leather and experiment on this first. As the leather dries so can the heat of the tools increase a little, and after an initial quick application to 'set' the leather in the impression, the tool can be put down again and rocked slightly. This gives a polished surface as well as a darkened one, and is known as 'jiggering'. Where blind lines run across the spine the polishing is done by sliding a pallet along the lines, and where a fillet is used for long lines on the sides, a small wooden wedge is fixed between the fillet and its fork, so that instead of rolling along the line it slides along it in a fixed position. Blind tooling, properly done, can be very beautiful indeed. A cleaner finish is given to the sides of a quarter- or half-binding by running lines down the edge of the leather as shown in the diagram. These may be either blind or gold. Where a spine has raised bands a pleasing finish is obtained by continuing the tooled lines at the sides of the bands on to the sides and bringing them to a point. A sample or two of added decoration is shown here.

Finishing in Gold

The portions to be gilded are now painted in with glaire, using a fine sable brush. Unless the letters or other motifs are very small and close together, avoid going outside the impressions too much. The glaire would be apt to show on the leather after the book is finished. When this coat of size is dry apply a second one and allow that to dry also. Take up a little Vaseline, sweet oil of almonds, or coconut oil on a wad of cotton wool, and rub it over the back of the left hand. This action distributes the grease evenly, and ensures that only the minimum shall be applied to the book. Too much grease is fatal to good tooling and also detrimental to gold rubbers. Rub over the glaired impressions; the purpose of applying this thin film of grease is to retain the gold leaf on the leather while the tooling is done.

Have the gold cushion and knife to hand, and take the book of gold in the left hand. Hold the knife blade outside the under page to support it, and let the pages go under the thumb one at a time until it is possible to see the coming of a gold leaf. This will occur two or three pages before the actual leaf comes to light.

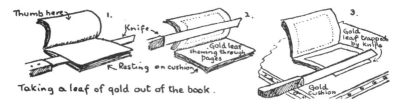

Taking a leaf of gold out of the book.

Transfer the knife to position 2 until it rests below the page next to the gold. Lower the book to the cushion; take out the knife and with it tap very gently under the book. If the gold is loose it will slide down a little on to the cushion. Trap this portion of the leaf very gently with the knife blade, and withdraw the book. Breathe very lightly indeed directly over the middle of the leaf, when it should flatten out evenly on the cushion. When the beginner acquires more skill, he will, no doubt, learn to lift out the gold on the knife, and turn it over on the cushion, but great care must be exercised until such experience is gained.

The gold is cut into pieces by keeping the knife blade in a perpendicular position, and cutting forwards and backwards with a steady pressure. This cutting should be done according to the requirements of the tooling, avoiding undue waste. For lettering it could be cut into strips $\frac{1}{4}''$ wide, and then across in the other direction four times, thus giving pieces about $\frac{3}{4}''$ by $\frac{1}{4}''$. Ribbon gold in transfer form may be applied direct to the leather where long lines occur. A piece of clean cotton wool is used to pick up the gold from the cushion; it should be formed into a fairly hard pad, especially under the first finger. A wipe over the grease on the back of the left hand will be sufficient to ensure that it will pick up the leaf. If brought over the first piece and pressed gently it will pick up the gold. The writer prefers to wipe this pad down the hair behind the right ear as an alternative means of giving it picking-up power.

The pieces of gold are put down on the impressions, and

pressed in until the tooling shows clearly under the leaf. No side or rubbing movement must occur, but only a straight up and down pressure. If any breaks in the gold are visible, pick up a piece, breathe on the gold already on the book, and put down the new piece very quickly. Each fresh piece put down should over-lap the previous one a little.

Meanwhile the tools should have been heating on the stove, and now require to be tested for heat on the wet pad. No hard and fast rule can be laid down on this matter. If the tool is too hot the gold looks 'frosted', and if the heat is not sufficient the gold will not adhere in the impressions. Damp leather will require less heat than leather which has become dry. The best method is to have a scrap of waste leather on which tests can be made. In practice, good tooling can be done if the heat is just sufficient to make them hiss slightly on the pad. When properly tooled the impressions should be clear and bright. Blood albumen glaire needs less heat.

Each tool must be brought over the impression in a perfectly upright position and guided by the left thumb. It is put down smartly and taken off again without hesitation. Where pallets and gouges are being used the flat side of the tool should be 'sighted', and these tools must always be used at right angles to the body. This will necessitate rotating the book to the correct position for each tool. Above all things, every tool used must be rubbed on the flesh side of a piece of spare leather to clean it before putting it down. Dirty tools will never give beautiful tooling.

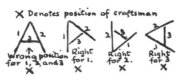

When the tooling has been done clean off the surplus gold with the gold rubber, and closely inspect the work. If one or two small places are defective, re-glaire once, allow it to dry, grease it, and lay on the gold; then re-tool it. If there are many defects it is easier to glaire all again and give a second coat of gold throughout. Double gold always looks richer and brighter, but of course entails more time and cost. A rub over with a little benzine on cotton wool will remove grease and the small bits of gold still adhering. If a piece of clean flannel is damped slightly and rubbed over the work it will clean off any surplus glaire lying outside the impressions, and the whole can then be polished with a clean soft duster.

Finishing Full Leather Bindings

The usual order for the finishing of such books is the completion of any tooling inside the boards first; then the outside of the covers and the spine, and finally the edges of the boards. If any tooling is done inside the boards it will now be seen how advantageous it is to defer pasting down the board papers until all the finishing is done. A simple line or lines round the board paper is a clean and effective finish. No paper pattern is needed, for if the corners are lightly marked and a straight-edge used to join them, a fillet can be run along; but it must stop within $\frac{1}{8}''$ of the further corner. When all four have been run in blind, the fillet must be used in the opposite direction, the mitre being used to complete each corner.

The back and sides will need patterns. The design should be worked out roughly at first on a separate piece of paper, and when a satisfactory one has been drafted it should be carefully drawn on a piece of thin bank paper which has been creased round the cover to obtain the exact size of the book side. When drawn, the tools must be tried out on the pattern, and the necessary adjustments made. If a system of numbering all pallets and gouges is used, a note of the tool number must be made on

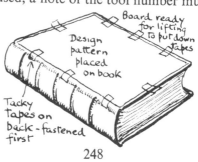

248

the pattern in its appropriate place. Only the position of the ends of long straight lines need be marked at this stage.

For blinding in the design, the pattern is cut down to the size of the cover, and provided at intervals down the spine side with pieces of tacky tape. Place in position on the book and fasten it down the back edge. Place similar pieces of tacky tape down the fore-edge and, lifting the board, turn them in. If necessary add pieces at the head and tail. Closing the board will tighten the pattern over the book.

Go over the whole design with warm tools and, if it is a complicated one, very light pencil ticks can be used to indicate the completed lines as the tooling proceeds. When the pattern is taken off, look over the design very carefully for any parts that may have been missed, and complete any long lines whose ends only have been marked through the pattern. When the student becomes more adept in the use of the tools it is possible to complete portions of the design after the pattern has been removed, provided the main guiding points have been marked through the pattern. If the same pattern is to be used on the reverse cover, its removal from the front should be carefully carried out. New pieces of tacky tape may be required.

Patterns and toolings on the spine are carried out in the manner employed for half-binding.

Lettering and Design

The earnest student would do well to take a course in lettering and design as a completion to the craft, and the writer has, of set purpose, avoided any suggestions for design in these pages. A study of historical examples is necessary as a background, and in order to be able to trace the way in which tooling has developed up to the present day. The methods of building up pattern, design, and arrangements of lettering are more than adequately dealt with by craftsmen like Douglas Cockerell in his *Bookbinding and the Care of Books*, and Alex. J. Vaughan in his *Modern Bookbinding*. In such cases there is adherence to the English tradition revived under William Morris and carried forward by Cobden Sanderson. But there is a large

249

field of study available now in the styles evolved in France and Germany. These are freer and more daring in conception, and have, under craftsmen like Le Grain and Bonet, exploited the large possibilities for design to be found in gouges and pallets, in beautiful inlays and built-up lettering.

With such a study as a background the student should endeavour to create an individual feeling in his designs, with a freedom circumscribed only by the nature of his tools and materials, and the fact that he is working upon a book which limits him by its shape and purpose. As far as he is able to overcome these limitations without violating the essential nature of the book, so far will he become a designer-craftsman.

Inlays

No description of book decoration would be complete without some mention of the fascinating subject of inlays on Morocco bindings. The work falls into two main divisions:

(a) thin inlays which are really 'onlays', and

(b) inlays proper.

(a) In the first case thin leather is placed over the existing leather, and a more correct term for it would be 'onlay'. This adding of different coloured leathers to a book gives it a richness and interest unattainable by tooling alone. When small onlays are used it is best to have hollow steel punches made exactly to the size of the brass tools. Small flowers and leaves are common forms used in this work. The leather chosen for the onlays must

be pared very thin indeed, and this can be achieved more easily if the leather is damped slightly. The shapes are then punched out of the pared skin with the steel punch, and placed upon a pasted sheet of paper. Very tiny motifs will have to be lifted off this sheet, when required, by means of a needle. Meanwhile the design has been blinded in with the brass tools and the onlays put into position and gently pressed down with a fine folder.

The board of the book is then placed between heavy chromium or aluminium pressing plates, and put under pressure until the onlays have set. The whole book must not be pressed or the spine may be crushed. When the onlays are dry the impressions must be tooled again, and if gold is to be added it will cover the edges of the onlays which have been put down into the tooled lines.

If steel punches are not available such a lack need not deter the student. The brass tool can be used to make an impression on the pared leather and the pieces cut out with a fine stencil knife or a pair of small scissors.

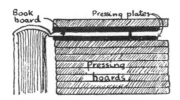

When larger shapes are to be inlaid the leather must be pared very thin, as in the case of the small ones, but when the leather comes to be pasted it is essential that it shall retain its shape in order to fit the portion of the design for which it is intended. To prevent expansion when wet, it should be placed upon a piece of thin pasted tissue or sulphite paper, the face side of the leather to the paste. Allow this to dry under a light weight and then mark and cut out the desired shapes. Go round the edges with an ordinary paring knife until no thickness of leather is to be seen; then paste them and lay down in position on the book. Place it between plates, as described above, and allow to dry in the press. A careful damping of the tissue paper will effect its removal, and a gentle sponging will take away any paste remaining on the inlays. Tooling is then carried forward in the usual way.

(*b*) Inlays may be put on books by actually cutting out the leather already on the book and inserting another colour, in a fashion similar to that used in woodwork. Some such inlays may form an integral part of the book cover in the sense that they are

251

part of the actual covering process, and the whole design for such a cover must be worked out carefully before any covering is done. The simple example shown is really a development of half-binding, but the material is all leather. It will be necessary to pare the turning-in at each end in the usual way, but not along the lines A and B in either colour unless the Morocco is very thick; in such a case a little may be taken off along the edges. The cover pieces of colour (1) are put on first and allowed to dry. The piece of colour (2) is cut out large enough to overlap the first colours about $\frac{1}{4}''$, and is pasted on and allowed to dry. Using a very sharp knife and a straight-edge, cuts are made through both pieces of leather in the centre of the overlaps along A and B. These cuts are continued round the edges of the boards and on the insides too. It is very important that this cutting should be done at an angle, as shown in the diagrams.

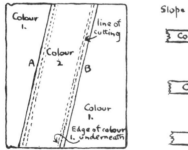
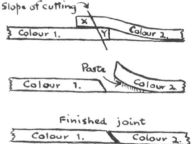

Damp along the cuts with a sponge until the spare piece (X) can be removed; carefully raise the edge of colour (2); damp and remove the waste piece (Y), and paste under colour (2) with the finger. Put the leather down again with a folder, removing the paste which squeezes out by sponging. While drying, it must be attended to at intervals to prevent any opening of the joint due to contraction. It is not possible to tool along such joints with safety, nor are they intended to be so tooled; but lines of design can, of course, cross them.

Where such inlays do not form part of the covering process, but consist of patches of colour in the design, they should be cut out a little larger than the intended finished shape; then they are pasted and laid down in position upon the existing cover, pressed lightly, and dried. The exact shape is marked out and a sloping cut made through both leathers along the marked lines. Damp the whole inlay and remove the waste around it; then lift the inlay itself very carefully to avoid stretching it, and damp and remove the piece underneath. It remains now to repaste the inlay, place it in position, and go over it with a folder. Press it, and attend to it round the joints, at intervals, until dry. The underpieces need not be wasted as the paste can be sponged off and the pieces used for other inlays. Onlays may be used in conjunction with this method where several colours may be involved, as a study of modern French bindings will reveal.

Still another method consists in making a stiff card template of the piece to be inlaid. The template is tipped on the book, with small spots of paste, in the desired position and a cut made at an angle, as before, round the edges of this pattern. Template and the leather underneath are then removed and the former placed on the leather to be inlaid. Cut around this in the same manner; paste the pieces thus cut out; place it in position on the book and press under chromium plates. This method does away with any risk of the leather being stained by paste present at X in the diagram.

Opening up and Pressing

After all the finishing operations have been completed the book should be opened up. This process is described at the close of Chapter 17. Finally the book should be placed between clean pressing boards and left under moderate pressure in a press for as long a period as possible.

CHAPTER 20

Case-binding

Practically all modern editions are case-bound, i.e. the book is sewn, cut, and generally forwarded by machinery, and fixed in a case already made to receive it. Without such rapid methods of production we could not hope to have the cheap and varied reading available today, but the hand-binder must of necessity always regard such case-binding as a temporary measure in the case of valuable books, keeping them clean until they can be bound in a permanent fashion by hand.

Nevertheless there are many books which do not warrant fine bindings, but could be recased with advantage, and books with paper covers which need a stiffer binding to lengthen their lives. But it cannot be emphasized too strongly that such work should not form part of the regular scheme for schools; it should be viewed as an occasional method to be used only when necessary. It is better to concentrate on the hand-craft itself, and case-binding will then fall into its proper place and perspective.

It is not easy to carry out case-binding properly without a guillotine, and this is far too dangerous an instrument to have around with young pupils present. It would mean that, for safety's sake, all the cutting would have to be done by the teacher, and with it there creeps in the evil of becoming a slave to it and employing it in the better forms of binding. This machine, or rather its misuse, has done more during the past century to wreck the very large numbers of fine books which came to be re-bound than any other single agent. Many an ample margin has disappeared at the hands of the guillotine operator without thought of the irreparable damage done. A very excellent thing to remember is that this machine may on occasion be a good servant, but is always a bad master.

Consider now two types of book which may have to be case-bound, viz.,

(*a*) Books which are pulled and resewn.

(*b*) Books which are cased without pulling.

The first type should be pulled, guarded, pressed, and sewn on tapes in the usual way. A decision must be made whether to use sewn endpapers or stationery ends, i.e. those tipped on with paste. If sewn-on ones are needed to give a somewhat stronger binding, use the 'W' type. If stationery types are used they should be made as in the diagram, and run down with $\frac{1}{8}''$ of paste, placed on the book, and allowed to dry under a weight.

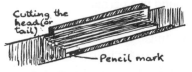

The book is glued up and all three edges cut while the back is still flat. If no guillotine is available mark out the fore-edge in the usual way, and cut it in the plough. Square the head and tail with a try-square and, keeping the back square, place in the plough. The book should have a piece of waste board at the front and a similar piece to act as cut-against at the back. In order to keep the book perfectly square it is advisable to leave these boards $\frac{1}{8}''$ short of the spine on both sides. If this is not done, the swell due to the sewing in the backs of the sections will cause the book to slip sideways when the press is tightened, and so throw it out of 'square'. The cutting completed, rounding and backing will follow, and then the cutting and squaring of the boards, leaving enough on them to allow for the 'squares' at the head, tail, and fore-edge. The back is glued, the muslin attached and glued down to the waste sheet; a hollow back may be fixed, but this is not essential; if a hollow is used its ends should be trimmed off level with the head and tail of the book. The boards are tipped with two small spots of glue near the back edges, and placed in position on the book. It is sufficient to leave the whole under a moderate weight until the boards are temporarily attached.

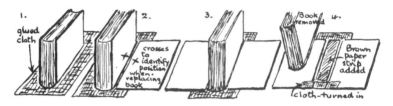

Cut out a piece of cloth, as for quarter-binding; glue it and lay it down on the bench. Place the book in the middle (Fig. 1) and lower the right-hand board (Fig. 2). Still keeping the book upright, lower the left-hand board (Fig. 3); mark the waste and board with a pencilled cross, and detach the book carefully (Fig. 4). If no hollow back has been fixed, take a strip of brown paper which has been previously measured to fit the book back in width, but as long as the boards, and place it on the glued cloth between the boards. There should be a small gap of cloth showing on either side of this strip to form 'joints'. Turn in the cloth at the head and tail, and generally neaten with a folder. Trim the cloth equally on each side and cover with paper, as is done in quarter-binding. If half-binding is desired, the corners must be fixed before putting on the paper sides. The 'case' has now been made, and when it is dry it is ready for fixing on the book.

Lay the case down open on the bench, and place the book in position on one side, being careful to have the side with the cross matching the cross on the board. If a hollow back is present, glue an inch of the waste sheet and about half-way across the hollow back, as indicated in the diagrams. For books which have no hollow back, the side only is glued an inch down the waste sheet.

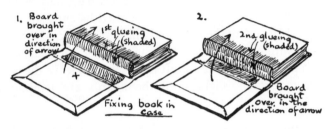

Make sure that the book is exactly in position on the underside by checking the 'squares' at the head, tail, and fore-edge; then bring over the other side of the case. Rub it down over the joint and turn the book over, opening the second board out flat. Glue again as for the first board, bring over, and run down and neaten the cloth at the head and tail. Place in a press, pressing boards up to the groove only, and leave all until dry. It only remains to tear off the wastes, paste down the endpapers 'shut', and press.

The second type concerns books which are fairly new and are not to be pulled. Take off the cover and remove the endpapers, replacing them by new ones of the stationery type. These endpapers should be a little larger than the book, and when attached they must be trimmed down to the size of the book. This is done by placing a thin straight-edge between the last page and the endpaper, having all placed upon a cutting card. If such a book has not been rounded and backed it is better to do so at this point. Damp the back a little with paste. When it is sufficiently moistened, clean off the paste and round it gently. If backing is also to be added it should be done immediately after the rounding.

The boards are cut out, and where only rounding has been given, they should be made to come within $\frac{1}{8}''$ of the back. The procedure then follows the same order as is outlined above for the first type of case-binding.

The Binding of Single Sheets without Guards

Occasions arise when it is necessary to bind a number of single sheets into book form in order to keep them neatly for reference. Such examples as theses come under this category; another is found in a book of very poor quality paper where the backs of the sections are in a very bad state; yet another occurs when a book has to be re-bound in the original cover. In the first two cases, guarding the leaves together would give far too much swelling in the back, and make binding operations extremely difficult, if not wellnigh impossible. In the third case a considerable amount of discretion must be used. If it be thought at all possible to guard the leaves together without causing too much swell, this must be done; especially is this the case when dealing with a book of value.

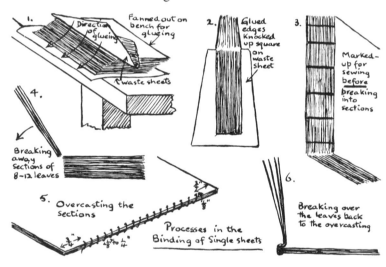

Processes in the Binding of Single sheets

Wherever possible, the back edges of the sections, or single sheets, must be trimmed off slightly in the guillotine or plough, in order to have a perfectly smooth block-like edge. If typewritten sheets are being dealt with, it will often be found that it is only necessary to knock them up square at the back edges. Two sheets of clean paper, similar to that which will be used for the endpapers, must be taken and placed one at each end of the book. The whole is now knocked up square at the head and back, and then fanned out slightly. Place the back along the edge of the bench, and glue the fanning out with thin hot glue. Immediately this has been done the whole of the book must be picked up carefully and knocked square again at the back on a clean sheet of waste paper. Place the sheets between boards in a press, putting only a light pressure on them. They are left thus until the glue is dry.

It is obvious that at this point the book must be marked up for sewing, as this cannot be done after the sections have been overcast. This marking-up should be done for sewing on 'sawn-in bands', and then the book is broken into suitable sections. The number of leaves allowed for one such section varies according to the thickness of the paper. Eight to twelve leaves may be taken as a suitable number. As each group of leaves is broken away from the body of the book it must be numbered with a pencil in the top right-hand corner to facilitate collation, and gently hammered down the glued edge to make it thinner. This is done on a knocking-down iron covered with clean paper.

Take a piece of waste strawboard and lay on it the first section. Using a fine awl, make a series of holes along the back edge of the section. These holes must commence about $\frac{3}{4}''$ from the head and finish the same distance from the tail, and should be $\frac{1}{8}''$ to $\frac{1}{4}''$ apart in a line $\frac{1}{8}''$ away from the back. Fine thread is used to overcast each section; ordinary white sewing cotton about number 36 is suitable. The diagram indicates the manner in which the sewing is done. A very gentle tapping of the stitching upon the knocking-down iron will flatten the stitches and close up the holes made by the awl, but it *must* be gentle, otherwise the hammer will cut the threads. In all books bound in this manner stiffness in the opening is always a difficulty, and in order to lessen this trouble each section must be treated in the following way. Commencing at the front, and taking one or two leaves at a time, bend them over up to the sewing until the centre of the section is reached. Turn it over and commence the same process again from the other end until the middle is reached again.

CASE-BINDING

These overcast sections are now sewn 'all-along' in the usual
way, and it is best to do this on sawn-in bands; this allows a
much better gluing up of the sections when bound. Very special
care must be taken in gluing up the back after the sewing has
been done. It may even be necessary to give a second gluing
after the first has set, for if this work is badly done the sections
tend to break away.

The fore-edge is cut before the glue hardens. Rounding and
backing is difficult, but can be done if great care is exercised.
The book can be left, however, with a square back, and in such a
case the boards will be set in $\frac{1}{8}''$ from the back and given a small
bevel. Stationery endpapers are used as a rule and these are
added before the fore-edge is cut.

The forwarding from this point follows that used for case-
binding, or, alternatively, that employed for hollow binding in
cloth.

CHAPTER 21

A Selection of Simple Exercises Leading up to Bookbinding

The principle underlying the following exercises lies in the fact that in each piece of work some definite process is present which will be used later in the craft of bookbinding; to this is added practice in the use of the tools and materials which the student will meet as a binder. In some cases this is the sole reason for the presence of such an exercise, whereas in others there is also a definite utility value for the object made. There is a slight increase in difficulty as the exercises proceed, and it should be clearly understood that they are by no means exhaustive. Rather should they be accepted as typical samples and suggestions of the lines which should be followed in this type of work; the teacher should endeavour to formulate similar exercises himself, keeping ever in view the ultimate goal, which is bookbinding proper.

Neither do I think that a great length of time should be expended on this type of work. Much of it could be done in the top class of a junior school, and it need not occupy a whole year's work in the first form of a secondary modern school. In the latter case, it can be completed in two terms where classes have three or four periods per week for craft. Good material is often wasted and time spent unprofitably on numerous exercises called 'Bookcrafts', which appear to have no end in view beyond a certain amount of activity on the part of the class. The pupils tend to become bored; the teacher becomes weary of the constant stream of useless 'models', and the whole exciting craft of real bookbinding has been entirely missed. For these reasons I outline these exercises with very great reserve, and trust they will serve as a beginning, and not as an end in themselves.

Care and Cleanliness in General

Whatever the age of the student, teaching must be given upon the subject of cleanliness in working; indeed, in bookbinding it really is next to Godliness, and needs constant watchfulness on the part of the teacher. A certain number of students have to be constantly reminded of the importance of tidiness in the make-up of any would-be craftsman.

First comes the care of the paste-pot. It is astonishing how many students there are who do not seem to be able to cultivate a habit of keeping the paste pot clean and tidy; students who will persist in wiping the paste-brush on the side or edge of the pot when lifting it out. Not only does this habit make a mess of the brush handles, but the paste dries on the side of the pot. This dried accumulation is difficult to remove without pieces dropping into the paste, and no clean pasting can be done with bits present in this way. If it can be demonstrated to students that surplus paste on a brush should be brushed out on the piece of material about to be used, and not on the pot itself, this trouble will be greatly lessened. A piece of string or some form of bar across the top may be used as a brush wiper, but this is a nuisance when making fresh paste, unless it be made removable. At the end of each day's work brushes should be washed clean and put aside to dry.

The glue pot also claims attention. It would be very unwise to use a fully loaded glue brush, as it is when lifted from the pot, and a wiper is therefore essential. If a piece of copper wire is stretched tightly across from side to side, using the lugs to which the handle is attached, a very good wiper is provided; its great advantage lies in the fact that surplus glue falls straight back into the pot and so does not 'gather' on the sides. A frequent fault to be found among beginners is a habit of allowing the water in the outer pot to boil too fast. The water either boils over or is left to boil dry; both faults are bad for the glue. The water should only just simmer gently, and the consistency of the glue itself should be checked at least once a day, as it tends to become too thick owing to evaporation. A very good electric glue pot is on the market; it is 'waterless' and, although expensive, is worth the outlay.

A good supply of newspapers should be kept in stock. Even these should be treated in a craftsmanlike manner, and before work is begun one or two should be prepared for use. They should be opened out and torn down twice, and placed in a pile ready to hand. Some periodicals only need opening and the staples removing. It is a common habit amongst beginners to waste a whole newspaper by failing to open it out properly. The habit of getting rid of a pasted piece of waste paper by folding it should be cultivated at all costs if clean work is to be produced at all. If space permits in school, it is advisable to provide a special table for pasting and gluing; this should be furnished with paste pots and brushes, and a neat pile of prepared newspapers. If it can be placed within reach of the glue kettle so much the better.

Exercise 1

A small square (or rectangular) mat

Bookbinding points: Squaring, cutting, and covering.

A piece of thin strawboard (1 lb. thickness) is roughly cut out $5\frac{1}{2}''$ square. A line is drawn about $\frac{1}{8}''$ inside one of the sides and a cross marked as shown. With a knife and straight-edge cut off this small strip, and so provide a straight base line from which all measurements are now made. Along this line mark off 5", roughly centred on the card, and from these points erect perpendiculars, using a try-square. Along these lines mark off 5" from the base; join the points thus made, and proceed to cut out the whole square. When cut, it should be checked with the try-square for accuracy, and inspected for clean cutting. This cutting is done on a piece of waste strawboard and NOT ON TINS. Select a piece of cover paper, placing it face side down on the bench; place the squared board upon it so that at least 1" of paper is protruding all round. Run a pencil round the board, and then measure and draw lines parallel to the pencilled square at a distance of $\frac{3}{4}"$ all round. Cut out the square of paper thus made, place it in the middle of a piece of newspaper, and paste it all over; the pasting should be done by working outwards with the brush for every stroke, never allowing the paste-brush to stop moving during any one stroke until it has reached the newspaper and is clear of the cover paper. The paper must be held firmly by the finger and thumb of the left hand during the process. Pick up the pasted paper, and fold over the soiled newspaper so that the surplus paste is covered. Place the piece of strawboard in position on the cover paper and turn in all four sides in the middle of each side. Nip up the corners neatly to approximately 45° and cut them off smartly with the scissors.

For each cut the scissors should *rest on the board* at the corner, and the handles be raised just enough to allow the thumb and fingers to grip. The expert may have other methods of cutting such a corner, but the method outlined here is easy and safe for the beginner. It is a waste of time to try cutting off the corners before pasting is done, as there are factors such as the expansion of paper which call for skill and experience beyond the capacity of pupils at this stage.

When the corners have been cut off, lift up the paper on one side, and tuck in the small portion at the corners round the edge of the board; do this with the thumb- or fingernail, and bring down the lifted side again. Repeat in the same way for the opposite side and go over all the work with a folder, squaring the paper over the edges of the board. The process just described is known as 'covering'. The board should be allowed to dry for a little while, and should then be placed under a light weight.

After drying is complete take a suitable piece of paper and place the covered board on its wrong side. The wrong side of a piece of paper is usually identifiable by the appearance upon it of a very fine 'netting' caused by the mesh of the paper-making machine. Draw a pencil line round the edges of the board, and *inside* this square draw another square $\frac{1}{4}''$ away from the first one. Cut out the inner square with a knife and straight-edge. This is the 'liner'; later on its counterpart in a book is known as the 'board endpaper'. This liner is pasted and laid down on the uncovered side of the board so that an equal margin of the cover is seen all round it. After it has dried for a little while it should be placed between boards and left under a light weight.

This is one of those occasions when the possession of a number of old flat irons is a great asset. Even in this first exercise the pupil begins to appreciate what pasted paper can do in the way of 'pulling' a board, and he begins to learn how foolish it would be to put down the 'liner' whilst the 'cover' is still wet, for all control of the board would be lost. If the cover be left to dry, it will curve the board and the addition of the liner should pull it back again. It is in such matters that experience must be gained in the ways which differing papers react to pasting. If a board is left out on the bench to dry out, it will curve so much that no liner will be able to straighten it again; it is for this reason that it should be placed under a weight before drying is complete.

Interest would be added to this exercise for younger pupils if a rectangular board were cut instead of a square one. It could be finished off by adding a picture and a small calendar; two holes punched at the head would provide for hanging it.

Exercise 2

A miniature chess or draughts board

Bookbinding points: As for Exercise 1, with the addition of accuracy and practice in cutting guards.

Rough cut a piece of 1 lb. strawboard approximately 6″ square, and square and cut it to $5\frac{1}{2}''$ square. Cover it and leave it to dry under a weight. This merely repeats Exercise 1, but the liner is not added.

Cut out and square accurately a piece of coloured paper 5″ by 5″. Mark two lines at the top and bottom parallel to the sides and ½″ inside them. Set a pair of dividers exactly to ½″ and mark out points along the two lines just drawn. These points should not be joined by pencil lines as this is an exercise in cutting guards, and guards are never marked in such a way. Place a straight-edge along the respective points and carefully cut from A to B in each case. All this work should be done on the reverse side of the paper.

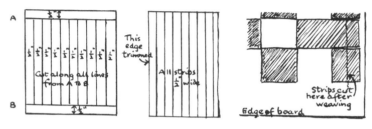

Take a piece of paper, contrasting in colour with the one already marked out. Cut out a piece about 5″ by 4½″, and trim off one long edge. With the dividers still set at ½″, mark off points along the top and bottom beginning at the trimmed edge. Cut through these points, thus giving eight strips ½″ wide. These are now woven into the first piece of paper to form a chess board. As the strips are threaded they must be carefully and persistently pushed up, with the back of a knife, until no space is left between them. When the sixth one has been inserted add the next one using the same weave, and push it to the bottom to make number 8 strip; then insert number 7 last. If number 8 is left until the last it will be exceedingly difficult to thread it in. All the work must be done on the reverse side. Bring all the ends of the strips to the reverse side and trim them off with scissors about ¼″ in from the edge of the woven board. The piece of work now completed constitutes the liner for the 5½″ board already made; it should be well pasted, laid in position and given a quick nip in the press to flatten it. Allow it to dry for a time on the bench and then place under a weight until the drying is complete.

Exercise 3

A blotter or writing-pad

Bookbinding points: As for previous exercises, with the addition of making corners involving the use of glue and cloth.

The dimensions of the blotter depend entirely upon the amount of stock available. If strawboard is in short supply it will be advisable to make a small 'sample', as it is not the blotter itself which is important so much as the processes involved in its construction.

Cut out and square a rectangular board to the size decided upon and line it on one side, leaving $\frac{1}{4}''$ border of strawboard all round the liner. Take a piece of bookbinder's cloth a little longer than the length of the board and about $4\frac{1}{2}''$ wide. Cut from it four long strips $1''$ wide, and fold them all down the middle, the face side of the cloth being outwards. Cut two of them exactly the same length as the board, and the other two the same as its width. The longer ones are glued on waste paper and laid on the bench. Bring the board, lined side downwards, over a glued strip so that its edge lies along the crease of the strip, and bring over the remaining half on to the board. Repeat on the opposite side. Fit the shorter pieces before they are glued, and mark the mitres. Remove the strips, cut the mitres and glue them into position. The board has now been provided with a border of passe-partout.

When corners are required in bookbinding a paper pattern must always be made first. Turn the board, unlined side upwards, and mark off with dividers, at one corner, the position for the cloth corner, as at A and B. The size of such a corner will be determined by the size of the blotter. Place a piece of paper under the corner, having a straight edge coinciding with the points A and B. Hold it down firmly and crease it with the finger from underneath, on both sides of the corner. Allow $\frac{3}{4}''$ outside these creases for turning in, and cut off the point to within $\frac{1}{4}''$ of the creased corner. This piece is cut off in the interests of economy when using the pattern to cut out the cloth. With the aid of this pattern, mark out and cut four cloth

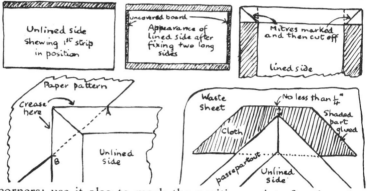

corners: use it also to mark the position points for the other three corners on the blotter. Place a cloth corner on a sheet of waste paper, and bring over one of the board corners into position. Holding the board down firmly, glue the exposed cloth and turn in both sides over the board. Cut off the surplus with scissors in the usual way, lifting up one side, tucking in and putting all down in a neat fashion. When all four corners have been completed, select a piece of lining paper, mark round the blotter upon it, and trim $\frac{1}{4}''$ inside these lines; paste the liner and lay it in position on the back of the blotter. When the paste has set sufficiently place the whole under a light weight to dry out.

Exercise 4

A folding note-case

Bookbinding points: Squaring and cutting boards in a cutting press.

For this exercise two thicknesses of boards are used, viz., 1 lb. and 8 oz. Roughly cut out two pieces of 1 lb. board, and two pieces of 8 oz. board, each piece being approximately $6\frac{1}{2}''$ by 4''. All four boards must now be temporarily fastened together for cutting purposes. Lay one board on the bench, and place very tiny smears of glue near the head and tail. Lay the next board upon it and repeat; lay the third board over the second and repeat with the glue, laying the fourth board finally down on this. Pick them up, knocking them square on one long edge and place them between boards in the press.

When the glue has set, place behind the knocked-up edge a piece of cutting board, and lower all into the cutting press until only $\frac{1}{8}''$ of the boards is showing above the front cheek. Screw up the press and plough this small strip off. This operation is fully described at the beginning of Chapter 9. The cut edge is now the usual base line from which to do the squaring and cutting. The size is marked out 6" by $3\frac{1}{2}''$, and the remaining three sides ploughed. The lines on the boards must be exactly level with the front cheek of the press when cutting is done.

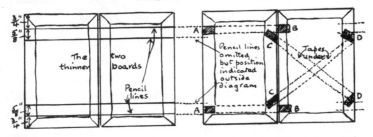

Four boards have now been cut exactly equal in size and they should be taken apart; any roughness, caused by the spots of glue, is sandpapered to remove it. All four are now covered, but it is more interesting if the two thin boards are done in a different paper from the two thick ones. When they are dry the two thinner ones are placed side by side and marked out, as shown, with pencil lines. Then take two pieces of $\frac{1}{2}''$ silk ribbon, $5\frac{1}{2}''$ to 6" long, and thread them under one board. Put a spot of glue at A, A; bring the end of the ribbon over the edge and let it touch the outer pencil lines. Allow it to set a minute or two, and then, holding the second board close to the first, glue down the other ends at B, B. Two further pieces of ribbon, a little longer than the first pair, are now threaded under the second board, and glued down as at C, C and D, D. The two thicker boards are glued, and set aside for a few minutes until they become tacky; then they are placed exactly over the thin boards, thus incorporating all the ribbon ends. Place all very carefully between boards, and leave in a press until drying is complete.

A SELECTION OF SIMPLE EXERCISES

Exercise 5

A folding chess board

Bookbinding points: 'Made' boards, cutting, single-hinge joint, covering in quarter-binding.

When thicker boards are required in bookbinding it is usual to glue pieces of board together until the required thickness is attained. Such boards are known as 'made' boards. A chess board having a single hinge joint requires thicker boards, so that for this exercise a pair of 'made' boards will be needed. The size of the board depends again on the supply of strawboard available, and it will be sufficient for school purposes if a chess board having 1″ squares is made. A pair of boards about $\frac{1}{8}$″ thick will be adequate, so that four pieces of 1 lb. strawboard roughly cut to $9\frac{1}{2}$″ by 5″ will be required.

Glue one side of each board all over, and put them together in pairs. They should be left in the press as long as possible; indeed it is a wise plan to attend to this during the carrying out of the previous exercise, so that they may remain in the press until a subsequent lesson. When dry, they should be tipped together with two tiny spots of glue ready for ploughing; the finished size after ploughing is 9″ by $4\frac{1}{2}$″.

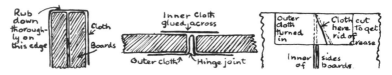

Cut out a piece of cloth approximately $2\frac{1}{2}$″ wide and $10\frac{1}{2}$″ long, and glue it. Pick up the boards, keeping them together square and true, and place them edgeways in the middle of the cloth. Lower them carefully on one side, and pull the cloth over tightly. Smooth it down on both sides; stand the boards on the fore-edge, and rub the cloth down over the back-edges until it adheres. This is most important, for nothing further may be done until this portion has begun to stick. Open the boards very carefully, keeping the cloth folded between them in the joint. Turn in the head and tail. It will be found advisable to cut the cloth with the scissors to get rid of the crease which forms in the joint. Close the boards again as soon as possible, and go over the back-edges again with a bone-folder. It should now be left undisturbed until there remains no doubt about the cloth having adhered to the back.

Another piece of cloth of the same colour, 1″ wide and $8\frac{3}{4}$″ long, is then glued down the inside of the joint, and rubbed down flat. Covering is the next process, and this is described in Chapter 15 under the heading 'Covering in quarter-cloth and paper'. There is little need to describe the lining pieces in detail; they are two pieces of paper, $8\frac{1}{2}$″ by $4\frac{1}{4}$″, ruled into 1″ squares with $\frac{1}{4}$″ margin on three sides of each sheet. The squares are painted in waterproof inks in two contrasting colours; then they are pasted and laid in position forming the endpapers (or liners).

Exercise 6

Case-covers

Bookbinding point: Quarter- and half-binding for case-work.

This exercise is not only an introduction to case-binding, but has a definite utilitarian value as a case-cover made to take magazines, periodicals, and the like.

The size of the book or magazine for which the cover is intended should be ascertained in three dimensions, i.e. the length, width, and thickness. To determine the size of the boards for the case-cover add $\frac{1}{2}$″ to the length of the book, and $\frac{1}{4}$″ to its width. Rough cut 2 lb. strawboards rather larger than the above dimensions, and square and cut them to the finished size. Cut a piece of manilla, or stout brown paper, as long as the boards and as wide as the thickness of the book or magazine.

The cloth for the back should be $1\frac{1}{2}$″ longer than the boards and as wide as the manilla slip, plus $\frac{1}{4}$″, plus 2″ to 3″. The two joints which constitute the $\frac{1}{4}$″ may vary, as the width of each joint should be equal to the thickness of the boards. In this case $\frac{1}{8}$″ is regarded as a minimum for each joint. Mark out the cloth as shown in the diagram; glue it and place the boards and manilla strip in position. Turn in and rub down the cloth at the head and tail. A piece of cloth for the inside is cut out $\frac{1}{4}$″ less than the length of the boards, but it need not be as wide as the outer cloth. This is glued and laid lightly down on the inside. Commence the rubbing down at the left-hand side. When the cloth has been put down in the left-hand joint, put a ruler or a straight-edge into the joint, holding it down while rubbing the cloth into the other joint.

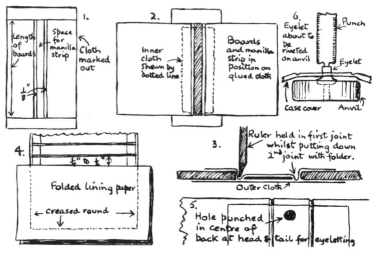

The outer cloth is then trimmed, and the boards covered in quarter- or half-binding—see Chapter 15—and allowed to dry standing on end. Place under boards and light weights to prevent too much curling.

For the linings sufficient paper is cut out so that when folded it is a little larger than one of the boards. Place the fold of the paper $\frac{1}{4}$" to $\frac{1}{2}$" away from the joint, and crease round the edges of the board, holding all firmly while it is being done. Inside these creases mark lines parallel to them and a little over $\frac{1}{8}$" away. Cut along these lines and finally trim off the fold of the paper. Paste both pieces, and lay them down in position as endpapers.

If a cord is required to hold the magazine in position, eyelets should be added near the head and tail. The holes must be punched as shown, and eyeletting tools may be purchased in complete sets from handicraft suppliers, such as Messrs. Russell Bookcrafts, of Hitchin.

Another exercise could be inserted at this point, namely, the loose-leaf file. I have omitted it because it is very similar to a case-cover, and the student having made the latter will have little difficulty with the former.

Exercise 7

Portfolios with wing flaps

Bookbinding point: As for case-covers—its utilitarian value is obvious.

The question of supplies again prevents large ones being made by every pupil, but small samples may be made which contain the same principles and processes; they can be used effectively as note-book holders or cases for collections of postcard reproductions. These are measured in the same way as that adopted for case-covers, and suitable amounts added to arrive at the size of the folio required.

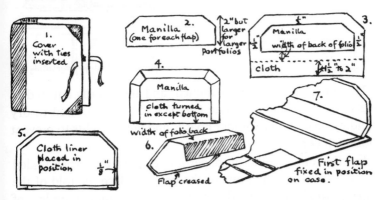

Proceed first to make a case-cover, but omit the manilla strip, and do not line the insides of the boards. At this point cut two slits about ½" from the fore-edges of the boards, and in the middle of the length. They should be long enough to take a width of ribbon for the ties. This ribbon, which should be about 6" long, is threaded through the slits, and ½" of it glued to the inside of the boards. When the glue is dry both slits should be closed neatly by tapping with a backing hammer on the knocking-down iron.

Cut out three pieces of thin manilla about 2″ wide. One should be as long as the case-cover less $\frac{1}{16}$″; the other two as long as the width less $\frac{1}{16}$″. Two corners on each piece must be trimmed off as shown in the diagram. Pieces of cloth are then cut with $\frac{1}{2}$″ margin on three sides, and 1″ to $1\frac{1}{2}$″ plus the width of the back of the case-cover on the base sides. Glue the cloth, place the manilla in position and turn all the sides in except the wide one at the bottom.

Liners of cloth should then be cut, leaving $\frac{1}{8}$″ margin all round. They are glued and placed in position, thus completing the flaps. Before they are attached, the wide piece at the bottom should be creased twice—one crease along the edge of the manilla lining and the other the width of the case-cover away from it. Glue the part shown shaded and fix the long one in position on the case. Mitre the other two, glue them, and fix in position. Place in a press a little while until they are set. The board papers for the inside are now cut out, pasted, and put down on the boards in the same way as lining the case-covers.

Exercise 8

Unsewn albums with single or double guards

Simple case-binding begins with this exercise. Simple small albums can be made from cartridge paper in order to teach the method. The same procedure is used for better materials such as manilla and cards of various thicknesses. For thinner sheets single guards are used; card sheets require double guards.

Albums with single guards

Select about 12 to 16 pages of good cartridge paper, or thin manilla, a little larger than the intended finished size. Knock them square on one short edge and trim a little off in the plough. From the same material cut guards 1″ wide and the same length as the edges just trimmed. The number of guards required is one fewer than the number of pages, and they must all be creased in the centre down the whole length.

Take a guard, flatten it on a sheet of waste paper and glue it evenly and thinly. Lay it on the bench, and place the straight edge of a page up to the crease in the guard. Turn it round and add another page to the remaining half of the guard. Rub it down thoroughly under a sheet of clean paper and fold back the pages, leaving the guard inside. Insert a slip of clean paper inside the guard to prevent the pages sticking together as there is always a slight squeezing out of the glue at the edges.

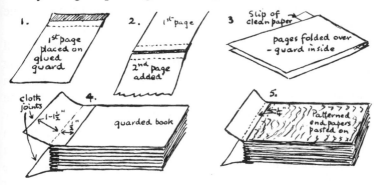

Glue another guard and place the whole of the completed pages half-way on it; add another page to the other half, rub down, and bend over again with the guard inside. Continue this process until all the pages have been added, keeping the back as square as possible throughout the whole operation. An alternative method is to guard the pages in pairs; then guard the pairs into fours and so on. Do not use paste for this work; it contains too much moisture. Two cloth joints as long as the back and $1\frac{1}{2}''$ wide are cut out of the material intended for the outer cover, and these are creased, right side inside, a third of the way across the width. This $\frac{1}{2}''$ is glued and the joints fixed on the book, the crease lying flush with the back edge of the pages. Four single sheets of thin patterned endpaper are required, each the same size as the book, and a straight edge must be trimmed on each sheet. Two of these must be put away safely, as they are not required until the book is nearly finished. The other two are pasted and laid on the outer leaves of the book, the straight edges coming within $\frac{1}{4}''$ of the crease in the cloth joint. These are left to dry, the book standing on its edge, and when they begin to curl drying must be completed between boards under a light weight.

Before the edges are cut, the book must be packed with waste paper. Sheets of newspaper are cut a little larger than the pages and inserted between them, up to, but not past, the edges of the guards. Sufficient sheets should be added to make the general thickness of the book throughout equal to that of the back, to compensate for the presence of the guards.

Mark a point X to denote the width of the book after it has been cut. This should be only as far inside the edge as will trim all the pages. Transfer this measurement to X1, taking it from the back of the book, and join X and X1. Place a try-square on the back, and square a line at the head (as at A), allowing enough inside the edge to trim all the pages. Turn the book over and repeat this for the tail. The book is then ploughed along these

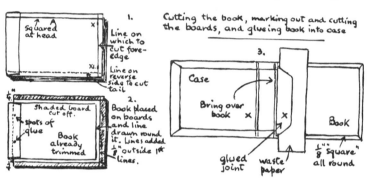

Cutting the book, marking out and cutting the boards, and glueing book into case

lines, having a cutting board behind the line in each case. It is most essential that the book be square in the press before any cutting is done.

Two boards are now cut out and squared, the book being used as a template. To do this the boards are roughly cut a little larger than the book, fastened together by two tiny spots of glue, and trimmed along the edge intended for the back of the book. Place the boards on the book so that the straight edge is within $\frac{1}{4}''$ of the back. In this position, run a pencil line round the head, tail, and fore-edge; add outside these lines three more lines $\frac{1}{8}''$ away, but parallel to the first lines; cut the boards along these outer lines. If the boards are thick, they should be bevelled slightly all round. This may be done by wrapping sandpaper round a bandstick or ruler and rubbing down the edges, keeping the angle as constant as possible.

Two small spots of glue are then put on the cloth joints, and the boards placed in position, being sighted all round to check the 'squares', i.e. the amount of board ($\frac{1}{8}''$ in this case) which projects beyond the book at the head, tail, and fore-edge. A light weight is placed over the book until this glue has set. Very little glue must be used—just two small smears on each joint— for it must not be forgotten that this is only a temporary fixing of the boards.

The binding may be in full, half, or quarter cloth. Cut out a piece of cloth, allowing $\frac{3}{4}''$ for turning in, and the instructions for case-binding are followed in the covering. These are found at the beginning of Chapter 20.

When the case has been made the book must be placed on one side of it, and a piece of waste placed under the cloth joint, which is then glued. It is usual to mitre the ends of the joints before gluing, and if the book is a thick one and appears to need strengthening, it can be lined with thick brown paper. After gluing the joint, replace the waste piece of paper by a clean piece to prevent any possibility of soiling the endpapers. Bring over the case, keeping it tight over the joint, and rub well down when closed. When both sides have been done the back should be attended to down the edges of the boards, using a bone-folder until the glue has set.

The two sheets of patterned endpaper which were put aside are now trimmed to fit the insides of the boards. If the straight edge of the paper is put down within $\frac{1}{4}''$ of the joint, and the paper held firmly whilst it is creased round the edges of the board, then $\frac{1}{8}''$ is marked inside these creases and trimmed off. They are then pasted and placed in position to form the 'board papers'. Leave the book standing open until the drying is nearly complete, and then leave in the press. Any lettering or decoration should be done before taking out the waste paper used as packing between the leaves.

Albums of thicker card having double guards

Each card should have a strip cut off the back edge. The

width of this strip varies with the size of the album. A small book would only need ½″, whereas a large album would have strips up to 1″ wide. Guards of white linen, or thin cloth, are prepared, and the width of these also varies with the width of the strips. Roughly speaking, they should be 1″ plus twice the width of the card strips, e.g. if the strips are ½″ wide then the guards will be 1″ plus 1″, i.e. 2″ wide. These guards are folded down the middle as in the previous exercise.

When a guard has been glued, a strip is placed on each side of the centre crease, and a page added at each side, leaving a small gap of ¹⁄₁₆″ between the strip and the page to form a hinged joint. They are folded with the guards inside, and strips and pages are added until the book is complete.

From this point the procedure is the same as that for albums with single guards. Heavier books of this nature must be strengthened down the spine with a liner of brown paper or thin linen, glued on and well rubbed down. A hollow back may be added to stiffen the covering cloth if it is thought necessary.

Exercise 9

The binding of a few single sheets

This is an exercise designed to teach stabbing and overcasting, and this method can be used to bind short theses, sheets of notes, and typewritten matter which will not be in constant use, but which need keeping in a tidy form for reference only. Such bindings naturally open 'stiffly' in the back owing to the nature of the sewing.

Stabbing

This is a very ancient form of binding. There is in existence an Indian palm-leaf book many centuries old which was bound by this method. Two types require to be described here, and the simpler one is dealt with first.

278

To each end of the book add a sheet of good endpaper and trim all the sheets true and straight along the back edges. Sometimes this is very difficult owing to the presence of written matter close to the back edges. Fan the pages slightly, and glue with hot thin glue. Knock the edges square again *immediately*, and nip in a press between sheets of waste paper until the glue has set.

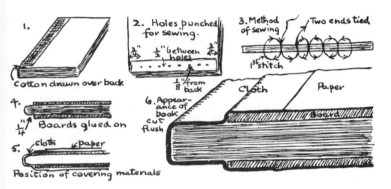

Take a piece of cotton cloth, jaconet, or thin linen, of sufficient width to extend round the back of the book and project on each side about $1\frac{1}{2}''$. *Paste the cotton* and draw it over the back and sides, and set it aside to dry. Then, using a fine awl, prick holes through the binding; the holes must be about $\frac{1}{2}''$ apart and $\frac{1}{8}''$ away from the back edge. The holes nearest the head and tail must be no less than $\frac{3}{4}''$ from the extremities of the book. The number of holes required is decided by the size of the book. Sew through these holes, beginning and finishing at the centre; tie a knot with the two ends, and tap the sewing down very gently on a knocking-down iron.

Two thin boards are now needed, and they must be cut to a size equal in height to the distance from head to tail, and $\frac{1}{4}''$ less than the width of the book from back to fore-edge. Glue the boards all over, and set them on the book $\frac{1}{4}''$ in from the back edge. Place between boards in the press and leave until dry.

Take a piece of bookbinder's cloth equal in length to the height of the book, and wide enough to come over on the sides about 1''. This cloth is glued and fixed on the back of the book, care being taken to rub it well down with a folder. The cloth is trimmed in the usual way to an equal width on each side. Cut out the paper sides of such a size that they just cover the portion of the boards still exposed. Glue these on, and leave in a press until drying is complete.

The edges of the book must now be cut. If the book is a very thin one, the cutting can be done with a knife and rule, the alternative for thicker books being of course the plough. The method adopted in binding this book will leave no projection of the boards beyond the pages (commonly known as the 'square'), neither will the edges of the boards be covered, and this type of binding is known as 'cut flush'.

The second and slightly stronger type of binding for a few single sheets is done in the following way.

Again a sheet of good cartridge paper is added to each end of the book. Trim the sheets straight on the back edges. Now take two strips of cloth as long as the height of the book, and $1\frac{1}{2}''$ wide. Two strips of cartridge paper of the same length but $2''$ wide are also required. Glue $\frac{1}{2}''$ of the cartridge strips and attach them to the end sheets of the book. In a similar manner glue the strips of cloth on top of the cartridge strips, being careful to have the face of the cloth outwards. When the glue is dry, fold the strips thus added right over upon the end sheets in such a way that the fold is perfectly flush with the back edge of the book.

Knock the whole of the sheets up square at the back, fan them out slightly, and glue all the back edges. Knock up square again and leave between boards in the press until they are dry. Turn back the strips into the original position, and make holes for the sewing in exactly the same manner as used in the first method. The stitches should go through the glued portion of the strips, and after the sewing is completed it must be tapped down on the knocking-down iron.

Take four single sheets of thin coloured paper to serve as end-papers. Thin paper is used so that the endpapers of the book do not become too thick and clumsy. Place two of the pieces on one side to serve as board papers at a later stage. The other two are pasted and placed on the end sheets of the book nearly up to the back edge, so that the sewing is now completely covered. If the sheets have been cut approximately to the size of the book, it may be that they will overlap a little at the edges after pasting; this does not matter for the book has still to be trimmed. Allow the pasted ends to dry, first in the open, and then under a light weight.

The book is now carefully squared and cut. Every effort must be made to ensure that it shall be done accurately, as endless trouble will ensue in fitting the boards if the cutting is done in a careless manner.

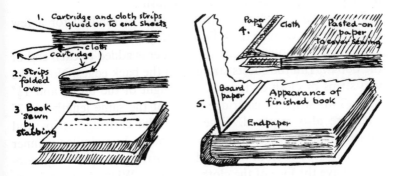

Cut out two thin boards and square them so that they are as long as the book plus two 'squares', and in width equal to the width of the book plus one 'square' but MINUS $\frac{1}{4}$", because the boards do not come right up to the back of the book. Glue each board along the back edge so that the glued portion is about $\frac{1}{2}$" wide. Fix them to outer strip of cartridge, and set the squares very carefully. Put between boards in the press, and, when dry, open the boards and cut down with scissors at the head and tail. This means cutting the cartridge slips a matter of $\frac{3}{4}$" down the back edge of the boards. Failure to do this means that the covering material cannot be turned in.

The method of covering has already been given in Chapter 15. It should be noted that this alternative method for a few single sheets is not really a case-binding, but it falls naturally into this chapter.

A variation of the above method consists in leaving out the cartridge slips, and after cutting the book and boards to size, each linen strip is touched with two spots of glue and the boards placed in position temporarily. Then the method is the same as that adopted for the albums, i.e. a case-bound book.

General Notes on the Foregoing Exercises

In all the above exercises ample scope is to be found for an imaginative approach to simple forms of decoration, and the treatment of cover and endpapers. Decoration may be carried out by brush, pencil, or pen, and some experiments made in the use of simple tools with tooling leaf. There is also a wide field to be explored in the making of decorated endpapers through free brush or pen patterns, potato cuts, marbling, and paste-comb graining, but such decoration must never be overdone at the expense of good craftsmanship in bookbinding.

CHAPTER 22

Single-section Books and Pamphlets

The group of exercises outlined in this chapter should follow those given in the previous chapter, and they form the link between those preliminary exercises and bookbinding proper. A series of seven examples has been selected as a representative collection covering the differing types of single-section binding. They are actually made of plain paper capable of being used for various purposes, e.g. notebooks, but the methods described cover the binding of single-section pamphlets, and include at least one type used in whole leather binding of illuminated addresses.

Number One

Take a sheet of paper and fold it to form a single section. A convenient size to use is demy or large post. The folding must be

1st fold
Right to left

2nd fold
Head to tail

3rd fold
Right to left. etc.

1"
Folds at head
3 stitch
Begin here
Two loose ends tied over long stitch
1"

Folding a sheet to make a section

done in the proper bookbinding manner, as an introduction to the process of 'pulling' a book. First fold from right to left, then from head to tail, and again from right to left, and so on. Further details are found in Chapter 1.

A piece of cover paper is folded round the section, and the whole knocked square at the head. The sewing is then done in a three stitch. If desired, the first and last pages may be pasted and the cover sheet put down on them and pressed until dry. Squaring and cutting follows. The fore-edge is marked out parallel to the back and the head and tail squared with a try-square, remembering that cutting is always done from the back to the fore-edge. This will mean marking the head on the front side, and the tail on the reverse side of the book. The cutting is done with a knife, but the board cutter may be used as an occasional alternative to give experience in its use. No more should be trimmed off than is necessary to trim all the pages. This type is known as 'sewing to show'.

Number Two

A sheet is folded and sewn straight away in a three stitch. Take a piece of cover paper large enough to go right round the book; fold it, open it out again and paste it all over. Lay the book down upon it, its back along the crease in the middle, and pull the cover over. It may be left under a weight after it has dried a little time. It is then squared and cut, and this type is called 'sewing not to show'.

Number Three

Fold and sew a sheet using a four-stitch. Cut out two thin boards the same length as the book, but $\frac{1}{4}''$ less in width. Mark pencil lines parallel to, but $\frac{1}{4}''$ away from, the back on each side. Glue the boards all over and place them up to these lines. Leave all in the press until dry, and then cover in quarter-cloth. The cloth and paper sides are only as long as the book, as there is no turning-in for this type. Covering in quarter-cloth is detailed in Chapter 15. Rub the cloth well down the edges of the boards at the back. When all is dry, squaring and cutting is done. This particular binding is called 'a book cut flush', i.e. no cloth or paper is turned in, and no boards project beyond the pages.

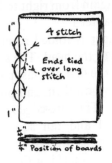

Number Four

Fold a sheet, and add to it an endpaper folded right round. If a patterned paper is chosen, the decorated side is inside when folded. Add outside this a folded sheet of waste paper. This need not extend the whole way across the book—half-way would be adequate. Knock all square at the head and sew in a four stitch. Cut out two thin boards and mark the book ¼" from the back in the same fashion as Number 3 book. Glue only 1" of the

boards, setting them in position on the book, and pressing until dry. Tear down the unglued portions of the waste sheets, cover in quarter-binding not turned in, and set aside to dry. Place a piece of waste paper larger than the book under each endpaper, and paste the latter. Shut down the boards on the endpapers, and leave in the press until dry. The book is finished by squaring and cutting flush.

Number Five

Fold a sheet and place round it a folded endpaper. Add to this a cloth joint 2" wide. This is for strengthening purposes and is cut the same length as the book, and folded down the middle. Add outside these a folded waste sheet, and knock all square at the head. This type is sewn in a multiple stitch, and the stitches should be about $\frac{1}{2}"$ long. Square and cut the book at this stage. Then cut out two boards allowing $\frac{1}{8}"$ 'square' beyond the head, tail, and fore-edge, and $\frac{1}{4}"$ inset at the back. Glue 1" down the

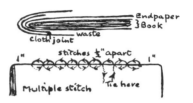

back edges of the boards, fix in position on the wastes, and place in the press to dry.

This book must be properly covered—not cut flush—and this should be done in a half-binding. The turning-in at the head and

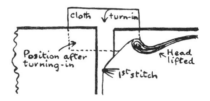

tail is done by lifting the book slightly as shown in the diagram. When all is dry, paste down the endpapers 'shut', and allow it to rema n in the press for as long as possible.

Number Six

There is little difference between Number Five and Number Six, and if time presses Number Five book could be passed over. In this type a double endpaper is used. Two folded sheets are placed round the book instead of one, but the face sides of the endpapers should be together.

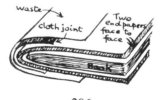

This book may be covered in full cloth. It is sewn in the same way as Number Five. If the endpapers are very thin, the inner fly-leaf can be pasted to the first and last leaves of the book. In the case of a printed pamphlet this would necessitate the addition of a clean piece of paper round the book before the endpapers are added. The board endpapers are pasted down shut.

Number Seven

This type of single-section book is often used for the binding of vellum addresses, and may be regarded as a branch of fine binding. If the student wishes to do it in the best style, very good hand-made paper can be used to take the place of vellum. This is used for the endpapers and the pages, and the cover and joints should be in Morocco. The following outline is merely a sample of the method, and not of the materials.

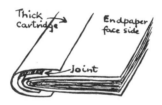

Fold a sheet and round it place an endpaper with the right side *outwards*. A joint 2″ wide is folded and placed over the endpaper. This is of the same material as that intended for the cover. A waste of strong Kraft paper or thick cartridge is added, and the whole sewn with silk to match the colour of the covering material. The stitch is the multiple one. When leather is used the knot should be tied outside the book and the loose ends frayed out finely. The book is now squared and cut.

A pair of *split boards* is required. Information on the making of such boards is given in Chapter 9. After squaring and cutting these boards to size, as in Number Five exercise, they are bevelled all round. The splits are opened out, the waste cut down to fit them and glue applied to the insides of the split portions. Then the boards are placed in position having the waste flaps inside the splits. Press thoroughly, having clean pressing tins inside the boards and pressing boards on the outer sides. Cover with the same material as the joints in a full binding. When dry, paste down the joints and trim out and fill in the boards in the manner described for full binding in leather in Chapter 16. Two 'board' endpapers are cut to size, pasted, and laid in position. After they have been drying open for a while, the book should be placed in a press under light pressure, and left to dry out completely.

Short poems written by pupils are excellent subjects for binding in the above fashion. They can be illustrated, and given hand-decorated ends, together with suitable simple tooling on the covers.

APPENDIX

Recipe for Bookbinder's Paste

1 cupful of white flour.
1 teaspoonful of ground alum.
3 cupfuls of water.

Mix the flour and alum together in one cupful of the cold water, and beat it until a smooth cream is obtained. Add the remaining two cupfuls of water, and place in a double pan on a stove. Bring the outer water jacket to the boil, stirring the paste all the time. Allow it to go on boiling until the paste has thickened; this actually takes about five minutes after the water has come to the boil. Take off the stove and cover the surface of the paste with a thin film of cold water to prevent the formation of a 'skin' as the paste cools. When cold, pour off this surface water and beat into the paste two or three drops of oil of cloves or formalin (40 per cent solution) to preserve it. The paste is then ready for use.

Following upon some research, very kindly carried out by Mr. W. H. Langwell, F.R.I.C., the above quantities were found to be:

Flour	4 oz.
Water	$1\frac{1}{2}$ pts.
Alum	$\frac{1}{6}$ oz.

The use of alum in the recipe is to prevent reversion. Without it the paste would lose its consistency and become thin and watery if kept for long; at the same time alum is, according to Mr. Langwell, detrimental to paper and he recommends that, while the paste is cooling, $\frac{1}{4}$ to $\frac{1}{2}$ oz. of precipitated chalk or whitening be added and stirred in to neutralize the free acidity due to the presence of alum. When cold, the addition of formalin, mentioned above, will preserve the paste for a considerable period.

Paste made from Cold-water Paste Powders

This is a very convenient form of paste for use in schools. It is best to make it in small quantities, and thus cut out waste. Place in a jar or some such receptacle about half-a-pint of cold water and begin to add the paste powder a little at a time whilst constantly stirring it. When it begins to thicken do not add any more paste powder until it has been given a thorough stirring. If it is not then thick enough more powder must be added, but in very small amounts. When it reaches the stage of being just a little thinner than is desired, set it aside, as it thickens a little more during the following ten minutes.

The Preparation of Cake Glue

When cake glue is employed for bookbinding, it should be wrapped in a cloth, placed on a firm surface, and hammered until it has been broken into small pieces. The purpose in using the cloth is to prevent the pieces from scattering when struck by the hammer. Place pieces in the glue kettle until it is just a little over half full, and then cover it with cold water. It should be allowed to soak in this fashion overnight, and then the heating can be commenced.

Glue which has been continually reheated for some length of time loses its nature, and when this occurs it is better to clean all out, and begin with fresh glue. When glue pots become very dirty and covered with old glue round the edges, they should be placed in a bucket, half full of hot water, and boiled steadily for some time until all the old glue has disappeared.

Information on the use of prepared flexible glues is given on p. 128.

APPENDIX

B. S. GLAIRE

Yet another glaire has been successfully made by Mr. Peter Waters, A.R.C.A., of 'Roger Powell Bookbinders', The Slade, Froxfield, Petersfield, Hampshire, who markets it under the name of 'B. S. Glaire'. It is based upon similar preparations in use by French finishers but is much clearer and therefore cleaner to use, especially on white leather. The temperature required for tooling can be much lower and there can be a delayed pressure rather than the usual quick impression. No PREVIOUS PREPARATION of the leather, such as washing-up, etc., is necessary or advisable and work, having been prepared with two coats of this glaire, can be put aside for a week or more before the tooling is carried out. The tooling should not begin for at least an hour after preparing and the tools should be bright and clean. It is a very excellent medium in all respects.

BIBLIOGRAPHY

Cockerell, Douglas, *Bookbinding and the Care of Books*
Cockerell, Sidney, *Marbling as a School Subject*
Vaughan, Alex. J., *Modern Bookbinding*
Zaensdorf, *Bookbinding*
Prideaux, S. T., *Bookbinders and their Craft*
Horne, H. P., *Bookbinding*
Plenderleith, H. J. (British Museum), *The Preservation of Leather Bindings*
Langwell, W. H., *The Conservation of Books and Documents*
Matthews, W. F., *Bookbinding*
Cockerell, S. M., *The Repairing of Books*
Mason, J., *Paper Making as an Artistic Craft*
Middleton, Bernard C., *A History of English Craft Bookbinding Technique*

INDEX

293

INDEX

INDEX

Marbling, 76–87
  colours, 77
  combs, 80
  troughs, 79, 80, 82
  with Linmarblin, 86
Margins, proportions of, 27
Markers, fixing of, 184
Marking-up for sewing, 92–103
  for books cut 3 edges, 93
    ,,   ,,   ,, head only, 94
    ,,   ,, trimmed only, 94
    ,, flexible binding, 102–3
    ,, four or more tapes, 99–100
  sawn-in bands, 100–1
    ,, three tapes, 95–9
Mason, J., 291
Materials, general list, 23–4
Mats, square, 263
Matthews, W. F., 291
Mending tears, etc., 38–9
  vellum, 39
  worm holes, 39
Middleton, Bernard C., 291
Mull, 24
  fixing, 160

Needles, bookbinder's, 22
  whipstitching, 22
Netting twine, 101

Octavo, crown, 25, 29
  · folding, 28–9
Oilstones, 23, 134–5, 198
Opening-up, 228, 253
Overcasting, 259, 278
Oxgall, 82, 83, 86

Pallets, 229, 231
Paper, blotting, 36, 39, 48, 68
  board, 68, 265
  coloured cartridge, 24
  covering, 24
  dyeing and staining, 89
  foxmarks in, 38
  inlaying, 47
  large post bank, 23, 40, 184, 239
  Kraft, 81, 189
  marbled, 62, 76–87
  mending, 38
  Michallet and Ingres, 62, 68
  offset cartridge, 24, 53
  sizes, 25
  sizing, 79, 35–6, 82

washing, 36–8
waterproofing, 89
Whatman's 13 lb. bank, 23, 40, 296
white cartridge, 24, 53, 60, 61, 189
Paring, leather joints, 63
  for quarter and half leather, 199–202
  for whole leather, 202
  knives, 23, 135, 198
  stones, 23, 63, 199
Paste, brushes, 22
  flour, 24, 289
  graining, 87
  making, 289–90
  pots, 22, 262
  powder, 24, 290
  washing, 244
Pasting up, 124
Pasting down, open, 227
  shut, 69, 223–6, 257–8
  fly leaves, 17
Payne, Roger, 231
Penknives, 22
Petrol, 35
Plenderleith, H. J., 213, 291
Plough, 22
  knife, 133–5
Polishing iron, 220
Portfolios, 273
Presses, cutting, 132, 157
  finishing, 22, 240
  lying, 34, 125
  nipping, 20, 51
  sewing, 22, 104–5, 113, 116
  standing, 20, 50
Pressing, boards, 20, 49
  book sections, 49–51
  tins, 20, 49, 171
Prideaux, Miss S. T., 76, 291
Pulling, 31–3
  books in parts, 32–3
  valuable books, 33

Quarter binding, 28, 192–5, 199, 205–9, 244
  section, 43
Quarto, folding, 29
Quires, books in, 25, 28, 35

Rebinding, first stages, 31–51
Reef knot, 113

296

INDEX